POINT LOMA RAILROAD COMPANY
TIME TABLE No. 16 (WEEK DAYS)
Effective October 10, 1915

WEST BOUND					**EAST BOUND**		

BALLOON ROUTE EXCURSIONS
VIA
Los Angeles & San Diego Beach Ry.
SAN DIEGO
TO
LA JOLLA
GOING COUPON Not Good if Detached from Return Coupon.
C. C. Pillsbury, Mgr.

BALLOON ROUTE EXCURSIONS
VIA
Los Angeles & San Diego Beach Ry.
GOOD FOR ONE PERSON
LA JOLLA
TO
SAN DIEGO
Expires Six Months from Date punched in margin.
Conductor on Going Trip will Punch Here on the Date Going Coupon is used

No. 16924

JAN. FEB. MAR. APR. MAY JUNE JULY AUG. SEPT. OCT. NOV. DEC.

1 2 3 4 5 6 7 8 9 10
11 12 13 14 15 16 17 18 19 20
21 22 23 24 25 26 27 28 29 30
31   1918–1919

S0-BEQ-983

The San Diego Electric
RAILWAY NEWS
San Diego, April 1, 1919
OFFICE, 2A UNION BUILDING
No. 4

FORGOTTEN ON THE CARS BUT NOT LOST

A woman stepped from one of our cars at Fifth and streets last month. After getting half way to the curb she hurried back to board car which had started and she had to board car which had handle. The car stopped immediately, when the woman got aboard uninjured. Conductor Fred R. Crane asked for an explanation. "I forgot my child, who is still on the car."

TOMMIES FIRST

Point Loma Railroad Company

Time Table No. 16
(WEEK DAYS)

Effective 2:00 A. M., October 10, 1915

FOR THE USE OF EMPLOYES ONLY

Read carefully special rules on back of this time table.
These rules are for the operation of trains on the Point Loma Railroad, and are in addition to the Rules and Regulations for Conductors and Motormen of the San Diego Electric Railway Company.

M. J. PERRIN,
Superintendent.

San Diego Electric Ry. Co.
GOOD FOR
CENT Fare
Inner & Outer Zones
Vice-President.
484012

ic Ry. Co.
t Fare
Outer Zones
sident.
484012

San Diego Electric Railway Co.
TRANSFER.—Good only for this current trip SEE OTHER SIDE
from point of transfer to line punched on first car after time cancelled.
W. CLAYTON, Gen'l Manager.
030643

1	2	3	4	5	6	7	8	9	10	11	12	13	14	15	16		A. M.
Jan.	Feb.	Mar.	April	May		July	Aug.	Sept.	Oct.	Nov.	Dec.						First
17	18	19	20	21	22	23	24	25	26	27	28	29	30	31			Fifth

1 2 3 4 5 6 7 8 9 10 11 12
5 10 15 20 25 30 35 40 45 50 55

3 ZONES
AUG.

$ **269** $
SAN DIEGO ELECTRIC RY. CO.
4:01 A.M. ... ly 17 ... :00 A.M., J... 24,
WHEN ... TIRE FA... O ... PASS ... ARER BE... EEN ... POINT ... N THE ... NNER AND ... UTE ZONES DU...
W. P. 1
No. 28962

INSPECTION OF HAND BRAKES
SAFETY STOPS
trains will make safety stops as follows:
Fourth and Broadway, San Diego.
Fourth and F Streets, San Diego.
Third and F Streets, San Diego.
First and Broadway, San Diego.
State and Broadway, San Diego.
Broadway and Kettner, San Diego.
Fe crossing, between Gilmore and La Playa Jct. all trains will proceed only on signal from flagman. If no flagman on duty, conductor will flag crossing.
Highway crossing at Turquoise Street, Pacific Beach, all trains will sound crossing whistle, stop not nearer than crossing, then sound Two long blasts of whistle and proceed over crossing with caution.

SPEED RESTRICTIONS
not exceed 18 miles per hour around curves on Kettner Boulevard and Hancock Street, and through trailing switch
not exceed 15 miles per hour through turnouts on sidings.
D. & A. Ry. Oil Supply House on Northbound track between Broadway and C Streets with caution account of nger to workmen or accident with S. D. & A. Ry. Gas Electric cars at that point.

MISCELLANEOUS
signals and Marker lamps are kept in box at 4th and Broadway. On outbound trips crews will supply them-essary lamps early enough that they may be used by sunset.
also be kept at La Jolla, but these must not be used except in emergency.

RAILS
OF THE
SILVER
GATE

RICHARD V. DODGE

JOHN D. SPRECKELS

The Great Builder

RAILS OF THE SILVER GATE

RICHARD V. DODGE

SILVER GATE

The Spreckels San Diego Empire

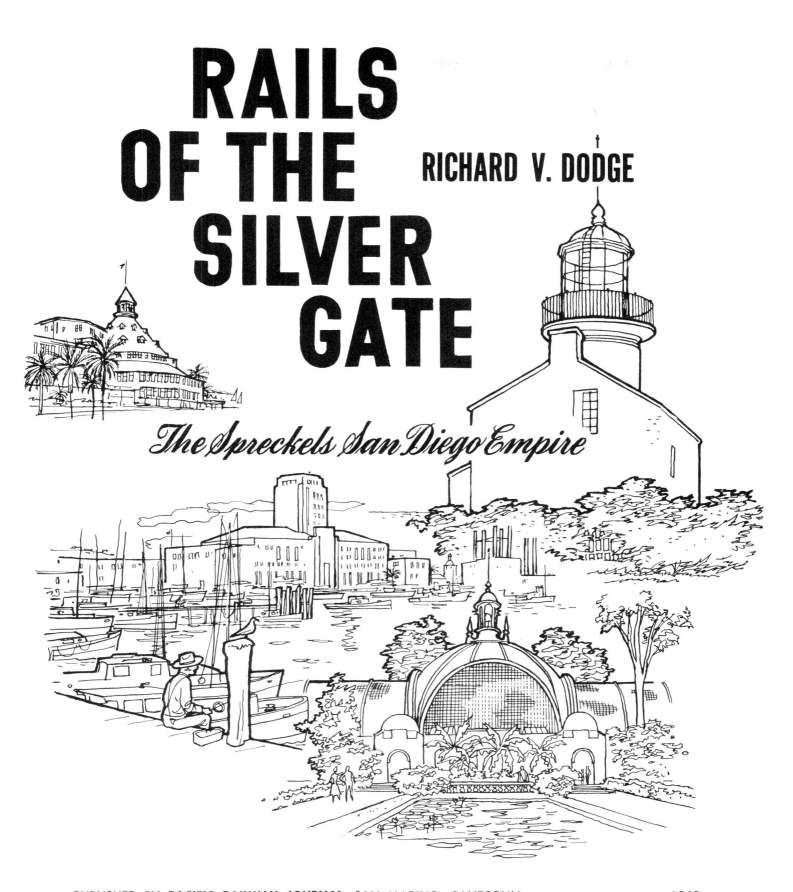

PUBLISHED BY **PACIFIC RAILWAY JOURNAL**, SAN MARINO, CALIFORNIA **1960**

RAILS OF THE SILVER GATE

Copyright 1960, by Pacific Railroad Publications, Inc., all rights reserved. No part of this book may be reproduced in any manner without permission in writing, except in the case of brief quotations for review.

Published by the Pacific Railway Journal,
a publication of Pacific Railroad Publications, Inc.
2304 Melville Drive, San Marino, California

Printed and bound in the United States of America

Library of Congress Catalog - Card No. 56-12943.

1st printing - September, 1960

Foreword

Over the centuries California has proven to be a land of adventure and romance, and blessed by a bountiful nature with a wealth of natural resources.

Down at its southernmost tip, eternally kissed by the sparkling waves of the blue Pacific, lies sunny San Diego, the delightful locale of this book. Civilization in California had its beginnings in San Diego.

First voyageur to arrive by sea was Juan Rodriguez Cabrillo. His small caravel first sailed into the harbor of San Diego on September 28, 1542.

Sixty years later, in 1602, Don Sebastian Viscaino, exploring the New World for Spain, sailed into the same bay and established a settlement. He changed its name from San Miguel, so called by Cabrillo, to San Diego de Alcala. In 1769, Padre Junipero Serra founded Mission San Diego de Alcala there, the first of the chain of 21 built along El Camino Real.

In 1822, California came under the rule of Mexico. But in 1846 the Bear Flag of the California Republic was raised at Sonoma and 23 days later, on July 7, 1846, California became the 31st State and a full-fledged member of the United States of America.

From then on San Diego attracted land seekers, and the boom was on. By 1885 it boasted 40,000 residents (although five years later, in 1890, this dropped to 17,000 when the rush collapsed).

One who came was John D. Spreckels. He sailed through the Silver Gate into San Diego harbor aboard his yacht Lurline in July, 1887, a man made wealthy by vast sugar holdings. Under San Diego's blue sky he decided to make his home.

The years passed. The trails once trod by the brown-robed Franciscan padres gave way to shining steel rails. A major railroad, trolley lines and even steam tramways speeded the growth of the city. The town grew and prospered, so that smaller towns sprang up around it, yet dependent on it, for life.

Spreckels used his wealth to build great hotels, expand transportation facilities, expand its business district and to develop its cultural features.

Under San Diego's cerulean sky a metropolitan city blossomed. Thrice blessed by a landlocked harbor which became a port of call for ships of all the world and, even more important, home base for the Pacific Fleet, San Diego in truth was — and is — the city by the Silver Gate.

This book, Rails of the Silver Gate, recounts the role played by public transportation in the growth of San Diego.

Donald Duke, Editor
September, 1960   Pacific Railway Journal

Acknowledgements

Railroading is a relaxing hobby for some people, an absorbing passion for others and a full-time business for still others. But all three groups find pleasure in the past — in reminiscing and comparing yesteryear's railroads, interurbans and trolley lines.

Much has been written on the part played by the large railroads in building California but precious little on the smaller lines. Yet each of these started out with the same hopes and dreams, the same determination to serve, build and, eventually, to expand, as did the giants.

Many fell short and are all but forgotten. Others were absorbed by larger systems and lost their identity. Only faded file records tell of their early beginnings. This book tells the enjoyable story of the several small railways which, jointly, helped build and make San Diego the city that it is today — San Diego, the city by the Silver Gate.

The author was not alone in compiling this volume. His major tasks were to assemble and to present in readable style the wealth of historical data gathered together by himself, acquaintances and a number of capable historians. So, in many respects, this book is as much theirs as mine.

I am indebted, first, to my friend Frederick W. Reif of San Diego for research assistance and illustrations from his fine collection of historical photos. I suspect, without Fred's help, this book would not have been written.

My thanks, too, to the employees of the San Diego Transit System for their co-operation, particularly to Chief Engineer H. E. Rowe, Equipment Superintendent Farrell Tipton, Purchasing Agent George Roxburgh and Editor Lauran G. Clapp of "Transit Topics."

I am grateful to Val H. Adams for excerpts from the biography written by his father, the late H. Austin Adams, titled "The Man—John D. Spreckels."

I acknowledge the help given by Gerald F. MacMullen, director, and James R. Mills, curator, of the Junipero Serra Museum, operated by the San Diego Historical Society. Its files of the "San Diego Union," the "Evening Tribune" and the "San Diego Sun" were of great help, as was the Public Library.

For photographs used in this book I want to thank the Union Title Insurance Co. of San Diego, Randolph Brandt, Donald Duke, Al Haij, R. P. Middlebrook, Douglas Duncan, Eric Sanders, Ira Swett who also prepared an article on the San Diego Electric Railway, and John H. Andert whose collection of timetables helped preparation of the section on Car Route Changes.

The colorful jacket illustration was done by Artist E. S. Hammack whose reputation among railroad fans is tops. And special thanks are due John Hungerford and Richard Ritterband for typography, A. E. Barker for equipment drawings, and Al Rose for lithography and fine book production.

And last but not least, I express grateful and heartfelt appreciation to Donald Duke for preparation of the manuscript for publication and production details. He conceived the idea for this book.

Richard V. Dodge

San Diego, California

Ferry - The Silver Gate

Table of Contents

CHAPTER I
The Great Builder

" He's a fool, anxious to part with his money!' croaked the pessimists, 'for no other capitalist nor syndicate of capitalists in the country would do what he's doing! "

" He's a far-seeing Empire Builder, retorted the optimists, 'betting on his own vision of the future; and such faith can remove mountains. "

The foregoing paragraphs are direct quotations from a life story written by H. Austin Adams entitled: *THE MAN JOHN D. SPRECKELS.* Without J. D. there would have been no San Diego Electric Railway.

Forebears

In Europe, in the germanic kingdom of Hanover, there lived a family with the surname *Von Spreckelsen.* Adams explains that *. . sen* shows that the family came, originally, from Norway. The prefix *Von* indicates that they were granted a patent of nobility. However, for many generations, the name had been simplified to plain *Spreckels,* a family of "hard-working farm folk".

Sufficient traits and characteristics of certain members of this branch of the human race will be brought out to form a personal background for this composite history of the San Diego Electric Railway Company, That is: first preliminary explanations and historical preludes will be given so that the reasons for the bringing of the SDE Ry. into existence will be understood. Then its story will be tied in with other enterprises, events and developments as it progresses. Brief accounts will be included covering all the other "legitimate" railways in the San Diego area.

The Father

Claus Spreckels was born in Lamstedt, Hanover, in 1828. He inherited the qualities of his ancestors: "adventurous daring, stubborn determination, absolute self-reliance and genius".

During his childhood and youth, his native country was torn by political upheavals. So, at the age of 17, he decided to emigrate to the United States of America, the land of golden opportunities. He landed in New York speaking no English and with only the equivalent of "six bits" (75 cents) in his pocket.

He found work and by "Work, work, work" soon started and carried to a successful conclusion several grocery stores in various eastern localities. His mottoes became: "Cut out the frills!" and "No nonsense!".

But the "Go West, young man" urge of the period was irresistible. Married and with a young son, he did just that in 1856, coming by sea to San Francisco.

There he established another grocery, started a brewery, became interested in sugar refineries, then plantations, railroads, electric power plants, etc. At the time of his death, in 1908, he was universally known as *THE SUGAR KING OF SAN FRANCISCO.*

Eldest Son

That first child was born on August 16, 1853 in Charleston, South Carolina, and was given the name *John Diedrich.* The boy was brought up strictly "no nonsense".

During his youth he was taught the principles of obedience, honesty, thrift, simplicity and thoroughness. He inherited many of the family traits. Add to these, a natural love of the sea and an insatiable love of music, good music.

He became a great dreamer and a builder who made his dreams come true. He did big things, so many big things. Scarcely was one project organized and started, when a bigger one would be envisioned. Those who ever expected him to surrender and quit did not know J. D.

He had married Lillie Sieben in October 1877 in Hoboken, New Jersey. There were four children: two sons who were named John D., Jr. and Claus; two daughters, Grace and Lillie. Claus later became associated with the San Diego Electric Railway.

By the time J. D. entered the local picture, he had already built a great empire in the north and in Hawaii. He owned and operated sugar plantations and refineries, fleets of steamships and tugboats, office buildings, banks, a San Francisco newspaper — *The Call* and many other commercial concerns.

He was "simple, sincere, fun-loving and lovable".

Other Eleven Children

The marriage union of the father and the mother produced eleven more

Adolph B. Spreckels
Brother and business partner—F. W. Reif

children but only four of them lived to reach maturity. Of the latter, one son is of particular interest in connection with the San Diego Electric Railway story. He was named *Adolph B.*

A. B. became the life long pal of J. D. and the two were business partners until separated by the death of A. B. on June 8, 1924.

Adams reports that their financial discussions would be somewhat along this line:

"Oh, by the way, A. B., I think of putting a few millions into so and so."

"Sure! Go ahead, J. D., Fifty-fifty, of course, as usual!"

Such was the confidence one brother had in the integrity of the other.

Early horse car plods north along dusty 5th Street at "D" (now Broadway). Note the tall electric arc light mast used for early day street lighting.—Union Title

CHAPTER II
Through the Silver Gate

Someone left the ice box door open! This occurred, accidentally, aboard J. D.'s schooner yacht, the *Lurline.* He had purchased the boat in 1883 and, at the time, a balmy day in July 1887, was enjoying a cruise to nowhere in particular. But the lack of refrigeration had caused much of the stored food to spoil.

The *Lurline* was then off Pt. Loma so Skipper Spreckels decided to put into the Port of San Diego, in order to replenish the larder and to take on a supply of water.

The Great Land Boom of the Eighties was at its peak just then. The population of San Diego was estimated to be between 35,000 and 50,000.

Tourists flocked in, expecting to buy lots one day and to sell them the next at inflated prices. The professional boomers had taken over. Prices sometimes doubled over night. But stringencies were beginning to appear in the money market.

When it became known that one of the Spreckels millionaires was in town, the slickers immediately began plying their trade. One type of bait was to offer the promising prospect a city franchise of some kind. So, when J. D.

came ashore, he was greeted by a welcoming group, shown around the "City of Promise" and offered an extraordinarily valuable franchise. Again quoting Adams:

"What sort of a franchise?"

"A wharf franchise."

"A wharf franchise! My God! A wharf for what?"

But J. D. had already had a dream. He was thinking of an essential commodity of the period — *coal.* So he accepted the franchise.

The J. D. who sailed out of the *Harbor of the Sun* was not the same man who had entered it a few days before.

He came, he saw, he visioned. That vision was the turning point of his life. He had dreamed of seeing a big, beautiful city rise on the shore of San Diego Bay.

First Investments

During his stay in port, J. D. had become acquainted with Elisha S. Babcock, Jr., organizer and president of the *Coronado Beach Company.* Babcock had come to San Diego from Evansville, Indiana, in 1884 in search of health. He,

also, was a man of courage and vision.

With Hampton L. Story and others, he had purchased the North and the South Islands and the "Peninsula", the latter now known as the *Silver Strand.* These divided the ocean from San Diego Bay. The two islands were separated by a body of shallow water, called "Spanish Bight", with only a sand spit at the ocean front connecting them.

Selecting South Island, which they named *Coronado,* meaning the "crowned", a residential real estate development was started. The land was cleared and shrubs were planted. The *Coronado Beach Railroad,* with tracks from the bay front to the ocean beach on what is now Orange Avenue, was constructed. Horse power was used until a Baldwin steam dummy was received. It had been ordered as University Heights Motor Road No. 1.

The *San Diego & Coronado Ferry Company* was formed. A steam launch *Della* (Mr. Story had it shipped out from the east) which towed barges was first used. Then landing slips were built and the new double-end ferry boat *Coronado* was delivered and put in service. Another ferry, much larger than the

The Strand below Hotel del Coronado in the nineties. In the foreground is Coronado Railroad coach No. 11 standing on a spur track. The boat house is directly above the coach and the original bath house to the right. Bath house was later moved to Tent City and a new Bath House built on the ocean front.—Union Title

Hotel del Coronado as it neared completion in 1888. The power house is in the foreground, at the extreme left is a double deck Coronado Railroad car.—Union Title

and tracks were built from the ferry landing, around the south end of San Diego Bay to 5th and L Sts., in San Diego. It was known as the Coronado Belt Line.

But Babcock and his companies were hard pressed financially so he turned to Spreckels, hoping to interest him in the projects, which also included water developments on the Otay River. J. D. did come to the rescue and bought into the Coronado Beach Company, which owned all the subsidiaries. Within a year, he had bought out H. L. Story's shares and obtained a controlling interest. Within five years the Spreckels Brothers were the sole owners.

With the acqustion of the Story holdings, a one-third interest in the *San Diego Street Car Company*, which operated a system of horse car lines. was obtained.

Thus J. D. was already in the real estate business, hotel operations, rail and ferry transportations, water development, ice manufacturing, distribution of electricity, bath house, boat house and zoo management and other allied undertakings.

Coronado, was built on the Coronado shore and was named *Silver Gate*. Instead of side paddle wheels, it had propeller drives. But the craft proved to be slow and unwieldy. After it had badly damaged itself and wrecked the slips on both sides of the bay and drifted out of control several times, it was taken out of service. To relieve the desperate situation, a small ferry with paddle wheels and walking beam drive, the *Benicia*, was purchased, second hand, in the north and brought down.

The first auction sale of lots was held on November 13, 1886 and it was a tremendous success.

Babcock then proposed to build the world's largest seaside hotel and work was started on the foundations for the magnificent *Hotel del Coronado* in March 1887. Construction was well advanced at the time of J. D.'s visit.

The hotel was to be brilliantly illuminated with electric lights, so a power house and generating station were built south of the hotel. Ice manufacturing equipment was included in the power house.

The hotel, still unfinished, was formally opened February 1st, 1888, just as the Boom was about to collapse.

A bath house company was included in the development plans and a fine salt water plunge was built below the bluff, south of the hotel. And there was a pool for seals, a monkey house and an ancient turtle. A boat house was constructed on the bay side, the arm being called Glorietta Bay.

The *Coronado Railroad* was organized

First double end ferry Coronado enroute to Coronado. (Below) Coronado Beach Railroad steam dummy No. 1 at the Hotel del Coronado site in 1886.

Coal Bunkers

When that wharf franchise was presented to him, J. D's. thoughts turned to the inefficient way in which coal was being handled and rehandled. Coal was then the chief fuel used in industries, railroad locomotives and general heating.

It was brought into San Diego Harbor from New Zealand and Australia and British Columbia in sailing vessels. The practice was to unload it onto lighters, then hoist it to storage piles on the dock. From the piles it was loaded into coal cars. Much coal was lost in these operations.

J. D. knew that there was a better way. He would build a modern coal handling wharf at the foot of G St. in San Diego and he did. It was a wide one, with wood plank deck supported on wood piles. It was angled to provide easy berthing of the ships at the outer end.

On the central portion was built a long wooden structure high enough to provide sufficient storage space and to permit loading into cars or wagons through chutes by gravity. On top of the bunkers were tracks on which dump cars were operated back and forth by means of cables. At the outer end were towers which could be adjusted to the hold of the ship. The towers were fitted with hoisting apparatus. Steam engines furnished the power for the hoisting and cable operations.

Thus the coal would be loaded in a dump bucket in the hold; the bucket would be hoisted to the tower where it would be tripped, dumping its load into the cable car. The car then would be moved towards shore to the proper bin, dumped and hauled back.

A boiler on the wharf under the towers supplied the steam needed for the engines.

Railroad spurs extended along each side of the bunkers and, on the north side, out to the end of the wharf, several car lengths beyond the boiler.

The bunkers were a land mark for several decades.

To manage the business, the *Spreckels Brothers Commercial Co.* was formed. Lines of building materials and general merchandise were handled. Cement in wooden barrels was brought in from Europe and other places in sailing ships, which would be unloaded at the outer end of the wharf using a donkey engine (vertical boiler and steam operated winch). A profitable business was carried on.

When the Southern California Railway, originally the California Southern Rail Road, and its parent company, the Atchison, Topeka & Santa Fe Railroad, were financially embarrassed in the early nineties and threatened to discontinue service, J. D. kept the trains running by furnishing coal on credit.

The wharf also served the useful purpose of providing good fishing stands free to young and old for many years.

The Nineties

With the collapse of the Boom in 1888, the population of San Diego dropped rapidly. More than one-half of the town's people departed. The 1890 Census revealed that only 16,159 persons remained.

The Boom had brought many substantial improvements, including numerous commercial buildings and residences, a well designed sewerage system and horse car and steam motor lines to furnish transportation. But much of the construction was shoddy. Many cottages and stores were "California" type: boards with joints concealed with battens, the interior finish being wall paper on cloth backing.

Gasoline stoves were in general use for cooking and "coal oil" (kerosene) lamps and stoves for lighting and heating. Disastrous fires were frequent occurences. Only the plutocrats used open jet manufactured gas flames or the unreliable electric lamps for lighting.

General illumination for certain areas

Fifth Street, looking south as it appears in 1892—H. R. Fitch

of the city was provided by means of batteries of six electric carbon arc lamps mounted at the tops of 125 ft. high steel masts, installed at widely spaced intervals.

Most of the streets were unpaved, dusty in summer and morasses of sticky mud when it rained. Cement sidewalks were just coming into fashion, replacing planks or earth.

The early nineties were depression years. The Atchison, Topeka & Santa Fe Railroad became bankrupt in 1893 and passed into receivership. In settlement, the present company, The Atchi-

The Coal Bunker wharf was the first Spreckel investment in San Diego—Union Title

son, Topeka & Santa Fe Railway, was formed. Bank failures were frequent, with great losses to the depositors.

There was a band stand in the Plaza at 3rd and D (now Broadway) Sts. One of the principal entertainment features of the times was to listen to excellent concerts given by the City Guard Band.

One of the usual nocturnal adventures was: to get up, light the gas or lamp and hunt for fleas.

Water was scarce, as usual.

This was the town which J. D. Spreckels had resolved to build up into a prosperous city and began to spend million after million dollars to accomplish it.

He added to the list of his investments in 1890 by purchasing the newspaper, *The San Diego Union*, from Col. J. R. Berry.

Steamer Queen of the Pacific prepares to leave Pacific Coast Steamship Co.'s wharf at the foot of Fifth Street. Note steam dummy and Santa Fe boxcars on wharf.—R. V. Dodge

Get Water First

A l w a y s farsighted and thorough, Spreckels followed a logical development plan by saying: "Get your water first, for without water you get your population under false pretenses and they quit you when the water runs dry."

Babcock had started construction of the Lower Otay Dam as part of his Coronado project but had to get help to complete it. He got it from Spreckels.

But early in the nineties, there was a drouth and the Otay Dams were almost empty. The use of water had to be restricted.

To prevent a recurrence of this intolerable state of affairs, Spreckels and Babcock organized the *Southern California Mountain Water Company*, went 60 miles east into the mountains to get a safe yield and built the big Morena Dam, together with a conduit through the mountains and hills to make the water available.

Water was first delivered, under a contract, to San Diego City's mains on University Heights in August 1906.

Spreckels had plans prepared for a second large dam at Barrett, when the City of San Diego purchased the entire holdings in 1912.

The Spreckels' policy of keeping well

in advance of demand proved to be the savior of San Diego in the Flood of 1916. Lower Otay Dam failed completely, due to the undermining of the spillway, pouring death and devastation into the lower Otay Valley. Without the water from Morena, the City would have been in desperate circumstances.

Next: Transportation

Second in importance is Transportation. "Before you can hope to get people to live anywhere, . . . you must first of all show them that they can get there quickly, comfortably and, a b o v e all, cheaply." That was the Spreckels' theory.

Let us take a look at the local rail facilities that were available in 1890.

First, the main line railway was built by the California Southern Rail Road from National City, via Temecula Canyon, to Colton in 1882, to San Bernardino in 1883 and to Barstow, connecting with the Atlantic & Pacific Railroad, in 1885. The "branch" line from the junction north of Oceanside to Los Angeles opened in 1888. In a consolidation with other roads, the name was changed, in 1889, to *Southern California Railway*. These were all subsidiaries of the Atchison, Topeka & Santa Fe Railroad. Trains

were operated to Los Angeles, San Bernardino and Escondido. In 1891 the track through Temecula Canyon was washed out and it never was rebuilt between Fallbrook and Temecula stations.

Then, there was a short rail line on the *Pacific Coast Steamship Company's* wharf at the foot of 5th St. Steam dummies were used, starting in 1882, to haul passengers and freight, in cars, from ship to shore and vice versa.

Next, came the *San Diego Street Car Company*, with a system of horse or mule car lines, in 1886. It was cheap, perhaps, fairly comfortable but not quick.

Also Babcock and Story's *Coronado Beach Railroad* started operation in July 1886, from the ferry landing to the site of the hotel. In 1889, a horse racing track was built at the foot of 5th St., along Spanish Bight, and a branch rail line was laid on that street to serve it.

Later, the *Coronado Railroad* was constructed from the ferry landing, following the shore lines of San Diego Bay and Glorietta Bay, down the S i l v e r Strand, around the south end of San Diego Bay and up the eastern shore, passing through Chula Vista and National City, across Chollas Valley to San Diego to a terminus at 5th and L Sts.

It was known as the *Coronado Belt Line* and was opened in June 1888. For motive power it had 4 steam dummies which had been ordered for the University Heights Motor Road, another Babcock and Story enterprise, 4 little engines which had been purchased second hand from a New York Elevated line and an old Rogers American type (4-4-0) locomotive number 9.

For a time, excursion trains from Los Angeles were run through, around the bay, to the hotel.

Former New York Elevated No. 34 on the Coronado Railroad poses for wet plate camera in 1887. Engine became Coronado Railroad No. 5—H. R. Fitch

National City & Otay Railway train on Spring Canyon bridge near Sweetwater Dam about 1888.—R. V. Dodge

No smoking was allowed in the coaches, consequently the platforms would become dangerously crowded.

Trains were operated on the Belt Line intermittently during the nineties.

The *National City & Otay Railway* was built by the San Diego Land & Town Company, a Santa Fe subsidiary, and it also used 5th and L Sts. as a terminus. Steam motors furnished the power and trains operated through National City to Sweetwater Dam, starting in December 1887, and through Chula Vista and Otay to Oneonta January 1, 1888. Extensions were made to La Presa and to Tijuana, California.

There was keen competition between the Coronado and the N. C. & O. For a short time a total of 104 trains were operated between San Diego and National City daily by the two roads. By agreement in September 1888, the trains were alternated on a half hour basis. Shortly after that service was drastically curtailed.

There was also competition between engineers to determine which one could get first to the crossing at what is now 34th St. and Dalbergia St., in Chollas Valley. Following a near miss, restraining orders were issued.

The N. C. & O. built a short-lived feeder horse car line on 7th St. in San Diego from L to F Sts. and the Coronado Railroad operated one in National City.

The *San Diego & Old Town Railroad* constructed a line from D St., out Arctic St. (now Kettner Blvd.) to Old Town. Originally planned as a steam motor line, it was used as an experimental electric railway for the Electric Rapid Transit Company. The joint electric and steam dummy operation began on Nov. 19, 1887. It was the opinion that the electric motors started smoothly and are a great improvement over the steam dummies. Passengers marvelled at the brilliant sparks from the revolving wheels, the mysterious power coming through the overhead wire. The generating plant was located in a brickyard on India St., near Kalmia.

In mid-December, the poles and wires were taken down and all electric equipment was transferred to a new line of the E. R. T. on 4th St.

The steam road was extended to the college campus at Pacific Beach. A crossing was made with the California Southern RR. at Old Town and the new track was laid parallel with the latter's

San Diego & Old Town Railway's first engine was this steam dummy. Later corporate name was changed to San Diego & Pacific Beach Railway—H. R. Fitch

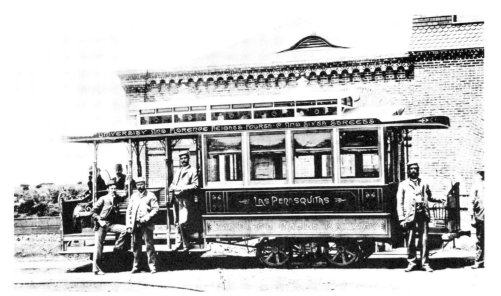

San Diego Cable Railway Las Penasquitas at the power house on the corner of 4th and Spruce about 1890.—F. W. Reif

ing, failed and the road was forced to close down after just thirteen months of operation. Sporadic attempts were subsequently made to run the cable cars.

Boom Failures

Three other railway projects, built and operated for a time during the Boom, are significant, as portions of their lines or franchises were later directly or indirectly utilized.

One was the *Park Belt Motor Road*, sometimes called the *City & University Heights Railroad* or *University Heights Motor Road*. This was one of the Babcock and Story projects, to further real estate development in Steiner, Klauber, Choate and Castle and other additions. It began at 18th and A Sts., to which point the San Diego Street Car Company's horse car line was extended; on D St. (now Broadway) from 12th to 16th Sts., to C St., to 18th St. to A St. The road then entered City (now Balboa) Park, was built up Switzer Canyon, then up the canyon over which the former 30th St. bridge spanned, to Bancroft and Upas Sts., twisted back then around and down to cross Wabash Canyon, up the east side, curving back and forth, finally following what is now Marlborough St. from Thorn to Steiner St. (now University Ave. in East San Diego) to a terminus which was soon called "Phantom City". It was just wild country.

Returning, the line followed Univer-

along the east shore of False (now Mission) Bay. A race track was built at the curve into Grand Ave. The name of the road was then changed to *San Diego, Old Town & Pacific Beach*. Two new steam motors were received from Baldwin Locomotive Works and trains started running to Pacific Beach April 16, 1888. The tracks were soon extended on Grand Ave. to the ocean front.

The final extension was made, in 1894, to La Jolla and the corporate name was changed again, to *San Diego, Pacific Beach & La Jolla*.

Construction was begun, in 1889, on what was expected to be the beginning of a new transcontinental railroad. It was given the name *San Diego, Cuyamaca & Eastern Railway*. Reports were that 675,000 ties, enough for a railroad to Yuma, and 20,000 tons of rails had been ordered, also, one locomotive. The road was opened from 9th and N (now Commercial) St. in San Diego to Lemon Grove, La Mesa and Lakeside on March 30, 1889, using engine number 106 which had been leased from the Southern Pacific and number 9 borrowed from the Coronado RR.

Sort of pseudonymous! The line was extended 3.3 miles up the river to Foster and that was as far east as it ever went.

Last, the *San Diego Cable Railway Company* was organized in 1889 with articles of incorporation for $500,000, to exist for 50 years. The tracks were 3 ft. 6 inch gauge with cast iron cable yokes on four ft. centers. The system was divided into two sections, with the power house located at the mid point, at 4th and Spruce Sts. The "town" section extended down 4th St., to C St., to 6th St., to a turn table at L St. The cable winder was designed for a speed of 8 miles per hour.

The "mesa" section was to be high speed — 10 miles per hour. It ran

north on 4th to what is now University Ave., to Normal St., passing the site of the San Diego College of Arts and Letters, to Park Blvd. to the "Bluffs" at Adams Ave., overlooking Mission Valley. Work was started on a recreation pavilion in a 5 acre park.

The line was single track with occasional turn-outs. The cable ran in both directions in the same slot.

12 double truck cars, including at least one open car, were purchased and were given names instead of numbers. Designed by Van Vleck, they were beauties, with stained glass in the clerestory windows, kerosene dome lights and electric buzzers.

Operation began on June 7, 1890 and it was expected that the loss would be $100 a day at the start.

But the California National Bank, which was providing the financial back-

San Diego Cable Railway car decked with bunting and brass band in celebration of opening day of the line.—F. W. Reif

University Heights Motor Road (Park Belt Line)—Jerry MacMullen

sity Ave., jogging and meandering up hill and down dale to Florida St., to Robinson St., where curves and trestles carried it on Essex St., to 5th St., to Fir St., again connecting with the San Diego Street Car system.

Four steam dummies had been ordered from Baldwin Locomotive Works for the University Heights Motor Road. The line was actually completed and the first trip, "girdling the Park", was made on July 7, 1888.

An open horse car on D St., at 5th St., bore a dash sign: "This car for Park Belt Motor Road." At 18th & A Sts., the horses were taken off and a steam motor took over, hauling the horse car around the portion of the loop to 5th and Fir Sts. There the motor cut off and horses finished the run to 5th and D Sts. The length of the line was over 10 miles.

But the Boom had collapsed and the trains soon stopped running, despite the contract to operate 3 trains daily for a period of 10 years. The motors were made the property of the Coronado Railroad.

Efforts were made in October 1889 to induce the Receiver to operate over a portion of the road, without success.

The *Electric Rapid Transit* has been mentioned as operating, more or less successfully, an experimental line on Arctic St., to Old Town. Contracts had been signed with the Henry Electric Railway Company to build several railroads, the principal one to be in San Diego. Professor J. C. Henry was the inventor of a system using a flexible cable to tow a "troller" to conduct electric current

from an overhead wire to the car motors. The troller consisted of a frame with a pair of grooved wheels placed horizontally on each side. The wheels were pushed by springs against the trolley wire. Two wires were required, the outbound cars using one and the in-bound the other.

Work had been progressing on lines on 4th St. and on G St. The company had a contract with the San Diego College of Arts and Letters to complete an electric line to the campus in University Heights by January 1, 1888. This was a physical impossibility.

So, the experimental line on Arctic St. was taken down and re-installed on 4th St., from the Pacific Coast Steamship depot, at the bay front, north as far as Fir St. The motor cars and trailers were transferred and service began on December 31st, 1887. It was pronounced a phenomenal success "despite the croakers". It was the first electric railway to climb 8 to 9 per cent grades hauling a trailer.

The route continued out 4th St. to what is now University Ave., to University Blvd. (now Normal St.), to at least as far as the road to El Cajon. Plans had been projected to extend the line to La Mesa Colony.

The operators were called "Motorneers" or "Motioneers".

Breakdowns and interferences were frequent, disrupting traffic. The road shut down for "two weeks" in June 1888 for alterations and repairs. It started up again 6 weeks later. It was down again in October on account of an oil famine. Notice was given on Dec. 5th: "Will not operate to-day on account of moving machinery."

Mischievous boys threw stones at the trolley wires. When there was a direct hit, there would be a resounding zing, much to the delight of the youngsters but scaring horses and disturbing the tranquility of nearby residents.

The company distributed electricity, in competition with the San Diego Gas & Electric Light Company, and lost out in a legal battle over the required height of poles for light wires. This was a staggering blow.

By June 1889, the losses were amounting to $20 a day and the line folded up.

Electric Rapid Transit dragging a four wheeled "troller" along an overhead wire on upper Fourth Street in 1888.—F. W. Reif

At the time, San Diego had a professional railroad promoter, named William H. Carlson. One of his prolific schemes, was to build a street car line from San Diego via Old Town to Ocean Beach. Soon it was decided to start at Old Town where it would connect with the San Diego, Old Town & Pacific Beach Railroad. As actually constructed, the *Ocean Beach Railroad* began somewhere in Roseville, on the bay side of Pt. Loma, climbed up the hill, probably via Wabaska Canyon, and down to the "Cliff House" resort, a hotel which Carlson and Higgins had erected, at Ocean Beach, the latter being more commonly known as "The Mussel Beds" in those days.

Having no motive power of his own, Carlson rented a steam dummy from the Pacific Coast Steamship Company. He wanted to transport the engine to Roseville on a lighter but the Steamship Co. said "No!". The motor had to be partially dismantled, loaded on a horse drawn dray and laboriously hauled over bad roads to the railroad. The dray mired down several times. This delayed the "grand opening" a few days.

The first train reached the Cliff House on April 16, 1888. Regular service was then inaugurated and it lasted for a short time. A ferry, probably a steam launch, was operated from the foot of H (now Market) St., San Diego, to Roseville.

Carlson did not pay the rent for the use of the dummy. The next time he went out to look over his railroad, he found that the rails had disappeared. The Steamship Co. had torn them up and hauled them to its warehouse for safe keeping.

California Southern Railroad Nos. 2 and 12 with picnic train at Oceanside in 1883. (Below) Opening day on the San Diego, Cuyamaca & Eastern at Lakeside in 1889, with borrowed Southern Pacific, Coronado Railroad and National City & Otay equipment.

CHAPTER III
San Diego Electric Railway Organized

Boiling down the foregoing, in the last quarter of 1891, the only rail transportation facilities in regular operation were the six steam lines and a limited horse car system. These fell far short of measuring up to the Spreckels' standard for promotion of civic growth and something had to be done to improve the situation.

Accordingly, on November 30th, the *San Diego Electric Railway Company* was incorporated. J. D. was named as a Director along with A. B. as President, Babcock as Vice President, C. T. Hinde and J. A. Flint as Treasurer and Secretary respectively. Flint was also general manager.

The purpose of the corporation was to construct, purchase, maintain and operate a street railway in the County of San Diego. Provision was made for the acquisition of the San Diego Street Car Company.

In a few years William Clayton became the General Manager, later earning the title "Vice President and Managing Director" of the Spreckels companies.

For some time Babcock acted as the Agent for the Spreckels Brothers in many transactions. In some cases it became difficult to determine if he was acting as J. D's representative or in his own behalf.

The fact that the name — San Diego Electric Railway Company continued unchanged from the date of incorporation in 1891 down to the time of the sale of the properties in 1948 is quite remarkable in street railway annals. Thus complex corporate entities generally associated in the characteristic financial maneuverings are absent.

Railway Absorbed

The *San Diego Street Car Company* had been incorporated in 1886. It had built lines on H (now Market) St., on 5th St., on D St. (now Broadway), on Arctic St. (now Kettner Blvd.), on Fir St., on First St., on 16th St., to South 20th St., (now 16th St.), to Milton Ave. (now National Ave.) to National Ave., to 31st., and on F St. For a time it operated on Atlantic St. (now Pacific Highway), on South 22nd St. (now Beardsley St.) and over Harrison Ave. to 28th St., after the National City & Otay Railway had abandoned its trackage there.

Laid with light, mostly flat iron, approximately 8½ miles of lines were in operation at the end of 1891.

The cars were typical of horse powered systems, single truck, seating capacities from 16 to 32, some closed, some open and a few of a semi-convertible type. Cars 1 to 6 incl. were built by Terre Haute Company, 7 to 12 incl. by The Pullman Company, 13 to 18 incl. by the J. G. Brill Company and 20 to 31 incl. by St. Louis Car Company. (No record of 19). They cost about $1,500 a piece.

The first car barn with stables, harness and blacksmith shops and a hay loft, was built at the southeast corner of 7th and H Sts., fronting on H Street. The capacities were 15 cars and 100 horses.

In 1888, larger facilities, of similar construction and including a corral, were erected at the south westerly corner of Arctic and D Sts. The car storage space, 36 feet by 150 feet, had rated capacity of 20 cars, the number of horse stalls being the same.

The grand opening on 5th Street had been a great event on July 3rd, 1886.

The Fifth St. line operated from a point between K and L Sts. north to Florence Heights at Fir St. Two horses were used up to the foot of the hill at A St. There a third horse was hitched on to drag the car up the grade. The tracks were extended on Fir St. to serve the renowned Florence Hotel, at 3rd St.

H. L. Story was given a citation on July 24, 1888 for allowing a car on 5th St. to speed exceeding 8 miles per hour.

Horse car at the foot of Fifth Street in early 1887. California Southern main line ran behind Pacific Coast warehouse.—H. R. Fitch

Poor horses!

But the transportation business did not prosper after the Boom had collapsed. Creditors filed claims in November 1889.

So, at a Receiver's sale, the San Diego Electric Railway bought the entire system on January 30, 1892 for the sum of $115,000. Included in the deal were: 30 horse cars, 148 horses, 40 sets of harness, 108 extra horse collars, plus horseshoes, hay, etc.

In addition to the horse car company, the San Diego Electric Railway acquired the trackage of the *Park Belt Line* or the *City & University Heights Motor Road.* Portions of the right of way of the *Electric Rapid Transit Company,* as predecessor of the San Diego Cable Railway and its successor, the Citizens Traction Company, were used later, as were those of the *Ocean Beach Railroad,* as predecessor of the Pt. Loma Railroad.

Conversion

Then came the task of changing over from horse to electromotive power. This involved the re-arranging and the relaying of the tracks with heavier rail, the laying of second tracks and extensions, the installing of overhead trolley wires with pole lines, span supports and feeders, the erecting and the equipping of a power plant, car house and shops, the purchasing of new cars and the adapting of old horse car bodies for electric operation and all the necessary auxiliary paraphernalia.

The Car House and Shops Building, 134 ft. x 106 ft., was erected at the northwest corner of Arctic St. (now Kettner Blvd.) and E St., with the Boiler Room, 58 ft. x 61 ft., and the Engine Room, 105 ft. x 62 ft, adjoining to the west, extending to California St., where the Southern California Railway's tracks were located. The brick smokestack was 125 ft. high.

The Car House was equipped with a transfer table for full utilization of the 8 stub storage tracks, holding 22 cars. The entrance door was located on E St., with a turn out from the Arctic St., track.

In the Engine Room was installed a Risdon-Corliss 300 Horse Power horizontal Steam Engine, 16" and 30" diameter cylinders x 42" stroke, with cam operated poppet valves, fly ball governor, 18 ft. diameter fly wheel and it was long belt-connected to drive two Thompson-Houston multi-polar direct current Generators, about 100 Kilowatt capacity (120 Horse Power) each. It was a fascinating sight to watch the rhythmic operation of such a piece of machinery. In 1893 a Ball tandem compound Steam Engine, 250 Horse Power, was

Early horse drawn tower car. (Below) Electric car No. 6 grinds north on Fifth Street. This was the first car to run over the new electric railway in 1892.—Both F. W. Reif

set up to drive two 90 Kilowatt Generators. (The record shows that a new Generator, 275 Horse Power was installed in 1896.)

The plant was "brilliantly lighted by 100 — 16 candle power" electric lamps.

There were three Babcock and Wilcox water tube Boilers, 103 Boiler Horse Power each, in the original installation.

During the conversion period, horse car traffic had to be maintained. Many of the proposed changes and extensions were delayed, waiting for street improvements to be completed.

The electrification started on Arctic St., at the car house, with the re-railing of the single track from E. St. to D St., and double track from E St. to H St. (now Market St.) with 30 lb. T rail. On H St., double tracks were laid

from Atlantic St. (now Pacific Highway) to east of 5th St., using 51½ lb. girder rail. From H and Atlantic Sts., 38 lb. girder rail was placed in the double track on the Santa Fe, formerly the Babcock and Story Wharf.

On H St., from east of 5th St., 30 lb. T rail was used in the double track to 16th St., to Logan Ave., to 20th St., single track to 26th St., double track to 29th St., on National Ave., and single track to the end east of 31st.

Next, on 5th St., double tracks were laid from L St. to Upas St., using 38 lb girder rail, and double tracks from Upas St. to University Ave., with 30 lb. T rail.

The system trackage aggregated, on December 31st, 1892, 16.70 miles of equivalent single track, of which 12.21

miles were electrified and 4.49 miles were horse car lines.

The San Diego Sun of September 19, 1892 reported: "Car No. 6 (as described in the next section) speeds over the electric line at 8:45 this morning with A. C. Jewett at the brakes." Many horses were frightened on the shake-down runs. In several places stops were necessary to clear the tracks which passing teams had covered. The plans were to start service the next day but a notice was posted "Not operating to-day. Men too inexperienced."

On September 21st double decker car No. 1 made a trial trip, carrying many of the City's notables.

D St. lines were electrified in 1893 from Arctic St. to 5th St. and the double track was extended from the car house to Front St., all with 30 lb. T rail. The portion of the D St. line from 5th to near 17th St. was also converted in January. Then the horse car connection to the defunct Park Belt Motor Line at 18th and A Sts. was abandoned. Horse car service was discontinued in 1st St. from H St. to D St. and on the F St. Line and the tracks were torn up.

Further expansion took place in 1895, by extending the D St. Line from 16th St. to 25th St., with 30 lb. T rail.

Due to the steep grades, the horse car line on 1st St., north from D St., could not operate north of Date St., so it turned off to Front St., to Fir St., to Union St. to Ivy St. The turn-off portion was abandoned and the excavation for a new line, continuing up 1st St., had reached Fir St. in the middle of June 1896. It was single track with 30 lb. T rail. The first electric car made the run to the terminus at Laurel St. on June 30th. With it went the horse smells and other things and the memories of boarding a car, then opening a slide in the front door and poking the

This double decker officially opened passenger service on the San Diego Electric Railway on September 21, 1892. Among the notables aboard are A. E. Horton, Mayor Sherman, J. C. Fisher, and representing the railway were E. S. Babcock, Jr., Capt. Hinde, H. L. Titus, J. A. Flint and M. J. Perrin—R. C. Brandt

driver to pay the fare or get change. When you wanted off, you pulled a cord which rang a regulation street car bell on the platform. Quite a thrill for the smaller fry!

The new cars had motormen and conductors.

The 1st St. and the D St. Lines were paired on December 23, 1896.

The second track on the Santa Fe Wharf was abandoned and a line change was made, taking out the curve to the west arm of the wharf and extending the electric car route to the new ferry building.

In August, 1896, a franchise was obtained for a new line on K St., from 16th St. to 22nd St. to H St., to 25th St., to D St. However, the track was laid from 16th and K Sts. to 22nd and H Sts. only and shuttle service was started in 1897.

The mileage at the end of 1897 totaled 16.70 equivalent single track, the same as in 1892, but all electric.

Rolling Stock

The more reliable pole trolleys had now outmoded the whimsical trollers of the Henry System.

Ten single truck, single trolley, open platform cars were purchased from the J. G. Brill Company, of Philadelphia, Pa., in 1892. The bodies were of wooden construction. The controllers or commutators and reversing switches were mounted under the floor and were connected by chains to a shaft and a tube in a vertical control column fastened to the dash. Thus, by means of two special handles at the top of the column, the motorman could control the speed or reverse the motion with his left hand while his right hand wound up or released the hand brake.

According to the records, the original electric equipment on all 10 cars and also on the 5 others to follow included Thompson-Houston type WP 30 motors, 15 horse power.

The cars were painted golden yellow and were attractively decorated with stencilled designs in gold leaf and brown shading.

Numbers 1 and 2 were double deckers while numbers 3 to 8 inclusive were of similar basic construction but single deck. Each had three windows in the central closed section with one transverse bench on each platform. On account of the space required for the winding stairways on the double deckers, stoop or platform extensions were

Early electric car at the Southern California Railway station.—R. V. Dodge

San Diego & Coronado Ferry Company's Benicia crossing San Diego Bay. The Benicia was used as a cattle boat on San Francisco Bay before coming to San Diego. Note the walking beam and the tall stack. A three master sits at anchor in the bay behind the Benicia.— Union Title

added to each end to accommodate the motorman and the controls.

The trucks on the double deckers were changed out to a heavier model with 2 General Electric No. 800 motors in 1896.

The bodies of cars numbers 9 and 10 were semi-closed type. As received, they had transverse seats, six large window openings with no glass and two small glazed windows on each side. A canvas roll-up curtain was provided, full length on each side, for weather protection. Soon the openings were glazed and the seats were changed to longitudinal. Then they were called "box cars" and the fresh air enthusiasts did not like them.

Car number 11 was also a closed box car. Entries indicate that, in 1895, the body of horse car No. 25, built by the St. Louis Car Company, was remodelled into seven openings, with glass, per side, retaining the open platforms. New doors, longitudinal seats, a pole trolley,

Array of electric cars at Fifth and H Streets. (Below) City Marshal, crew and passengers pose for the camera in 1892.—F. W. Reif

etc. were installed. One Peckham long wheel base single truck was purchased along with two second hand WP 30 motors and No. 168 WP 40 commutators.

Numbers 12 to 15 inclusive were evidently open horse car bodies, having 4 fixed double (back to back) transverse benches, mounted on Brill single trucks No. 10, which had been ordered for them in 1893. No. 13 was soon converted for service as "Wrecker" or "Tool Car."

Tongue switches were operated by the motorman using a long switch iron. The handle end hung on a hook on the dash, the lower part resting against the coupler, when not in use. Great was the admiration of the youth of the age when the motorman would take up the iron and, with marvelous dexterity, would throw the switch without stopping the car.

After a few years the "wind-up" type of controllers was changed to the conventional K-2 box type on all the cars.

Original Network

Upon completion of the conversion, the additions and the line changes, the electric lines consisted of the following routes:

Fifth St. and Logan Heights Lines From University Ave. on 5th St. to H St., to 16th St., to Logan Ave., to 26th St., to National Ave. to east of 31st St.

First and D Streets Lines From Laurel on 1st St., to D St., to 25th St., on Golden Hill.

Depot Line: From Pacific Coast Steamship, National City & Otay and Coronado Railroad depots at L St. on 5th St. to D St., to San Diego, Pacific Beach & La Jolla and Southern California Railway depots between Arctic and California Sts.

Ferry Line: From the landing on the Santa Fe Wharf (Babcock and Story built the wharf but sold it in June 1887 to the California Central Railway, an Atchison, Topeka & Santa Fe RR. subsidiary.) to H St., to Arctic St., to D St., to 5th St., to H St. to ferry.

K Street Shuttle: From 16th St., on K St., to 22nd St., to H St.

Without a doubt, J. D. had given San Diego one of the finest electric street car systems for a town of its size in the country. Later, J. D. explained his position by saying: "I made those larger investments to protect the investments I had already made. It was just plain business sense. The city would not grow without an abundant water supply and adequate street car facilities. If San Diego did not grow, my big investments would not pay."

Coronado Beach R. R. Electrified

Some of the Spreckels' companies were so closely interwoven, that they must be treated concomitantly. The San Diego Electric Railway, the San Diego

& Coronado Ferry and the Coronado Beach RR. were operated in conjunction to provide regular connecting service from 5th and D Sts., San Diego, to Hotel del Coronado.

Plans were made to convert the Orange Ave. line from steam to electric operation about the same time those for the San Diego Electric Railway were prepared.

Two cars were ordered from The J. G. Brill Company. They were numbered in the 40 series so as not to conflict.

No. 41 was a double truck, single pole trolley, open platform double decker, larger than the ones in San Diego. Stoops or verandas extended at both ends to accommodate the motorman and the controls. The central closed section had four windows and there were two benches outside at each end. Hand brakes were the dog and ratchet wheel type.

No. 42 was a single truck car similar to numbers 4 to 8 inclusive in San Diego.

The track was reconditioned and the overhead was installed. On October 6, 1893 "The electric car made a trial trip over Orange Ave."

The smaller car, 42, was used regularly on week days, while the double decker handled the crowds on Sundays and special occasions.

It was a treat to make the street car-ferry-street car ride on a Sunday afternoon and to play on the beach below the hotel.

Later a wooden car house was built at 1st St. and Orange Ave.

Dust Palliation

With unpaved streets and a dry climate, dust was a major nuisance most of the year. Streets had to be sprinkled frequently, using horse-drawn tank wagons fitted with two sprinkler heads at the back. The tank would be filled at the nearest fire hydrant. It was a slow process. The theory was that the electric railway could do it better, quicker and cheaper.

So, in 1898, a 5,000 gallon wide-throwing Street Sprinkling Car was received from Miller-Knoblock Company of South Bend, Indiana, at a cost of $3,100. It had double, long wheel base trucks with 2-27 horse power motors, motor driven pumps, a large sprinkler to cover the area of the roadway from the car to the curb, if any, and a small one to sprinkle the track area. It was equipped with "an elaborate system of brakes". It bore number 103.

An article in the San Diegan Sun furnished the information that 5,000 gallons of salt water, which weighs 8.43 pounds per gallon, made a total load of 42,150 pounds. The empty car weighs 10 tons, so that the weight when full is about 31 tons.

A storage tank was erected at the Power Plant and a connection was made so that the car tank could be filled at the foot of D St. As fresh water was generally short of supply, salt water from the bay was used.

On December 24th, the Sun reported "The big sprinkling car does some good work . . . E. S. Babcock decided he could make several people happy by running the big sprinkling car up and down 5th St. just about once. The work of the sprinkling car is very thorough and the street as wet down from curb to curb."

It was the plan to sprinkle all the streets traversed by car lines daily, during the dry season at least. These were listed as:

D Street, from foot (California St.) to	
25th Street	8,960 ft.
H Street	16,720 ft.
K Street	3,660 ft.
5th Street	14,060 ft.
1st Street	6,080 ft.

The hills on 5th Street, 1st Street and on D Street are quite steep and there was not sufficient motor power to operate with a full tank. A bid was offered on sprinkling the streets "where grades are not excessive" at 55 cents per 1,000 gallons. This was not accepted, at the time, by the Board of Public Works.

New trucks with 4 motor equipment, including GE No. 52 motors, were ordered and were installed in 1899 and the car was outfitted with an additional pump and large sprinkler. Then it could make the grades and sprinkle the entire roadway in one pass.

When barefoot, you could not roll up your short pants and follow in the

Coronado Railroad No. 41 was longer than San Diego double deckers.—F. W. Reif

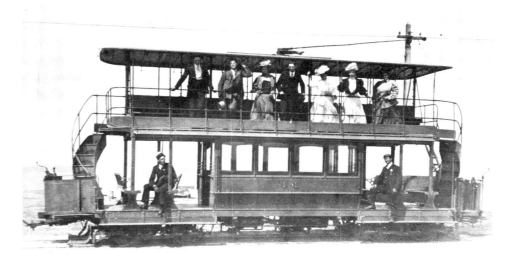

Coronado Railroad trolley at the end of the line at Hotel del Coronado in the 1890's.—R. C. Brandt

water gushing from the sprinklers or No. 103 like you could with the sprinkling wagons.

When concentrations of salt formed in the streets, drivers began to complain that the tires on their carriages or wagons rusted out quickly. After a few years, the sprinkling operations were discontinued.

While waiting for the new trucks and the pump equipment, the tank and the sprinkling apparatus had been removed and the chassis was used as a work flat car to haul track materials. After the sprinkling of streets was discontinued, the car was converted permanently into a Work Flat with open center controls and was used in the building of new car lines.

Citizen Traction Competes

Along in August, 1895, George B. Kerper, of Cincinnati, who had bought the remains of the San Diego Cable Railway for the sum of $17,600, came out to convert the line into an electric system and organized the *Citizens Traction Company*. On September 26th "The engines in the . . . power house were 'fired up' . . . to test the machinery."

After some legal entanglements were settled, a contract was signed for the setting of poles. Two Bi-polar Generators were installed to replace the cable winding equipment. The cable grips were removed and 25 Horse Power motors, controllers with wiring and single pole trolleys were added to nine cars.

Railway street sprinkler trying to keep down the dust in 1900—E. L. Whitson

Two were altered for trailer service. Since the motorman did not require as much room as the gripman did, the front seats were extended across the cars.

What a choice place to ride! Up in front of the motorman with the knobs on the dash simulating controls!

On July 24th, 1896, the first converted car ran the entire length of the line following the same route the cable cars did, namely: From the "Bluff" at Adams Ave., on Park Blvd. to Normal St., to University Ave., to 4th St., to C St., to 6th St., to L St. The line was opened on the 28th with five cars in regular service. The length of the road was 4.7 miles plus turnouts.

Work began on the restoration of the pavilion and grounds, now named Mission Cliff Park.

Kerper proposed to build an inclined railway, like the one on Mt. Lowe, to the floor of the valley, then run a car line out to the old Mission of San Diego de Alcala.

The cars, being double trucked, ran and rode much smoother than the single truck cars of the San Diego Electric Railway.

But, in January 1897, the Risdon Iron Works placed an attachment on the properties in the amount of $2,400. The Court appointed Mr. A. D. Norman as Receiver on February 12, 1897. In an effort to reduce the expenses, wages were cut. After 7 months' operation Mr. Norman died suddenly. Mr. A. E. Dodson succeeded him on September 17th. Dodson made a desperate effort to put the road on a paying basis. Oil burners were installed under the boilers, saving $20 a day by the substitution for the expensive coal. Wages were restored to a living basis. To keep the road in operation Receiver's Certificates were issued.

One day, when a payroll had to be met and there were $4,500 unsold certificates, the only prospective purchaser was the San Diego Electric Railway Co. An apparently reluctant sale was made, to keep the road running a while longer. But the daily receipts were not sufficient to pay the expenses, so the Receiver had to advertise the road for sale to the highest bidder.

In February 1898 the Citizens Traction Company was sold to E. S. Babcock and wife, as agents for the Spreckels' interests, for the amount of the Receiver's Certificates outstanding — namely $19,000 plus fees and costs. The San Diego Electric Railway Co. acquired the properties and franchises on March 23, 1898.

Included in the transaction were the tracks, overhead lines, real estate, a hotel the combination Power Plant and Car House, machinery and the rolling stock, 12 cars.

Deeds for the Power House block at 4th and Spruce Sts., 3 blocks, including Mission Cliff Park, on Adams Ave., plus two other parcels of land were obtained and equities in two contracts covering 550 lots were acquired.

The College Hill Land Association had entered into a contract by which it was to transfer to Mr. Kerper and Citizens Traction Company certain lots in University Heights as a subsidy and consideration of their operating their road in the face of an opposition line to sparsely settled country for a period of three years continuously.

As soon as the San Diego Electric Railway got control, they made a flat demand for the Kerper Subsidy, although they simply agreed to operate the line from 5th St. and University Ave. to Mission Cliff and abandoned the remainder. The Association's stockholders thought that they were being held up. Finally one of them said: "I move that we be robbed." Subsequently 327 lots were acquired by the San Diego Electric Railway Co. on account of the equities.

Thereupon, service was temporarily discontinued, the track gauge was widened to standard 4 feet 8½ inches from

Mission Cliff to 5th St. and University Ave., a connection was made to the 5th Street line and through service to the pavilion was begun.

The Power Plant and Car House were abandoned, also four of the cars.

J. D. had favored the name Mission Cliff Gardens for the park. It was developed into a refined recreation spot. There were games, magic lantern shows, soft refreshments and, on Sundays, concerts were provided. Summer houses were built at scenic points, over looking Mission Valley. Later there was an ostrich

farm and, at various times, children's playgrounds, merry-go-round, ferris wheel miniature Japanese gardens, a deer park, a bird house, a pheasant yard, a silk production exhibit and other attractions were added. The park was used for many picnics.

The abandoned tracks on 4th St., C St., and 6th St. were removed in 1903.

(Note: Cast iron cable yokes were unearthed on C St. during the laying of storm drains in July 1955. One is now on exhibition as a relic in the Junipero Serra Museum in Presidio Park.)

Chassis for street sprinkler was used as a work car. (Below) One of the cable cars converted to electric operation by Citizens Traction Company in 1896. Note the lever hand brakes on the car.—R. C. Brandt

CHAPTER IV
1900's - Era of Growth

Ring out the old, ring in the new! January 1, 1900 meant the end of the 19th Century. Or did it? Exceptions will, no doubt, be taken to this statement, as they were in 1900, when the consensus of opinion was that the ones who won were the Naught-y Ones. Anyway, the calendar changed from 1899 to 1900 on that date.

J. D. may have thought that he had already made large investments in San Diego and Coronado but he "hadn't seen anything yet". The first quarter of the 20th Century lay before him.

Despite the vast sums he had ploughed into San Diego, the town had not yet begun to grow. The 1900 Census listed only 17,700 inhabitants. As one native explained it. 'Yeah! The population stays 'bout the same. Seems like every time a baby is born, someone leaves town.'

Gas and electricity were coming into more general use.

Some downtown streets were being improved and paved.

A small theatre on 4th St., opposite the Plaza, had shown one of the first moving pictures "The Lightning Express". What excitement when the engine rushed down the track towards you, its wheels rotating backwards!

The automobile had not yet become a menace but a man in Coronado had rigged up a buckboard with a one cylinder gasoline engine drive and proudly drove his "horseless carriage" around the town. Soon the merry Oldsmobile would be on the way.

An elegant bath house, with a large plunge tank and also tub baths, had been built in 1897 by Graham E. Babcock on property leased from the San Diego Electric Railway Co. on the southeast corner of D and California Sts., across from the Southern California Railway (Santa Fe Route) depot. It was named *Los Banos.* Warm salt water came from the power house adjoining.

In addition to a slide and some spring-boards, there was a series of rings suspended by ropes over the deep part of the pool. Many were the demonstrations of feats of strength, swinging from one ring to the next over the water. Those not so strong, lost their grip and there would be a big splash.

J. D. purchased the San Diego newspaper, *The Evening Tribune,* in 1901.

Some inter-corporate manipulations by The Atchison, Topeka & Santa Fe Railway Company took place. A lease arrangement was made with the Southern California Railway Company in June, 1904. Then, on the 17th of January

1906, the Southern California Railway was "sold" to the Santa Fe. Since that date it has been Santa Fe all the way.

Tenting Tonight

Early in 1900, a development was worked out which became an immediate success. It was the unique *Coronado Tent City.*

The ground or sand on the Strand below the Bathhouse was leveled and enlarged by dredging on the bay side. Then several hundred tents and palm-leaf-covered cottages were set up. Permanent buildings, marked "Men" and "Women" alternately, were erected at frequent intervals throughout the "city".

A recreation center was constructed which included a restaurant, auditorium with a dance floor, and a band stand or shell. There were seat benches in front of the latter. There were tables and benches for picnickers, a shallow pool for children, stores and concessions.

Then the unfortunate ferryboat Silver Gate was made fast just off shore on the bay side and was converted into an attractive "floating casino".

The outstanding Ohlmeyer's Band gave regular free concerts afternoons and evenings.

"Here is boating, bathing, fishing and all the pleasures of camp life combined with most of the conveniences of life in the city."

Coronado Tent City was soon famed the world over.

To serve the new summer resort, the Orange Ave. electric line was extended from the Hotel terminal, down the hill to a junction with the Belt Line. The latter's track was converted for electric operation through the "city". A side track was put in at the lower end for switching.

Both cars 41 and 42 were used and on special occasion, when large crowds had to be handled, each pulled two Coronado Railroad open cars as trailers. It was a marvel that little 42 could make it up the hill with her train.

Los Banos plunge in 1897 opposite the Santa Fe depot—Union Title

Coronado Tent City in the early 1900's. The jetty at the left protects hotel from the ocean's erosive action. Bath house below hotel rotunda at left, note boat house on the bay. Doubledecker No. 41 hauls a trailer through tent camp bound for Hotel del Coronado.—Union Title

Coronado Tent City with Coronado Railroad electric car about 1905. (Below) The hull of ferry Silver Gate was fitted as a floating casino. (Lower) San Diego & Coronado Ferry Ramona.

To celebrate the Fourth of July at Tent City became an annual event. The crowds would be larger than could be handled by the ferry and the street cars, so steam trains would be operated around the bay. Naturally, most of the younger generation would choose the 20 mile train ride.

Later, when the Silver Gate was withdrawn, a large building was erected to house the casino facilities. It also had bowling alleys.

One summer the unusual happened. There was a near cloudburst. The ardor of the tenters was thoroughly dampened. Another time, during some swimming

events, a woman had been seen, sitting in the back of a row boat. The spectators were horrified when, suddenly, she fell over backwards and did not come up. Half a minute later, Mr. Kyle, who owned a bathhouse at the foot of 6th St., in San Diego, bobbed up, clad in a full regulation bathing suit of the period.

In July 1903, a new steam ferry boat, named "Ramona", was received. On the 7th it was put on the run and carried large crowds for the Tent City band concert. The following year the "cattle boat" Benicia was retired and dismantled.

Cars No. 16 and No. 50

On the 31st day of December, 1901, two "combination" car bodies were ordered from American Car Company. Combination evidently meant a closed center section with open end sections. The new cars were in the car house on January 26, 1902.

One was a 25 ft. 6 inch body for car No. 16. A single truck was ordered and, when received, the body was mounted on it.

The other was a 34 ft. body for car No. 50. A photograph of the latter shows that these were somewhat similar to the Brill 1892 bodies, the longer one having a five window closed section and two benches each in the open sections.

The deal on car No. 50 is somewhat clouded. Coronado Railroad records contain the following entries:

Sept. 1902: Motors and freight on material for Car No. 50 $1,194.84

Dec. 1902: To Car No. 50 from San Diego Electric Railway $2,706.66

Feb. 1903: Car No. 50 has old truck equipment of San Diego Electric Railway Co's. Sprinkler. Brill No. 27 trucks have an unusually long wheel base — 7 ft. Extra power necessary to operate Car No. 50.

May 1903: Car No. 50 fitted with new wheels, trucks and motors.

Feb. 1904: Car No. 50, originally owned by San Diego Electric Rail-

way . . . has been transferred back to San Diego Electric Railway Co. for $3,800.00

One offered explanation is: That the Coronado Railroad had planned to rebuild one of its coaches for electric operation and had ordered trucks and electrical equipment for it. Then the San Diego Electric Railway got a "bargain" from the American Car Company and bought the 34 ft. body. As previously set forth, it had been found advisable to replace the trucks and motors on the Street Sprinkler No. 103. When the body arrived, it was mounted on the old trucks from No. 103. After a few months' use in San Diego, the car was transferred to Coronado. There the trucks were changed out to the ones received in September 1902. In the meantime, a new car had been ordered from Brill for Coronado and, before it arrived, Car No. 50 was sent back to the San Diego Electric Railway.

Comment by the San Diego Union on the new cars had been: January 26, 1902: Car. No. 50, one of the two new cars recently purchased, was on the Coronado Ferry run last night. She is of fine appearance and larger than the average.

Car. No. 16, which is to be used from the pavilion to 31st and National, was out for a trial run on Friday evening. The officials of the street car lines declare her a beauty.

Car Remodeling

So fast was the stride of progress in electric traction that the cars and equipment purchased in 1892 and the two bodies just received were already obsolete. There was nothing to do but to pitch in and bring them up to 20th Century standards.

The true "California" type body had gained great popularity. This design had a closed center section, longitudinal seats, like the cable cars, in each open end section, lever hand brakes, "vestibule" (wood and glass) fronts and single trolleys.

A body shop was established in the car house on Arctic St., about the middle of the block. A paint shop was built on the southwest corner of Arctic and D Sts., after the old horse car barn had been moved.

Eight of the twelve former cable cars had been acquired, in fairly good condition, from the Citizens Traction Company. These were retired in 1901. Work was started in 1902 on the remodeling of four of them, parts being used from the other four, lengthening the frames, to produce the California type. On Nov. 1, 1902, "The long expected trucks arrived and will be installed on the four new cars."

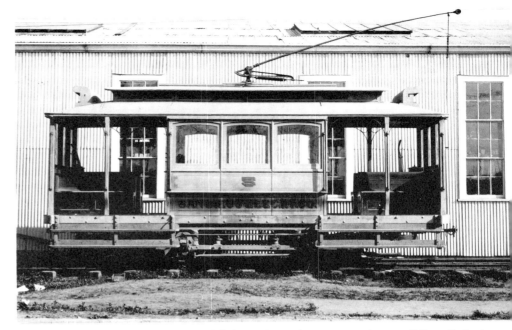

Electric car No. 5 as remodeled in 1904 at the temporary shops on Kettner Blvd. at E Street.—R. C Brandt

The cars were given numbers 51, 52, 53 and 54 and were completed in 1903.

These double truck cars were a big improvement over the four wheeled bobbers. The motorman had some protection from the weather. But there was one big disadvantage. He couldn't grab the switch iron and throw the switch. He had to stop the car and he or the conductor had to alight to perform the operation.

So an experimental electrically controlled switch was installed on the south track on D St., west of 5th St., one of the first. The primitive model did not function very smoothly and the manipulation of the controls by the motorman was a sight to behold. Sometimes he did not have to back up or throw the switch by hand.

Next the body of car number 3 was rebuilt and lengthened, modeled to match the first four, except as to roof design, double trucked and was renumbered 55.

Likewise, the body purchased for car number 16 was worked over, lengthened and given car number 56.

Car No. 50 was also vestibuled and

San Diego sported the derby hat and the full skirt too!!! San Diego also had quite a bit of street car traffic as evidenced in this 1904 scene.—Union Title

*San Diego Electric power plant and car barn about 1900. (Below) Car No. 1 after the upper deck was removed and ends vestibuled
—R. C. Brandt*

the seats were changed. It was equipped with air brakes in July 1906.

In 1904 cars number 1 and 2 were rebuilt, changing from double deckers to single, installing vestibules, and lever brakes, changing the seats in the end sections.

Cars numbers 4 to 8 inclusive received similar treatment, i. e.: vestibules, lever brakes and seat changes.

More Juice Needed

Motormen were complaining that they had to "fight the juice" all day long. Too many cars were climbing hills at the same time. The people were demanding more cars on the Mission Cliff line. Manager Warner said that added service to University Heights will be provided as soon as the new machinery is installed. At present there is not sufficient power to run extra cars.

So, in 1905, it became necessary to enlarge the Power Plant by the installation of:

3 — Keeler 250 Horse Power Water Tube Boilers.

1 — Westinghouse-Parsons Steam Turbine, 1,000 Kilowatt capacity. The

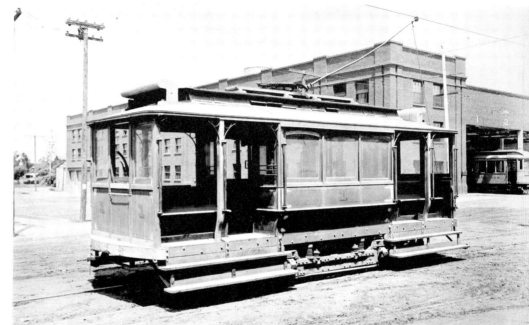

Street Railway Journal listed this turbine as direct connected to 2 — 500 Kilowatt, 600 Volt Direct Current Generators at 1,500 Revolutions Per Minute but a photograph taken after 1911 shows it to be reduction gear connected to a single Generator (Unit No. 1).

2 — Westinghouse-Parsons Steam Turbines each direct connected to a 500 Kilowatt 2,300 Volt Alternating Current Generator, on one foundation. (Units Nos. 6 and 7).

2 — 22½ Kilowatt Steam Engine Driven Exciters.

2 — Westinghouse 500 Kilowatt Induction Motor - Generator Sets. (Units Nos. 4 and 5).

Induction motors were then installed to belt drive the two original generators,

Looking north on Fifth Street about 1905— Security First National Bank of Los Angeles

replacing the old steam engines.

Commercial power was furnished by a Ball 75 Kilowatt Generator direct connected to a Ball 100 Horse Power high speed Steam Engine, providing service when street cars were not operated — mdinight to 5 A.M.

In 1908, 2 — Cahill 250 Horse Power and 2 — 400 Horse Power water tube Boilers were added. Then the 3 Babcock & Wilcox 100 Horse Power Boilers were retired from service.

Car Building Program

The remodeled cars had won public approval and construction of complete bodies began in 1904. This gave employment to local workmen.

Adopting practically the same design as was used for car number 56, 30 bodies 33 ft. long were built, equipped with double trucks, single pole trolleys, lever brakes, and were put on the road, as follows:

Nov.-Dec. 1904   Nos. 57, 58 and 59
July-Nov. 1905   Nos. 60, 61 and 62

The heart of the power plant. In the foreground is the Westinghouse-Parsons high pressure steam turbine and the 1,000 kilowatt direct current generator. (Below) Looking north on Fifth Street from E Street about 1912. Note 40 foot car No. 99 in the foreground and the various automobiles.

Apr.-June 1906	Nos. 63, 64 **and 65**
Nov. 1906	Nos. 66, 67 and 68
Apr.-June 1907	Nos. 69, 70 and 71
Nov.-Dec. 1907	Nos. 72, 73 and 74
Jan.-Apr. 1908	Nos. 75, 76, 77, 78, 79 and 80
July-Sept. 1908	Nos. 81, 82, 83, 84, 85 and 86

Second trolleys were added to all the cars, including the double truck remodeled ones in January 1911.

A glance at the construction rates reveals the fact that San Diego really began to grow in 1905. By 1910 the population had more than doubled, to 39,578.

More carrying capacity was needed, so longer bodies were designed and 24 cars, 40 ft. long, were built in 1910 and 1911. These were numbered 87 to 110 inclusive. The closed sections had 5 windows, they had 2 trolleys, larger motors and air brakes.

All cars were finished in standard yellow with the ornamental decorations in gold leaf with brown shading.

Passers-by would stop at the shop door, from time to time, and watch the growth of the cars. The millwork was contracted but assembled at the Shop. First the sills, then the skeleton frames, followed by the side panels, ends, roofs and so on, then the mounting on the trucks and the moving to the paint shop.

How we loved those cars! They were so convenient. You did not have to wait until they stopped to get on or off.

Coronado Betterments

To keep abreast of the changes in Coronado, other entries in the Journal of the Coronado Railroad give data on additional car transactions:

Dec. 1903 and Jan. 1904: Drawings for construction of Car No. 43.

Jan. 1904: Car No. 42 changed into vestibule car incl. lever brakes.

Mar. 1904: Car No. 41 (the double decker) equipped with rope brakes.

June 1904: New 43 ft. car No. 43, built by J. G. Brill Co., of Philadelphia, received on June 29th and put in service 2 days later.

May 1906: One of the single truck "box cars" (Car No. 11) was purchased from San Diego Electric Railway and transferred to Coronado for use on Race Track Line at a price of $1,100.
(Assigned Car No. 44)

May 1907: Equipped Cars No. 41 and No. 43 with air brakes.

June 1907: Equipping 4 trailers (Open Cars No. 12, 13, 14 and 17,

Car No. 66 is a handsome California type car built in 1906 by the San Diego Electric shops. (Below) The 87-110 class cars were longer, but equally attractive in appearance. No. 107 poses at the Imperial Avenue car barn.

used with electric cars) with air brakes.

June 1908: Rebuilding Car No. 41, changing same from double decker to single decker, changing seats, increasing length 10 ft. $406.81

New Car Lines

60 pound Tee rails on Redwood ties had now been adopted as the standard for track construction, except on principal streets recently paved with asphalt, where the track was placed on a concrete base. The relaying of old trackage had begun.

In April 1904, an application was made for a franchise for a car line on *M St.* (*Imperial Ave.*) from 16th St. to 32nd St. It was built in 1905. An additional franchise extended the construction on M St., from 16th St., to 10th St., to K St. to 5th St. in the same year.

Cars were then operated from 32nd and M Sts., to D St., to the Santa Fe Station. This eliminated the original "Depot Line."

This was the beginning of a large expansion program.

But some important and unexpected events occurred which interrupted the proposed plans temporarily . . .

Sickness Fells J. D.

Early in 1906, J. D. became desperately ill in his home in San Francisco. Unable to eat for several weeks, he wasted away, losing weight from 175 to 100 pounds. He was believed to be on the brink of death but had just begun to show faint signs of a rally when a violent catastrophe struck without warning . . .

Cataclysm

There was no way to broadcast news so rapidly in those days as now, with radio and television available. The first intelligence to most San Diegans that something dreadful had happened came with the cry: Extra! Extra! All about . . .

Then they read the news that early that morning, April 18, 1906, San Francisco had been practically destroyed by an earthquake and that both sides of Market Street were on fire. In San Diego there had been only a slight tremor felt later in the morning.

But in San Francisco there was wild panic with many exaggerated rumors being circulated. The sick man, J. D., heard that San Diego had disappeared, that Coronado and the Hawaiian Islands had been swept away by tidal waves. He believed that all his vast investments in San Francisco and the other places were lost. Instead of sinking in despair,

Coronado Transportation—Both photographs were taken at the Coronado Ferry landing. No. 42 as rebuilt in 1904, and double decker No. 41 and two trailers. (Below) Car No. 44 acquired in 1904, followed by No. 43 with two trailers.—Both F. W. Reif

the blow seemed to give him almost super-human strength. The dire emergency was the tonic which did what medicines had failed to do.

Soon, however, some order was restored out of the chaos and the losses and damages, while severe, were not nearly so huge as depicted.

J. D. immediately despatched one of his steamers to Coos Bay, Oregon, with

instructions to pick up all the food and supplies available and to return to San Francisco at once.

Then he made arrangements for another vessel to bring his family and all his personal friends to San Diego. Adams tells that when J. D. boarded the ship, he found it crowded with refugees. He did not recognize a familiar face. "Who are all these people?", he asked the Captain.

"I don't know, but they all said that they were friends of yours, sir."

J. D. and family found shelter in his own Hotel del Coronado. Quickly he regained strength and health and soon was ready for more punishment.

He had decided to make his home in Coronado and construction was started on a fine mansion, across the electric tracks from the hotel. It contained a large music room in which a pipe organ was installed. There, at the console, J. D. spent many an hour, the harmony swelling from the pipes and reeds acting as a safety valve for the pent-up emotions and terrific strains which he had to bear.

Railroad Promised

Ever since the former management of the Atchison, Topeka & Santa Fe Railroad double-crossed San Diego, by accepting the subsidies to make National City its western terminus and, then in 1889, moving the offices to Los Angeles and the shops to San Bernardino, the people had been clamoring for a direct line east.

Many had been the schemes proposed and the organizations formed to accomplish this purpose. All had ended in failures.

Headed by George W. Marston, the founder of the Marston Dry Goods Store, a committee was formed in 1900 to make another attempt to get a railroad. The San Diego & Eastern Railroad Company was organized and subscriptions to a $40,000 fund needed for surveys and purchases of right-of-way for the proposed line from San Diego to Yuma, Arizona, had been obtained. Chief Engineer H. T. Richards reported: "The Dulzura Pass is the hardest piece this side of the divide."

Estimates had been prepared of the cost of construction and equipment, amounting to $4,573,850.

The Spreckel mansion opposite Hotel del Coronado also faced on Glorietta Bay—Union Title

The corporation carried on but there was no indication that the road could ever be built.

When San Diegans went to bed on the night of December 13, 1906, there was practically no hope of obtaining a competing railroad. The next morning, when they picked up their San Diego Union, they gasped and rubbed their eyes. Yes. That is what the headlines read:

"RAILROAD FROM SAN DIEGO TO YUMA IS NOW ASSURED".

"NAMED SAN DIEGO AND ARIZONA RAILWAY"

"Line Will Be Built and Owned by Spreckels Interests".

The articles of incorporation of the San Diego and Arizona Railway Company bore the date of December 14, 1906. They covered the construction of a standard gauge railroad from San Diego by the most practicable route to a point at or near Yuma in the Territory of Arizona.

The incorporators were J. D. and A. B. Spreckels, J. D. Spreckels, Jr., William Clayton and Harry L. Titus.

The capital stock was fixed at $6,000,000, indicating the estimated cost of the road.

The rights-of-way and the franchises of the San Diego & Eastern were taken over. Then J. D. ordered that every subscriber to the San Diego & Eastern fund be reimbursed in full.

Collosal condemnation proceedings were begun to obtain a 100 ft. right-of-way through the city and for other parcels of land needed. These included areas for a roundhouse, shops and stores, a freight house, yard tracks, proposed depot grounds at India and H Sts., and all the property fronting on the easterly side of Arctic St., north to Date St.

J. D. later revealed that he had been acting as Agent for E. H. Harriman, President of Southern Pacific Company. Little did he realize what the outcome would be. He had promised the people that they would get a railroad.

S.P. & E.S. Absorbed

Before taking up the expansion of the San Diego Electric Railway Company's lines, it is desirable to sketch some other rail projects of the period.

One of these is the *South Park & East Side Railway.*

This was an enterprise growing out of the operations of the Bartlett Estate, under the presidency of E. Bartlett Web-

Cars Nos. 10 and 11 of the South Park & East Side Railway—F. W. Reif

South Park & East Side Railway No. 13 taken over by the SDE in 1909 and operated as SP&ES until 1915.—R. V. Dodge

ster. Property along the south and the east sides of City (now Balboa) Park was being developed into a desirable residential district, known as South Park. It was the intention to include Brooklyn Heights.

To serve the areas, an electric street railway was constructed starting in March 1906, from the end of the Broadway St. line, on 25th St., to B St., to 28th St., to Beech St., to 30th St., to Amherst (now Cedar) St. There the power house was built.

Two used single truck open cars were acquired, probably from Los Angeles, and were given numbers 1 and 2. Shuttle service was started.

Then the construction of a line from Broadway on 25th St., to F St., to 4th Ave., to C St., was begun.

Two other "new" double truck cars were purchased second hand. The first was received December 25, 1906. It was run up Broadway and hauled over to the South Park & East Side track on 25th St. The new green car had been shipped from Los Angeles and bore the marks of having come from the Pacific Electric (or Los Angeles Pacific). The fourth car was purchased on January 4, 1907. These two were numbered 10 and 11 and had four window closed sections with open end sections. They were equipped with air brakes and whistles.

Rumors were then current that H. E. Huntington was backing the Bartlett people.

Until the F Street line could be completed, free passes were issued to all purchasers of property in the tracts controlled by the Estate. Since transfer arrangements could not be made with the San Diego Electric Railway, this was to make the fare downtown 5 cents.

When the tracks were laid down F Street in 1907, 10 minute service was established to the center of the business district.

Other franchises were obtained, including lines on:

30th St., to El Cajon Ave., to the City Limits (now Boundary St.)

30th St., from Beech St. to N St. B St., from Arctic St., to 6th Ave., to F St.

Thus the South Park & East Side Railway was becoming a strong factor in local transportation.

Result: The outfit was purchased by the San Diego Electric Railway Company on May 27, 1909, total length — 3½ miles.

In August 1910, cars No. 10 and No. 11 were equipped with Brill trucks. No. 10 was renumbered second No. 12 and No. 11 became second No. 11.

N.C.O. Electrified

When an announcement was made, early in 1906, that a portion of the National City & Otay Railway would be electrified and a modern interurban service would be established, it caused some eye-brows to be raised. It did not conform with the conservative policies of the National City & Otay management. Did it mean competition with J. D's. expanding system?

As has been reported, the National City & Otay Railway was built by the

San Diego Electric 2nd No. 11 and former SP&ES No. 11, now sporting a golden yellow coat of paint.—F. W. Reif

NC&O interurban as rebuilt from a Coronado Railroad coach. View taken at Santa Fe station about 1908.—Doug Duncan

San Diego Land & Town Company, a Santa Fe subsidiary. Referring back to November 15, 1905, an article in the San Diego Sun was found to the effect that B. P. Cheney, president of the San Diego Land & Town Company, was here for a conference with E. S. Babcock. Negotiations for the sale of Sweetwater Dam and the National City & Otay Railway are all off.

Subsequent developments prove that this was a misstatement, as far as the railway was concerned, and that the Spreckels interests obtained control of the National City & Otay at that time or soon thereafter.

After years of stagnation, National City and Chula Vista were now showing signs of potential growths and, in keeping with J. D's. progressive transportation policy, it was natural that electric interurban service should be established.

Accordingly a series of "Job Numbers" (work orders) was set up in the San Diego Electric Railway's accounts on July 1, 1906.

Job No. 1 called for the construction of an overhead trolley line from 5th and L Sts. in San Diego, over the National City & Otay tracks, through National City to 3rd and K Sts. in Chula Vista, 10.3 miles, including bonding of track, feeder wires, etc.

No. 2 provided for the reconstruction of four Coronado Railroad's coaches numbers 1, 2, 3 and 37 for electric cars, exclusive of trucks, electrical equipment, painting, etc. An entry in the Coronado Railroad's journal for September 1906 shows these coaches "sold" to National City & Otay Railway Co. at $1,300 each. The four car bodies were rebuilt in shops in National City, into California type interurbans, similar to those in Los Angeles, except the sides in the open sections were panelled up to the sill height. They were lengthened to 51 feet — 6 inches, with a seating capacity of 56.

Before these jobs were completed, Job Number 17 was issued to construct a track and overhead connecting the National City & Otay Railway with the San Diego Electric Railway at the intersection of 13th St. and Imperial Ave., in San Diego. This changed the proposed routing from the terminal at 5th & L Sts. so that the interurbans could be operated downtown. The cars were brought to San Diego "for finishing touches."

Job Number 3 called for the equipping of the four car bodies with trucks, motors, air brakes, etc., while Job 4 provided for the painting. The cars were numbered National City & Otay Ry. No. 101 to 104. The first car was brought to San Diego in August 1907.

Electric interurban service started Sunday December 1, 1907 from Chula Vista and National City to San Diego, the cars turning from 13th St. in San Diego into Imperial Ave., to 10th Ave., to K St., to 5th Ave. to Broadway to the Santa Fe station (California St.). Electric energy was purchased from the San Diego Electric Ry.

When the double tracking in Third Ave. in San Diego was completed and the necessary curves were installed, the routing was changed to 5th Ave., to Market St., to 3rd Ave., to Broadway.

San Diego Southern R. R.

Since the Spreckels' interests now controlled the San Diego Electric Railway, the National City & Otay Railway and the Coronado Railroad, it was obvious that economies could be effected by changes in the set-ups. Accordingly a new corporation, named *San Diego Southern Railway Company*, was formed by J. D. Spreckels and others in January 1908. The articles of incorporation provided for a railroad from San Diego in a general southerly direction to a point at or near Ensenada in Lower California; to Coronado and a third via Sweetwater Valley to La Presa, Jamacha Valley and on to Lakeside. The third extension, if constructed, would severely compete with the San Diego, Cuyamaca & Eastern Railway.

Effective July 1, 1908 the San Diego Southern took over the steam divisions of the Coronado Railroad and the National City & Otay Ry. and the electric interurban line of the latter. At the same time, the electric division of the Coronado RR. was "sold" to the San Diego Electric Ry., it thus acquiring electric cars numbers 41, 42 and 43 and re-acquiring "box car" number 44. The four trailers, used with the electrics, were included, also one horse car and a small line tower car (non-electric).

National City & Otay interurban cars numbers 101 to 104 inclusive were re-lettered "San Diego Southern Railway", as were four coaches from the Coronado RR which were used as trailers.

Six new interurban type cars were purchased from the Niles Car Company in 1908. They were of California design but were a little shorter than the National City built cars. These were numbered 105 to 110 inclusive. Three of them, numbers 105, 106 and 107 were retained by the San Diego Southern. The other three were transferred to the San Diego Electric Ry. in 1909 and 1910. The numbers were changed, on the books, to 401, 402 and 400 respectively but not on the cars until 1911.

The Electric Division was extended from Chula Vista south to Otay, 2.1 miles, in October 1909. That was as near to Ensenada as the electric cars ever ran. Another change was made in 1910 when a connecting track was laid in San Diego by the San Diego Electric Ry. on 13th St., from L St. to K St., making the route of the interurbans from Newton Ave., on 13th St., to K St., to 5th Ave. and so on to the Santa Fe station.

The company applied for a franchise to operate an express service but the request became involved in the controversies of J. D. and the San Diego Electric Ry. versus the San Diego City Council over a 50 year term for street railway franchises and a two percent gross revenue tax, delaying the issuance of the permits. The company also petitioned for permission to operate a railway express service from the center of the city to Ocean Beach over the Point Loma Railroad. Finally the permits were granted, authorizing one express car to operate

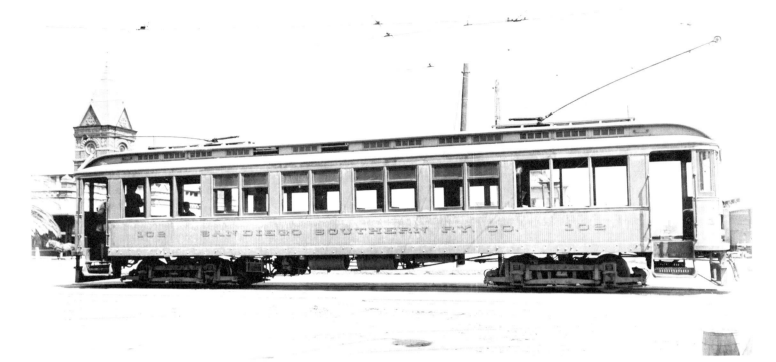

San Diego Southern Railway No. 102 at the foot of Broadway. Note the tall tower on the Santa Fe Railway station behind interurban.—R. C. Brandt

through the city making a limited number of trips.

Combination baggage and passenger car No. 5 of the Coronado RR. was rebuilt by the San Diego Electric Ry., converting it to electric, in March 1910. It was lettered and numbered San Diego Southern Railway No. 111.

Express service was started under the direction of Wells-Fargo & Company. One run to Ocean Beach was made daily except Sunday beginning in mid-July.

The San Diego Southern Railway was merged along with the San Diego & Cuyamaca Railway into the San Diego & South Eastern Railway Company in 1912.

Big Town

Back in 1867, when Alonzo E. (Father) Horton bought most of the present downtown section of San Diego at 25 cents an acre, he platted the tract, since known as Horton's Addition. He laid out the streets, mostly 80 feet wide, and named them so that any stranger could easily find his way around.

Beginning at the westerly line of the tract, the north-south streets were numerals: First Street, Second Street, et seq. Starting at "A" Street, the east-west streets were lettered: A Street, B Street, et seq. south to the bay. North of "A" Street, names of trees were used but they followed in alphabetical order: Ash Street, Beech Street, Cedar Street et seq.

But, now since the town was beginning to grow into a city, letters for streets became too plebian. They did not reflect individuality. So some were changed: "D" Street became *Broadway*, "H" Street

was renamed *Market Street*, "I" Street changed to *Island Avenue* (more to avoid confusion with 1st Street), "M" Street became *Imperial Avenue* and "N" Street *Commercial St.*

Then the word "Street" was found to be objectionable to some highbrows. It just wasn't euphonious. So, from First to Twelfth inclusive, they are now called "Avenues". Aven-ue-phoney-ous! Thirteenth *Street* is the next one after Twelfth *Avenue.*

Other changes were made for more logical reasons.

Atlantic Street, which was partly in the bay before the spoil from dredgings moved the waterfront out to the bulkhead line in 1914, is now *Pacific Highway.*

Grant Avenue has been renamed twice, spoiling an alphabetical sequence in that section. It was first changed to *Woolman Avenue* and now is Ocean View Boulevard.

Arctic Street was changed to *Kettner Boulevard* to honor a beloved Congressman, Bill Kettner.

Milton Avenue, from 16th St. to 26th St., is now *National Avenue,* again interrupting a sequence.

Similarly Oliver Avenue was changed to *Main Street.* Reason unknown.

Many changes were necessary when additions and tracts were annexed by the city to avoid duplications. For a few examples: Fillmore Street became *University Avenue,* University Boulevard became *Normal Street,* Carolina Street, from El Cajon to Adams, became *Park Boule-*

vard, Steiner Street in East San Diego became *University Avenue,* with an offset at 34th Street to the one in San Diego. Amherst Street is now a part of *Cedar Street.*

On the 1910 map, what had been Pierce St. is shown as Harasthy St. Now it is a part of the Washington Street Freeway.

In National City, all the numbered avenues have been given names. 8th Avenue is now Cleveland Avenue.

The information herein contained may be applied to the preceeding sections. Beyond this point the current street names will be used. This will be premature, chronologically, but will simplify the following through of the line construction projects.

Immense Rail Spread

"So I set to work to develop . . . a street railway system which would reach out to even the outlying section of the city." J.D.S.

Track construction was resumed following the subsidence of the earthquake scare period.

Each new line or extension was to be built up to its terminus for this era of expansion. All were single track at the start.

State St. — Old Town Line.

In 1906 — track was laid from Broadway on State St. to Ivy St. — 4000 feet, in December. Shuttle service was started.

1907 — extended on Ivy St., to India St., to Winder St. A crossover between

Immense rail spread saw track construction on University Avenue, east of Georgia Street in 1907. Note the barren land waiting for prospective buyers as soon as trolleys started running.—H. R. Fitch

the double tracks on Broadway between State and Union Sts. was put in. Cars then ran through to 3rd Ave. and Broadway, in May.

1910 — extended on India St., from Winder St., to Pierce St. (Harasthy St., now a part of Washington St. Freeway), to California St., to San Diego Ave., to Calhoun St., to Mason St. in Old Town. When completed it was joined with the Imperial Ave. line.

J. D. purchased the old adobe ruins on Mason St., known as the Estudillo House or Ramona's Marriage Place. The buildings were wonderfully restored and the patio was landscaped into a beautiful garden. Then it was called *"Ramona's Home"* and became a tourist attraction, creating fares for the street car company.

3rd Ave. — *Mission Hills Line.*

Also in 1906, rails were laid on 3rd Ave., from Market St. to Fir St., serving the Robinson Hotel, formerly the Florence. Car service began.

1907 — extended on Fir St. to 4th Ave., to Spruce St., passing around the old cable railway power house to 1st Ave., to Brookes Ave. It was necessary to build some wooden trestles to carry the line across gullies, then the track was extended to Washington St.

1908-9 — extended from 1st Ave. on Washington St., to Hawk St., to Lewis St., to Stephens St., Mission Hills. Combining with the Market St. Line, a route was formed from Stephens and Lewis to 25th and Market Sts.

In June 1910, additional service was provided over part of the route by operating every other car over the new K St. line. This made 10 minute service from 1st Ave. and Washington St. to

5th Ave. and Market St.

In 1913, the final extension was completed from Stephens St., into Fort Stockton Drive to Trias St., Mission Hills, Old Town.

Market St. Line.

Trackage on Market St. had been laid from the Coronado ferry wharf to 16th St. in the original network.

It was extended in 1907 from 16th St. on Market St. to 25th St.

In 1910 a route was formed from 25th and Market Sts. to Mission Hills by combining with the 3rd Ave. line.

University Ave. (City Heights) Line.

J. D. then prepared to build a car line out through lemon orchards and sparsely settled country to the same "Phantom City" of Park Belt Motor Line fame, in City Heights. (East San Diego).

As soon as the grading of University Ave. was completed, in 1907, work was started on laying track from Normal St. on University Ave. to Fairmount Ave. A photograph shows that flat body car No. 103, the chassis for the street sprinkling outfit, had been altered to a center control work car and was used to handle the track materials.

Shuttle service was started, connecting with the Mission Cliff-Logan Heights Line at Normal St.

This extension, in a few years, proved J. D's theory . . . "that transportation determines the flow of population" . . . to be correct.

As soon as reliable street car service was assured, the lemon groves around 30th St. and University Ave. were cut down, a subdivision was platted and soon North Park was booming. Similarly East San Diego developed rapidly.

The "antiquated" cars in shuttle service were nicknamed "The Flying Dutchman" and "The Loon".

An Observation Tower was erected near Fairmount Ave.

In 1916, the line was extended on University Ave. to Euclid Ave.

Adams Ave. Line.

Back in 1905, plans for a big development of the Gay Tract, out Adams Ave. way, were announced by D. C. Collier

Car No. 72 at the end of Route 2 on University Avenue near Fairmount about 1912. Note the observation tower behind trolley, also the real estate bargains on the sign at the left foreground.—H. R. Fitch

of the University Heights Syndicate. Preliminary surveys for a proposed electric railway from a connection with the San Diego Electric Railway's Mission Cliff line had been completed. The road was to be operated as an integral part of the San Diego Electric Railway's system.

Again construction was delayed, waiting for the City to grade Adams Avenue and to construct a high wooden trestle over the Sandrock Road (Texas St.) and canyon.

In 1907, the track was built, through wild country, to a point one mile beyond the City Limits (Boundary St.), total length 11,086 feet, by the San Diego Electric Railway and the costs were set up in its accounts. Soon shuttle service was established.

Before the line could be extended, another wooden trestle had to be erected, this one over Ward Road. When completed, in 1910, the tracks were continued on Adams Ave. to Marlborough Drive, Kensington Park.

A spur track was built on what is now 35th St., in 1907, north to a gravel pit, from which materials for ballasting were obtained.

A nice afternoon trek was to ride to the end of the Adams Ave. line, then walk across, passing orange groves, to catch the shuttle car on University Ave.

B St. Line.
In 1909, to provide service from the old Santa Fe Freight House and the La Jolla Line to the San Diego High School, a car track was laid on B St., from Kettner Blvd. to 14th St.

F St. Line.
Trackage had been obtained from the South Park & East Side Railway by purchase, on F St., from 25th St. to 4th Ave., in 1909. A connecting track was laid on F St., from 4th Ave. to the 3rd Ave. line.

When the then new Post Office (now Custom House and Court House) Building was erected on F St., between State St. and Union St., double tracks were installed on F St., from 3rd Ave. to State St., and a single track from State St. to Kettner Blvd. in 1913.

K St. Line.
In the 1905 construction, tracks were laid on K St., from 5th Ave. to 10th Ave. and, in 1910 for the San Diego Southern Railway's cars, from 10th Ave., to 13th St., to L St. Also, in 1910 — trackage was built on K St., from 5th Ave. to 16th St., making a second track from 5th Ave. to 13th St., and a single track from 22nd St. to 25th St. The stretch from 16th St. to 22nd St. was a part of the K and 22nd Sts. shuttle in the original network. Service on this section replaced the shuttle and the portion on 22nd St. was then abandoned. An extension was next made on 25th St., from K St., to Ocean View Blvd., to 30th St. in the same year.

A through route was then formed by combining this line with the 3rd Ave. line, via 5th Ave. and Market St. to 1st Ave. and Washington St. Every other Third Ave. car then ran out to 30th St. and Ocean View Blvd.

Imperial Ave. Line.
In the 1905 construction, tracks were laid from 5th Ave. and K St. to 32nd St. and Imperial Ave.

In 1909 — the line was extended on Imperial Ave. from 32nd St. to 34th St. Soon it was built out the roadway from 34th St. to Greenwood Cemetery east of 39th St.

In 1910, a route was formed from 39th and Imperial Ave., to Old Town, a long line.

Broadway — Brooklyn Heights Line.
The First Ave. and Broadway Line of the original network terminated at 25th St.

In 1909 the track of the South Park & East Side Railway from Broadway and 25th St. to 30th and Cedar Sts. was acquired by purchase.

In 1910, an extension was made on 30th St. from Cedar St. to Juniper St., using a private right-of-way to make the jog at Ivy St. When the 30th St. Bridge was completed, the line was extended to Upas St.

In 1911, the track was built on Upas to the offset 30th St., to University Ave.

The Broadway cars followed the extensions.

Miscellaneous.
Other additions were built as follows:

In 1909 — on 1st Ave., from Broadway to Market St. On State St., from Broadway to Market St.

In 1913 — Tracks were laid on 15th St., from K St. to Imperial Ave., to serve the new shops.

Trackage on 4th Ave., from C St. to F St., had been acquired from the South Park & East Side Railway. This was used jointly with the La Jolla Line.

The San Diego Electric Railway grew up fast.

Point Loma Railroad

Another electric interurban venture was the Point Loma Railway Company, formed in 1907 by Col. D. C. Collier, promoter, and associates. The purpose of the road was to develop the Loma Portal, Roseville and Ocean Beach areas of Point Loma. Surveys were started.

The plan decided upon was to build a railroad from the end of the State St. Line of the San Diego Electric Railway, then at India and Winder Sts., via Hancock St., to Barnett Ave. (originally Tide St.), crossing the tracks of the Santa Fe Railway at grade, to Lytton St., to Rosecrans St., to Macauley St. in Roseville, thence cross lots, using the roadbed of the old Ocean Beach Railroad up

Wabaska Canyon to Tennyson St., to a switch between Warrington and Worden Sts., thence cross lots to Voltaire St., to Bacon St., to Santa Cruz St.

From that point, a "South Loop" was to be constructed on Santa Cruz St., to Guizot St., thence cross lots to Orchard St., to the alley between Catalina Blvd. and Redondo St., to the alley between Catalina Blvd. and Wells St., to the switch on Tennyson St.

A reorganization took place in 1908 and the corporate name was changed to Point Loma Railroad Company.

Rails were ordered by Collier, as President and General Manager, in October. Collier then petitioned for a franchise amendment to use electricity, gasoline or steam. The franchise was awarded in November.

A construction and operation contract was made with the San Diego Electric Railway. Collier admitted that J. D's. endorsement made the line possible.

For passenger equipment, the San Diego Electric Railway bought Niles interurban cars No. 108 and No. 109 from the San Diego Southern Railway when they arrived in 1909. They were relettered Point Loma Railroad Co. Car No. 110 was also acquired in 1910 for use as a "sight seeing" car. To avoid confusion, the numbers were changed to No. 401, 402 and 400 respectively — on the books, but the cars were operated with their old numbers until 1911.

By May 1909 the first section of the track was completed to Ocean Beach

and service was begun on the first. The whole system was put in operation from and to India and Winder Sts. about July 3rd, around the scenic loop. The length of the road was 8.2 miles.

An amusement center was set up along the ocean front. It was named "Wonderland." Later the Silver Spray Plunge was built.

When Collier and associates met obstacles in financing in 1910, J. D. and A. B. stepped in and took the investment off their hands, hoping that some day it might make a reasonable return. They "assumed the responsibility in what they believed to be the very best interests of San Diego. In weaker hands, the company might have gone to the wall and become another landmark of failure. Failures do not build cities."

The cars were then operated through

over India and State Sts. to Broadway, to Third Ave., to Market St., to Fifth Ave. to L St. Later the route was shortened to loop downtown from Third Ave., to F St., to Fourth Ave. to Broadway.

"Balloon" sight-seeing trips, twice a day, were started on February 3, 1910, using car No. 400, originally San Diego Southern Railway No. 110, which was painted a chocolate brown color, according to recollections. The runs included Broadway and Brooklyn Heights to the end of that line at Upas St., Mission Cliff Gardens, Ocean Beach, making the scenic loop, and later, to Ramona's Home in Old Town.

In conjunction with the San Diego Southern Railway, Wells-Fargo & Co's. express service to Ocean Beach was started in July 1910 using car S. D. S. No. 111 with one trip daily.

Point Loma Railroad No. 402 purchased from San Diego Southern in 1909. This Niles built car was assigned to Point Loma operation.— R. V. Dodge

La Jolla line trolley on C Street near Second Avenue about 1905.—R. C. Brandt

In 1916 a branch was constructed on Rosecrans St., from Macauley, south through La Playa to the United States' Naval reservation and Fort Rosecrans. This trackage was operated as a shuttle from "Roseville" junction.

The Point Loma Railroad Company was kept entirely separate from the San Diego Electric Railway Company for accounting purposes and was always run at a loss.

By May 1910 more than 100 homes had been built since the completion of the line. The residents began to demand a five cent fare but the company was never able to make that reduction.

The Point Loma Railroad Company was officially purchased by the San Diego Electric Railway Company in 1922.

Los Angeles & San Diego Beach Railway

Los Angeles bound?

Sometime in January 1899, the steam motor road, San Diego, Pacific Beach & La Jolla Railway Company, was sold by Malcolm Forbes of Boston to Captain Charles T. Hinde and E. S. Babcock of Coronado. The San Diego Sun added to the report: "It is known, of course, that Messrs. Babcock and Hinde are not the real purchasers, but they represent the Spreckels Brothers, whose abiding faith in San Diego and the bay regions ap-

pears to be constantly on the increase."

" . . . the first move will be to electricize the entire road."

Be that as it may, the Coronado Railroad Company's journal has some pertinent entries:

Jan. 1902: To "La Jolla Car" No. 1
May 1902: Sale of electric car No. 1, known as "La Jolla Car", to G. E. Babcock $4,250

It was a double truck combination express and passenger type with drop (or droopy) platforms. It was stored in the car house at Coronado for sometime and was lettered "La Jolla Line".

In 1904 applications for franchises for an electric line in San Diego were filed. The route was from a connection with the San Diego, Pacific Beach & La Jolla Railway's track in Kettner Blvd. at C St., via C St., to 6th Ave., to the Tidelands at L St., thence, paralleling the Santa Fe's tracks, to 9th Ave. and Commercial St., to the San Diego, Cuyamaca & Eastern Railway's station at the foot of 10th Ave.

Work was started in October 1904 and the line was ready for operation by October 1905.

A one cylinder Gasoline Engine driving a Direct Current Generator was set up at the northwest corner of India and C Sts. as the power plant. A temporary wooden housing was erected around and over it.

A single truck open car with six benches was purchased, second hand, in Los Angeles. It bore No. 48 and became La Jolla Line No. 2. It was hauled over the new line by a team of horses and an express wagon on the 19th. The San Diego Sun reported: "Through the lettering on the car, which reads *Los Angeles & San Diego Beach Railway,* the old lettering can be distinguished. This reads: *Pacific Electric Railway.*" That settled it. H. E. Huntington was behind the new line. Further proof: Someone discovered that the linemen stringing the trolley wires were paid with Pacific Electric checks.

Babcock tried to explain everything. He bought a small car from the Pacific Electric and had it shipped to San Diego. Pacific Electric linemen were "loaned" to put up the wires.

Then they couldn't get the engine

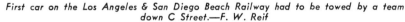

First car on the Los Angeles & San Diego Beach Railway had to be towed by a team down C Street.—F. W. Reif

started and had to await the arrival of a 10 Horse Power Motor. On the 20th, a trial run was made with only the crew on No. 48. The trip was completed "in brisk time and without a hitch", despite some trouble with the engine. It failed to develop the rated 50 Horse Power.

The cars were operated on a meet all trains basis to transfer passengers. Close connections were scheduled and La Jolla and Cuyamaca trains were held for the arrival of the electric cars.

In 1906, the new corporation was formed, using the name as lettered on the open car. The reorganization became effective April 1st with the same E. S. Babcock as President, his son, Graham E., taking an active part and E. A. Hornbeck, long associated with the National City & Otay and San Diego, Cuyamaca & Eastern Railways, as General Manager.

When conditions required another small electric car, San Diego Electric Railway's passenger car No. 10, retired in 1909, was used for a time, probably leased. California type passenger car No. 7 was purchased from the San Diego Electric Railway in 1913 and was renumbered La Jolla Line No. 3.

Since 1899, it had been the expectation to extend the road to Los Angeles. Numerous other proposals for such a line had been made. One was by the Keller-Kerckhoff Company, rumored to have represented the Pacific Electric Railway also. They had built the Stratford Inn at Del Mar (later Hotel Del Mar and presently being converted into a home for the aged). Franchises had been granted for an electric railway from San Diego to Del Mar and some roadbed

was built north of Old Town parallel with both the Santa Fe and the La Jolla Line. The franchises were forfeited.

J. D. also had aspirations for interurban service to some northern points. He stated publicly, about 1907, that he would build an electric railway to La Jolla. Surveys were made and plans laid out to extend the proposed Old Town Line. Then J. D. was asked by some of E. S. Babcock's friends whether or not he would buy the La Jolla Line. J. D. said that he had no desire to crush Mr. Babcock to the wall and, while his railroad did not serve the territory he proposed to open, he would be glad to consider Mr. Babcock's proposition. But Mr. Babcock said he did not wish to sell his road because his family thought he

ought to retain it to have something to keep his mind busy. When asked to name a price, Mr. Babcock suggested arbitration. J. D. declined to listen to this proposal.

Then, in 1910, Mr. Babcock informed J. D. that his family thought it would be better for him to sell his road. J. D. told him that he was already conducting negotiations for his own line to La Jolla. He could build his own road on a superior location for less money. He had petitioned for a franchise but it had become involved in the 2% gross income tax and the 50 year franchise arguments. One "anti-Spreckels" Councilman remarked: "I don't believe Clayton and his company (San Diego Electric Railway) ever intended to build that La Jolla road. It was nothing but a bluff to frighten competition."

The tracks of the San Diego, Pacific Beach & La Jolla Railway were never electrified but the Sun's article on January 11, 1909 contained the news that "the specifications have been drawn for four cars, longer and finer than the big car now in use on C and 6th Sts., to operate to Los Angeles."

However, 2 McKeen gasoline-mechanical Motor Cars had been ordered in 1905 and came out under their own power from Omaha, Nebraska, in 1907 and 1908.

The McKeens had 200 Horse Power 6 cylinder Engines and were geared for

McKeen motor car of the Los Angeles & San Diego Beach Railway pauses in front of Hotel Cabrillo enroute to Ramona's Home, Pacific Beach and La Jolla. (Below) McKeen motor again pauses at Hotel Cabrillo on a slow day. Note the large flywheel on the front power truck beside engineer.—A. E. Barker collection.

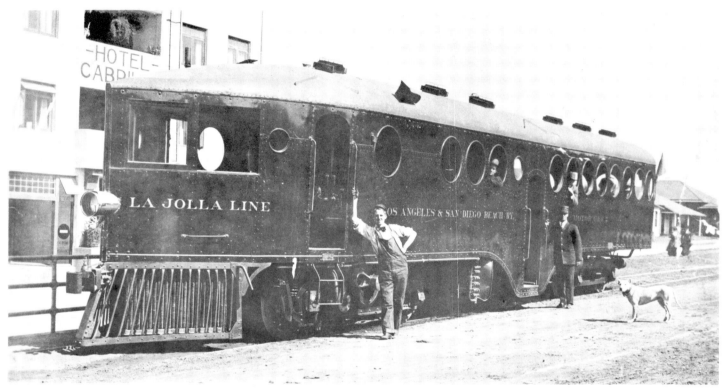

This odd looking gasoline motor car was built from an old Mack Truck. It provided additional service on the Los Angeles and San Diego Beach Railway.—A. E. Barker collection.

The San Diego, Cuyamaca & Eastern purchased a McKeen motor car to supplement service to La Mesa, Lemon Grove, Narragansett and Encanto Heights. Motor was later sold to the U.S. Reclamation District at Yuma, Arizona.—A. E. Barker collection.

Hewitt-Ludlow Car Co. of San Francisco built motor No. 31 for the San Diego & Southeastern Railway. Car was 25 feet in length, seated 32 and was powered by a 70 h.p. oil engine geared to the rear truck. (Below) National City & Otay No. 6, a 2-4-2 tank engine built by Porter in 1888.—A. E. Barker collection.

90 miles per hour, weighed 60,000 pounds and had an efficiency of 3 miles per gallon. The gear ratio was reduced to 65 miles per hour. Then they "pulled out the clutches" every three weeks.

The motor cars shared the runs with the steam trains. Soon they were nick-named *The Submarines.* Coaches were used as trailers until some special ones were built. The motors ran over the electric line and looped the business district after arrangements were made with the South Park & East Side Railway, returning via 6th Ave., to F St., to 4th Ave., to C St.

On the evening of May 29, 1911, a southbound San Diego Electric Railway car crashed into the side of one of the torpedo-shaped cars at the 1st Ave. and C St. crossing, knocking it off the track. Both vehicles were damaged considerably. According to the Sun, the First Ave. car had been delayed by a power failure and was being operated at high speed.

The McKeen cars lasted to about 1914.

Later a Mack Truck chassis was fitted with flanged wheels and a passenger body and made the runs through to La Jolla. It was numbered No. 51.

Additional steam locomotives had been added to the roster, all second-hand.

The company struggled along, never earning enough to pay more than the operating expenses, until 1919. Then it applied for permission to abandon the entire system. Despite considerable opposition, the authority to do so was granted on January 11th.

On the 17th, according to a newspaper article, "6,000 tons of steel from the La Jolla Railway will be loaded on the steamer Colorado Springs for shipment to Japan".

Four years later portions of the right-of-way were utilized by the San Diego Electric Railway.

Railway to Imperial Beach

One more local rail line should be listed to complete the picture.

A settlement had been started at Imperial Beach, at the southerly end of the Silver Strand. For its development convenient transportation of some sort was a necessity. The San Diego Southern Railway did not operate passenger service over the nearby Coronado Belt Line tracks except on special occasions.

In December 1908, the *South San Diego & Imperial Beach Railway Company* was incorporated to build an electric line from the south end of San Diego Bay to the beach, about two miles. The promoters were: G. Y. Gay, E. W. Peterson, R. B. Thomas and R. A. Smith. The firm represented was the South San Diego Investment Company.

Mexico & San Diego Railway's storage battery cars Nos. 1 and 2 were powered by the Edison System. The line operated from the NC&O Junction on the San Diego & South Eastern, over the Coronado Railway tracks to South San Diego, hence to Imperial Beach over its own rails.—R. P. Middlebrook

In the following year, a franchise was sought by Mr. Peterson to construct a railroad over certain highways.

Ferry or launch service was started in 1910 from a San Diego Landing to South San Diego, connecting with the car for the beach. But, the car, instead of being electric, was a small open one with a gasoline-mechanical drive.

A reorganization took place about 1912 and the corporate name adopted was *Mexico & San Diego Railway Company.* Ferry service was abandoned and joint use of the then San Diego & South Eastern Railway's track from South San Diego to National City & Otay Junction was arranged, 1.1 miles.

Thomas Edison had invented an electric car without a trolley. Two used single truck closed cars, 24 ft. long, each propelled by an electric motor pow-

ered by 200 cells of Edison batteries were purchased. 10 additional cells took care of the lighting requirements.

Operation began in April 1913. Then you could get to Imperial Beach by boarding an electric interurban car in San Diego and riding to 24th St., in National City. There you transferred to the steam motor train destined to Tia Juana. But you got off at National City & Otay Junction and changed to the Mexico and San Diego vehicle.

The flood in 1916 put an end to all this. The San Diego & South Eastern Railway was compelled to abandon the steam train service to Tijuana.

A little later, the two battery cars appeared on the Los Angeles & San Diego Beach Railway, so the Babcocks evidently had something to do with the line.

CHAPTER V
The Exposition - High Cost of Operation

Dark streets! Inconspicuous destination signs on the dash! Little wonder that you boarded the wrong car!

Efforts were made in 1907 to remedy the situation. Sheet metal hoods were fabricated and were mounted on the roofs of 29 cars, one at each end. Into these square wooden blocks or boxes, their faces being painted and lettered for a choice of four routes, could be slipped and turned to display the proper designation. Electric lamps illuminated the exposed face.

These were a big improvement but, as traffic increased, route identification that could be more easily discerned was desirable.

Early in 1910, it had been proposed to assign numbers to the street car routes and to install illuminated number boxes on the car roofs on the right front corners, according to direction of motion. The system became effective December first.

The original line-up was as follows:
ROUTE NO.

1 *Fifth Ave. & Logan Heights Line.* From Mission Cliff Gardens at Adams Ave., via Park Blvd., Normal St., University Ave., Fifth Ave., Market St., 16th St., Logan Ave., 26th St., National Ave. to 31st St.

Connections with City Heights (University Ave.) and Normal Heights (Adams Ave.) Lines.

2 *First Ave. and Broadway Line.* From Laurel St., via First Ave., Broadway, 25th St., B St., 28th St., Beech St., 30th St., to Upas St.

3 *Third Ave. (Mission Hills) and Market St. Line.* From Stephens St., via Lewis St., Hawk St., Washington St., First Ave., Spruce St., Fourth Ave., Fir St., Third Ave., Market St. to 25th St.

4 *State St. and Imperial Ave. Line* From Mason St. in Old Town (Ramona's Marriage Place), via Calhoun St., La Jolla Ave., California St., Washington St., India St., Ivy St., State St., Broadway, Fifth Ave., K St., Tenth Ave., Imperial Ave. to Cemeteries or Sierra Vista between 39th and 40th Sts.
Note: This car for Pacific Coast Steamship Co's. wharf, San Diego Southern and Cuyamaca Depots.

5 *Third Ave. and K St. Line.* From Washington St. via First Ave., following Route No. 3 to Market St., to Fifth Ave., to K St., to 25th St., to Ocean View Blvd. to 30th St. Note: This car for Pacific Coast Steamship Co's. wharf, and San Diego Southern Ry. Depot.

6 *F St. Line.* From Broadway via Fourth Ave., F St., to 25th St.

7 *B St. Line.* From 14th St. (San Diego High School) via B St., to Kettner Blvd. (Santa Fe Yards).

8 *Depot Line.* From Fifth Ave., via Broadway to La Jolla and Santa Fe Depots and Los Banos Baths.

9 *Coronado Ferry Line.* From Ferry Landing, via Market St., Kettner Blvd., Broadway, Fifth Ave., Market St. to Ferry Landing.

10 *Coronado Ferry Line.* From Fifth Ave., via Broadway, State St., Market St. to Ferry Landing.

The two shuttles were not assigned route numbers:

From Park Blvd., via Adams Ave. to Marlborough Drive.

From Normal St., via University Ave. to Fairmount Ave.

The San Diego Southern Railway was operating its electric line from San Diego to Chula Vista.

The San Diego Electric Railway operated the Point Loma RR. from India and Winder Sts., in San Diego, to Ocean Beach.

Over the course of the years there were many changes in the routes, mostly due to the growth of the territory served.

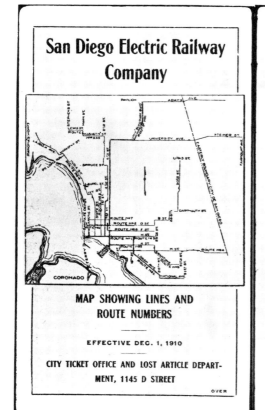

San Diego Electric Railway Company

MAP SHOWING LINES AND ROUTE NUMBERS

EFFECTIVE DEC. 1, 1910

CITY TICKET OFFICE AND LOST ARTICLE DEPARTMENT, 1145 D STREET

OVER

EFFECTIVE, DECEMBER 1, 1910
CAR ROUTE NUMBERS
ROUTE NO. 1.
(5th St. and Logan Heights Line.)
SOUTHBOUND—On 5th St., H St., 16th St., Logan Ave. and National Ave. to 31st St.
NORTHBOUND—On 5th St., University Ave. and Park Blvd. to Normal School, Mission Cliff Park and Ostrich Farm.
NOTE—Connections with City Heights and Normal Heights lines.
ROUTE NO. 2.
(1st and D Street Line.)
EASTBOUND—To Golden Hill, Brooklyn Heights and 30th and Upas Sts.
WESTBOUND—To 1st and D and 1st and Laurel.
ROUTE NO. 3.
(3rd and H Street Line.)
SOUTHBOUND—To 3rd and H Sts., out H St. to 25th St.
NORTHBOUND—To Hillcrest and Mission Hills.
ROUTE NO. 4.
(M Street Line.)
EASTBOUND—East on D St., South on 5th St. to K St., to 10th St., to M St. Out M St. to Cemeteries or "Sierra Vista."
NOTE—This car for Pacific Coast Steamship Co.'s wharf, San Diego Southern and Cuyamaca Depots.
NORTHBOUND—North on 5th St., West on D St., to State St., North on State St. and India St. to Ramona's Marriage Place, Old Town.
ROUTE NO. 5.
(3rd & K Street Line.)
SOUTHBOUND—On 3rd St. to H St., to 5th and H Sts., to 5th and K Sts., East on K to 25th, on 25th to Grant Ave., thence to 30th.
NOTE—This car for Pacific Coast Steamship Co.'s wharf and San Diego Southern Ry. Depot.
NORTHBOUND—North on 3rd St. to Hillcrest and Mission Hills.
ROUTE NO. 6.
(F Street Line.)
BETWEEN 4th and D Streets and 25th and F Streets.
ROUTE NO. 7.
(B Street Line.)
BETWEEN Russ High School and Santa Fe Yards.
ROUTE NO. 8.
(Depot Line.)
BETWEEN 5th and D Streets and Santa Fe and La Jolla Depots and Los Banos Baths.
ROUTE NO. 9.
(Coronado Ferry.)
To Ferry Landing via D St., 5th, 5th and H Sts.
ROUTE NO. 10.
(Coronado Ferry.)
To Ferry Landing via D, State and H Streets.

OVER

All these will not be listed in the texts unless significant changes in trackage are involved.

New Power Plant

The demands for electric energy kept constantly increasing to a point beyond the safe generating capacity of the small plant located west of the car storage and shops areas.

An entire city block at India and Ivy Streets had been bought in 1905 as a power plant and car house site but it had been decided not to use it for such purposes.

So, plans were drawn for an entirely new reinforced concrete building on the northwest corner of Kettner Blvd. and E St., where the car house was located. The use of the block diagonally across Kettner Blvd., a part of the San Diego & Arizona Railway's right-of-way, was arranged for. A temporary shed was erected for shops purposes and tracks

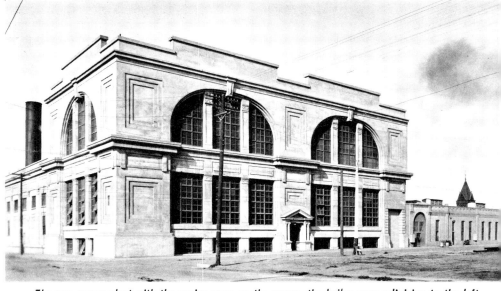

The new power plant with the engine room on the corner, the boiler room adjoining to the left. Car body and paint shop to the right of the engine room. Tower above shops is on the Santa Fe depot—R. V. Dodge

were laid for car storage in the open.

Then the old structure was town down and the erection of the building now occupying the northwest corner (1957) was started in 1910.

The generating equipment specified was extraordinary.

An order was placed with Allis-Chalmers Manufacturing Company for: One vertical cross-compound reciprocating Steam Engine, cylinders 28 inches and 60 inches diameters by 48 inches stroke, to develop 1,810 Indicated Horse Power, direct connected to one Westinghouse 1,200 Kilowatt, 600 Volt, Direct Current Generator, 80 Revolutions per minute, 160 pounds per square inch gauge steam pressure, and, in combination with, One Exhaust (Low Pressure) Steam Turbine, 3,600 Revolutions per minute, reduction gear connected to one Westinghouse 1,000 Kilowatt, 600 Volt, Direct Current Generator, 514 Revolutions per Minute.

These were known as Units No. 2 and No. 3.

The building was completed in 1911, Units No. 2 and No. 3 were installed in that year, then some of the old machinery was moved to the new engine room, including:

The 1,000 Kilowatt Turbo-Direct Current Generator, Unit No. 1,

The two 500 Kilowatt Motor-Generator Sets, Units No. 4 and 5,

The two 500 Kilowatt Turbo-Alternators, Units No. 6 and No. 7, including the Exciters.

The Allis-Chalmers vertical compound reciprocating steam engine dominated the interior of the engine room.—San Diego Gas & Electric

Adams Avenue Car Barn at Florida Street was completed in 1913. This view taken about 1929.—F. W. Reif

Two Aultman & Taylor 400 Horse Power water tube Boilers were added. In 1914 and 1915, two Babcock & Wilcox 400 Horse Power water tube boilers were installed.

About the same time, one 5,000 Kilovolt-amperes Westinghouse Turbo-Alternator with a 50 Kilowatt Exciter, 2,400 Volts, 1,800 Revolutions per Minute, was added as Unit No. 8, together with two 1,500 Kilovolt-amperes General Electric Motor-Generator Sets with 2,150 Horse Power Synchronous Motors 2,300 Volts, 360 Revolutions per Minute, direct connected to 550 Volt Direct Current Generators, Units No. 9 and No. 10.

In 1917, Motor-Generator Set, Unit No. 4, was transferred to the Substation Equipment Account. It was removed and used as a portable substation on the National City and Chula Vista Line.

The three 250 Horse Power Keeler Boilers were retired.

In 1920, the two Cahill 250 Horse Power Boilers were removed, along with Unit No. 5, the other 500 Kilowatt Motor-Generator Set. The 1,000 Kilowatt Turbo-Generator had been removed but not credited.

That was the situation on December 31st, 1920. Effective on New Year's Day, the property, including the Power Plant, and all equipment was sold to the San Diego Consolidated Gas & Electric Company. Thereafter the San Diego Electric Railway purchased the electric energy required.

All the old generating equipment except Unit No. 8 — Westinghouse Turbo-Alternator and Units No. 9 and No. 10 — General Electric Motor-Generator Sets were soon replaced with additional turbo-alternators and motor-generator sets.

New Facilities

The need for new shops and new car houses had been anticipated.

On June 19, 1909, the property on the westerly side of Fifteenth Street from K Street to Imperial Ave. was purchased, 600 feet by 200 feet.

The following December a contract was awarded for the construction of a reinforced concrete Car House, 195 feet by 276 feet on the block between L Street and Imperial Ave., 100 car capacity.

It had three bays with 15 tracks and was completed in April 1911.

The brick Shops Building on the northwest corner of 15th Street and L Street was being erected in 1912. When completed, the temporary facilities at Kettner Blvd. and E Street were removed. Tracks were laid on 15th Street from K Street to Imperial Ave. with ladder tracks into the shops and the yard in 1913.

In the latter year, a second Car Storage House of brick construction was built on property which had been acquired through acquisition of the Citizens Traction Company on the north side of Adams Ave., at Florida Street. With a capacity of 100 cars, it cost $145,000.

Build! Build! Build!

As Adams wrote, in effect,: Money, as such, meant little to J. D. It was just a means to an end. And the end was to Build!, Build!, Build!

Visualizing a group of substantial structures of blending architecture and uniform skyline, he had purchased all the property fronting on the south side of Broadway from Kettner Blvd. to Third Ave., 8 blocks.

Reinforced concrete construction was just coming into general use and it was adopted as the standard.

The first concrete structure to be erected was the easterly part of the six story *Union Building* at Third Ave. in 1908. It housed the offices of the many local Spreckels' companies and there were several floors available as rentals.

Then the magnificent *Spreckels Theater Building*, with its large auditorium and up-to-the-minute equipped stage to handle the largest road productions, together with many office suites was built at a cost of $1,000,000 on the block from First Ave. to Second Ave. It was dedicated on August 23, 1912.

The Second Ave. section of the Union Building was added in 1911.

The *San Diego Hotel*, on the block

Machine and repair shops about 1927.—F. W. Reif

Imperial Avenue car house about 1927.—
F. W. Reif

between State Street and Union Street, was begun in 1913.

Also J. D. purchased property at Fourth Ave. and G St. and put up the *Golden West Hotel.*

In 1914, a plant building for the two newspapers was erected on Second Ave., adjoining the Union Building.

In Coronado, in 1909, J. D. had built an attractive *Public Library* and presented it, including the park, to the people.

All these were in addition to the many San Diego Electric Railway Company's facilities.

In reply to some critics, J. D. said: " . . . if I have extended the street car lines ahead of population, . . . if I have built stores and offices and hotels and a theatre ahead of demand, I can see that this may be a reflection on my business sense; but for the life of me, I can not see that San Diego has any cause for complaint. Whether or not any investment paid me, I paid taxes on it."

"I build for the future, not for immediate returns."

Franchise Battle

Would you buy any street railway company's bonds having a term of only 25 years?

By the provisions of the City Charter, the granting of street car franchises was limited to a 25-year maximum term. J. D. had encountered great difficulties in financing improvements with this limitation. There was no market for such short term bonds.

To remedy the situation, in 1910, he sought to obtain a charter amendment, by means of the newly authorized "Initiative and Referendum".

The opponents rapidly sprang up, prepared arguments and organized "Anti-Spreckels" groups. Led by the afternoon newspaper, the San Diego Sun, which J. D. castigated as "scurrilous, unscrupulous and hypocritical", and demagogic politicians, much discontent was stirred up. It became a bitter campaign. It was: "To Hell with Spreckels. We are sick and tired of being a one-man town. If Spreckels wants 50-year franchises the down trodden common people must see that he does not get them."

The Sun kept harping on capitalistic greed, incapable management, poor service, old-fashioned cars, defective brakes,

flat wheels, overcrowding and what not. At one time, the Spreckels' corporations had been accused of being linked with "The Stingaree", San Diego's red light district. It was a general accusation that: "the public utilities of the City of San Diego had been helped, supported and protected by money filched from fallen women . . . ".

Just before the election, Austin Adams pitched into the fracas. He came out apparently opposing Spreckels, then, by clever sarcasm, of which he was a master, and the deadly *reductio ad absurdum,* refuted the misleading arguments. His version, in his inimitable style, is so cunning that it is worth repeating.

Quote: I went the "antis" one better in denouncing that ruthless and scheming enemy of the people, John D. Spreckels. They merely denounced him; I damned him up hill and down. I catalogued his heinous crimes against poor long-suffering one-man-ridden San Diego; I showed him up pointing to the fact that he had come to San Diego when everybody else who had the price of a railway ticket was leaving the busted village — that he had with diabolical malice aforethought invested millions here when everybody knew that San Diego was destined to remain forever a one-horse, not a one-man, town — that he had proved his heartless contempt for the rights of the workingman by keeping hundreds working for him at the highest wages when, as times were bad and money was tight, nobody else was cruel enough to exploit the wage-slaves by giving them work, but allowed them to be gentlemen of leisure and walk the streets — that his ulterior object in asking for long-term franchises was that he wanted to be able at any time to go on developing his one-man town — that he had already got a strangle hold upon us all by pouring million after million into our city — and, finally, that if we did not rally at the polls to put a stop to his outrageous policies, this dangerous man would go right on developing San

Looking west on Broadway from Fourth Avenue about 1925. The Plaza was a famous gathering place in San Diego. Beyond the Plaza is the Union Building (now Land Title Building). Next building west is the Spreckels' Theater Building. Note the many street cars and the motor bus on Third Avenue.—Union Title

Diego until his devilish dream of turning it into a real city was realized! End of quote.

"You can't fool all the people all the time".

The election was held on February 15, 1911 and the amendment carried by a ratio of over two to one.

Benefits From Longer Franchise

"Thanks to J. D's. willingness to invest hundreds of thousands of dollars in developing a superb street car system long before it was needed and before it could possibly pay", a broad program to improve the services rendered was undertaken.

William Clayton, Vice-President and Managing Director, set forth the details in October 1911 as follows:

Extend the Broadway - Brooklyn Heights Line on 30th St., from Upas St. to University Ave.

Then extend Route No. 2 from Upas St., to University Ave. and out University ave. to Fairmount Ave., cutting back the University Ave. shuttle to 30th St.

Double track along the greater part of University Ave., from 30th St. east.

Establish 10 minute service from University and Fairmount to Fifth Ave. and Broadway.

Change service on the Adams Ave. shuttle from one-half hour to 15 minute headway, connecting with the proposed 5 minute service on No. 1 Line from Mission Cliff to Downtown.

Extend the double track on the Third Ave.-Mission Hills Line from the Robinson Hotel (4th Ave. and Grape St.) to Hawk St.

Double track the State St.-Old Town Line from Broadway to India and Winder Sts. This will enable the Point Loma cars to operate without interference.

Extend the double track on the Imperial Ave. Line from Eleventh Ave. to 32nd St.

On No. 1 Route, establish 5 minute service from Mission Cliff Gardens to National Ave. (Logan Heights) as soon as cars are available.

Increase the frequency on the Point Loma Line from one hour and 40 minutes to 40 minutes.

Will order about 25 new cars.

He emphasized that "This does not mean that car service in San Diego with 40,000 to 50,000 people will be as frequent as that in Los Angeles with 300,-000".

Smokestacks or Geraniums

Not only were the citizens divided pro and anti Spreckels, but they became further split as to the ultimate development of San Diego.

One faction wanted *The City Beautiful.* They were called the "geraniums". The other was working for *The City Prosperous.* They were known as the "smokestacks".

The geraniums desired to turn San Diego into a sort of exclusive residential park. The smokestacks wanted commercial and manufacturing enterprises to build up large payrolls.

J. D. took the only sensible course, the middle of the road. "City Beautiful", "City Prosperous". Why not both?

In 1923, at a dinner gathering of San Diego business men, both pros and antis, J. D. bared his heart in an epochal address. He should have delivered it years before, but, as he always said: "I am a man of action, not words."

In this talk of simple eloquence, he lashed out. He told them just what was wrong with San Diego. Quoting, in part:—

A "one-man" town! My God! If you only knew how often I have turned heaven and earth to induce men of large means to come to San Diego. For thirty years I have hoped and worked for men with big ideas, big ability and big capital to get into our big game down here. God knows we need them! Would not such

an enormous influx of capital mean more to me than to anybody else?

Just see what brains and capital have done for Los Angeles. Why? Well, simply because Los Angeles business men see the need for wholehearted co-operation; and San Diego business men do not. — They pull together; we indulge in a tug-of-war. — They build; we tear down. End of quote.

And he had hit the nails right on their respective heads.

San Diego & Southeastern Railway

The San Diego Southern Railway, since 1908, had been operating the steam divisions of the former Coronado Railroad and National City & Otay Railway, including the electric interurban line from San Diego to National City, Chula Vista and, later, to Otay.

Since its incorporation, it had the right to build a railroad from San Diego to Lakeside, which would be in competition with the San Diego, Cuyamaca & Eastern Railway. But E. S. Babcock had been in control of the latter since 1904.

This simplified the acquisition of that railroad by the Spreckels interests and it was taken over in 1909. The corporate name was changed to *San Diego & Cuyamaca Railway Company,* with William Clayton as President.

Up to 1908 the Cuyamaca had operated steam trains only from San Diego to La Mesa, El Cajon, Lakeside and Foster. In that year a McKeen Gasoline Motor Car was received and it was given the name "Cuyamaca". An Automobile Rail Car with chain drives and a passenger body was also in use, bearing number 24.

Time Schedule No. 27, effective January 21, 1912, of the San Diego & Cuyamaca listed four passenger round trips daily between San Diego and Foster, one daily except Sunday, two Saturday only and one Mixed and one Freight trains daily except Sunday. There were notations that "Trains will be run with Locomotive or Gasoline Motor Car, as occasion may require." and "Company Reserves the Right to Vary from this Schedule at Pleasure." E. A. Hornbeck was the General Manager.

In order to effect the economies that would result through the merger of the Cuyamaca with the San Diego Southern, a new corporation was formed in 1912, immediately following Time Schedule

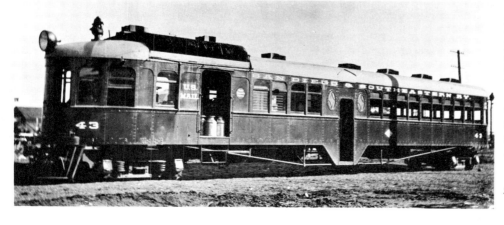

San Diego & South Eastern gasoline motor car No. 43.—R. P. Middlebrook

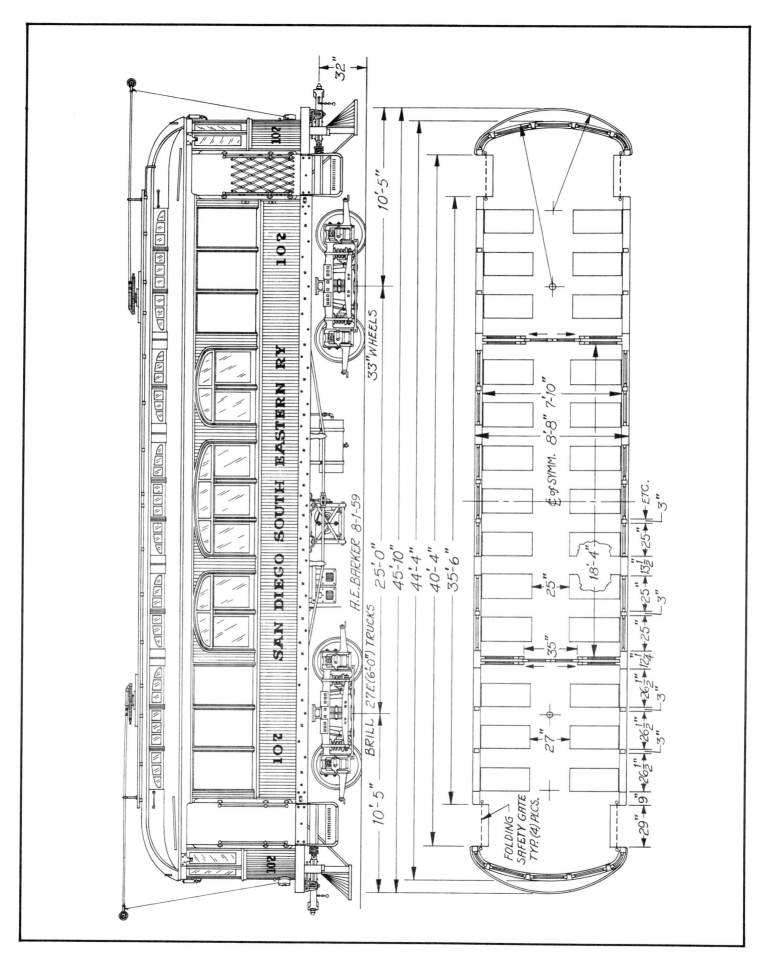

SAN DIEGO SOUTH EASTERN RY

102

101

102

101

102

A.E. BARKER 8-1-59

BRILL 27E (6'-0") TRUCKS

33" WHEELS

32"

10'-5"

25'-0"

45'-10"

44'-4"

40'-4"

35'-6"

10'-5"

℄ of SYMM. 8'-8" 7'-10"

18'-4"

25"

35"

27"

29" 9" 26½" 26½" 26½" 12¼" 25" 13½" 25"

3" 3" 3" 3" ETC.

FOLDING SAFETY GATE TYP. (4) PCS.

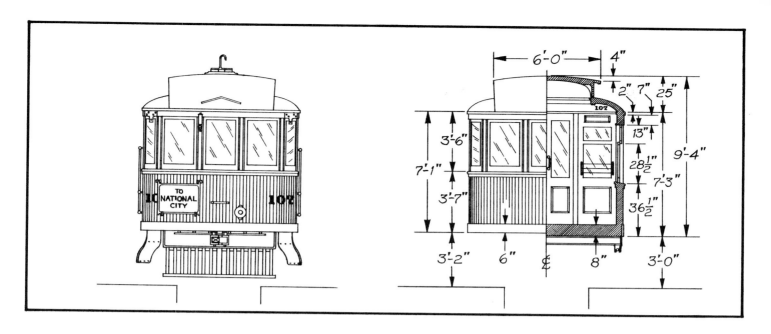

San Diego & South Eastern No. 101 and trailer car. This scene at 3rd Avenue and Broadway just before No. 101 was remodelled into a combination car.—R. V. Dodge

San Diego & South Eastern No. 101 and trailer car. This scene at 3rd Avenue and Broadway after No. 101 was remodelled into a combination car.—R. V. Dodge

No. 27, with the name *San Diego & South Eastern Railway Company.*

Operations were then divided into three divisions. The Cuyamaca became the Eastern Division, the Coronado and National City & Otay steam lines became the Southern Division and the interurban line the Electric Division.

Time Table No. 1 of the San Diego & South Eastern, effective March 31, 1912, indicates, by omission, that the use of the motor cars had been discontinued. The McKeen Car "Cuyamaca" was sold to the United States Reclamation District for the Yuma Valley Railroad, Arizona.

On the Southern Division, steam trains were operated from Sixth Ave. and L St., San Diego to Tijuana and to Sweetwater Dam. After the Cuyamaca station was moved from Tenth Ave. to 13th St. on Commercial St., only one steam train a day was operated out of San Diego, from 13th St., to National City, the others starting from 24th St. and Cleveland Ave., National City. Effective September 1, 1914, no steam train service was provided out of San Diego over the Southern Division.

The number of trains on the Eastern Division was reduced but the Electric Division was flourishing, using the rebuilt coaches No. 101 to 104 inclusive and the three Niles cars No. 105 to 107, the trailers, also the Express Car No. 111. These were relettered.

After car No. 101 had been damaged in a collision, it was reconstructed into a combination express and passenger car.

Injuries Galore

As the traffic of all sorts increased, so did the number of accidents. Many were ascribed to the California-type street cars, especially the 33 footers which had only hand brakes operated by a lever.

Here are a few that occurred in 1910:

February 2: Carl H. Heilbron, prominent electrical dealer and politician, was waiting for an inbound car at 22nd St. on Broadway. As the car approached, the lever brakes did not take hold on the hill and the car rolled on to 21st St. before it could be stopped. Mr. Heilbron attempted to board the car at the rear end when it whizzed by. He was thrown to the pavement and injured.

May 16: Hand brake lever strikes woman's head.

A boy was saved from death by a passenger on car No. 59.

April 5: Falls off, trying to save hat. Woman dies.

June 30: Two men fell off a Coronado car.

And, in 1911:

April 10: Man Struck by car. Near death.

April 29: A child was saved by the fenders.

July 10: Car at Fourth and Maple strikes a Flanders automobile carrying 13 persons.

July 23: Woman fell off University Ave. car, when reaching for her purse.

Woman loses grip on stanchion on car No. 76, on curve. Fatally hurt.

October 26: Boy attempted to get off a Brooklyn Heights car at 19th and Broadway at full speed. Right leg had to be amputated.

November 5: Man died after stepping from a moving car at 5th and Walnut.

December 12: Man fainted. Fell off open section of Old Town car going west on Broadway at Union St.

Many efforts were made to increase the safety of the open sections of the cars.

Meyer Rail Guards, consisting of counter balanced iron frames operated by the motorman or the conductor, were tried out on car No. 91. They prevented the patrons from alighting on the wrong side, since double track operations now increased the hazards, also prevented passengers from alighting until the car was stopped but many got their heads bumped.

Wooden skirts were attached to all the cars, as side fenders, between the step sections.

Modern Cars

The art of street car building had advanced beyond the home-made type. So, it had been decided not to build any more cars locally. The California design was now considered obsolete.

As more rolling stock was needed, 24 cars of a new type, Center Entrance, Pay As You Enter, were ordered from the St. Louis Car Company and were delivered in 1912. They were 43 ft. 7 inches long and the bodies had a closed section and an open section each. All had 2 General Electric motors as original equipment. They were assigned numbers 125 to 148 inclusive.

Subsequently, a classification system was adopted and these cars became Class No. 1.

In the same year, a larger car of similar type was ordered from American Car Company, as a trial. It was 48 ft. 7 inches long. This was in anticipation of the needs to handle the exposition traffic in 1915.

When received, this car was given number 149, a forerunner of Class No. 2.

As these new cars were readied for operation, most of the remaining original equipment, except the Coronado cars, were removed from passenger car service, in 1912 and 1913. Among the retirements were: No. 1 to 8 inclusive,

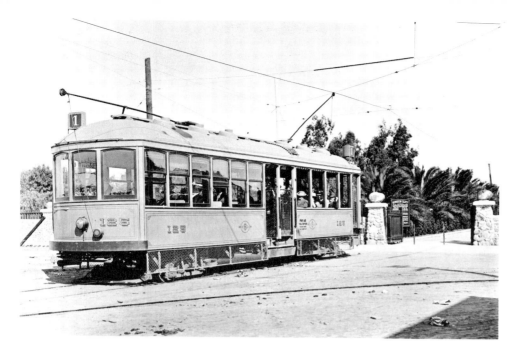

Pay-As-You-Enter car No. 125 pauses at the north end of Route 1 at Mission Cliff Gardens. (Below) A general view of the 1915 Panama-California Exposition in Balboa Park. The tall tower is the California State Building. (Lower) The terminal at the Exposition grounds in Balboa Park. Line made a loop at the extreme right.—Union Title

second No. 12, second No. 13, second No. 14 and California type 33 ft. Cars No. 51 and 53.

Second No. 12 was transferred to Service Equipment and was converted into Wrecker No. 54.

Panama-California Exposition

Along in 1909, someone came up with the brilliant idea that San Diego should put on a World's Fair. What better way could be devised to gain publicity for the fast growing town? The suggestion took hold immediately. Col. D. C. Collier became the chief promoter, soon acquiring the title of "Director General".

The numerous proposals and varied suggestions resolved into the date to be the year 1915 and the theme — to celebrate the opening of the Panama Canal, scheduled for completion in that year. The name selected for the big event was the Panama-California Exposition.

An exposition fund was started and, by the end of 1909, over half a million dollars had been subscribed.

Suddenly some San Franciscans decided that an exposition in 1915 was their prerogative as San Francisco, at that time, dominated the State. It would be named the Panama-Pacific International Exposition. This caused great consternation and anxiety among the San Diegans. Numerous meetings and conferences ensued between the parties concerned without agreement.

Then J. D. stepped in, in 1910, with a cash donation of $100,000. This clinched it. San Diego was determined not to be bluffed out. It had the backing of all the Southern California Counties. By April, over $750,000 was in the fund. All this was accomplished by a city of about 40,000.

A portion of a near-barren hilltop in City Park was selected as the site and the name was changed to Balboa Park. A bond issue by the City provided for major improvement and the attractive landscaping was started.

For access to the area, Laurel St. was extended east from Sixth Ave. and the graceful "El Puente de Cabrillo" (Cabrillo Bridge) was built of reinforced concrete to span the rustic canyon, now occupied by the Cabrillo Freeway. The extension of Laurel St. through the site was called "El Prado".

This exposition was going to be different. In the first place, it was to be open the entire year. Then the finest examples of Spanish-Colonial architecture were adopted for the exhibit buildings designs, all of temporary type except the

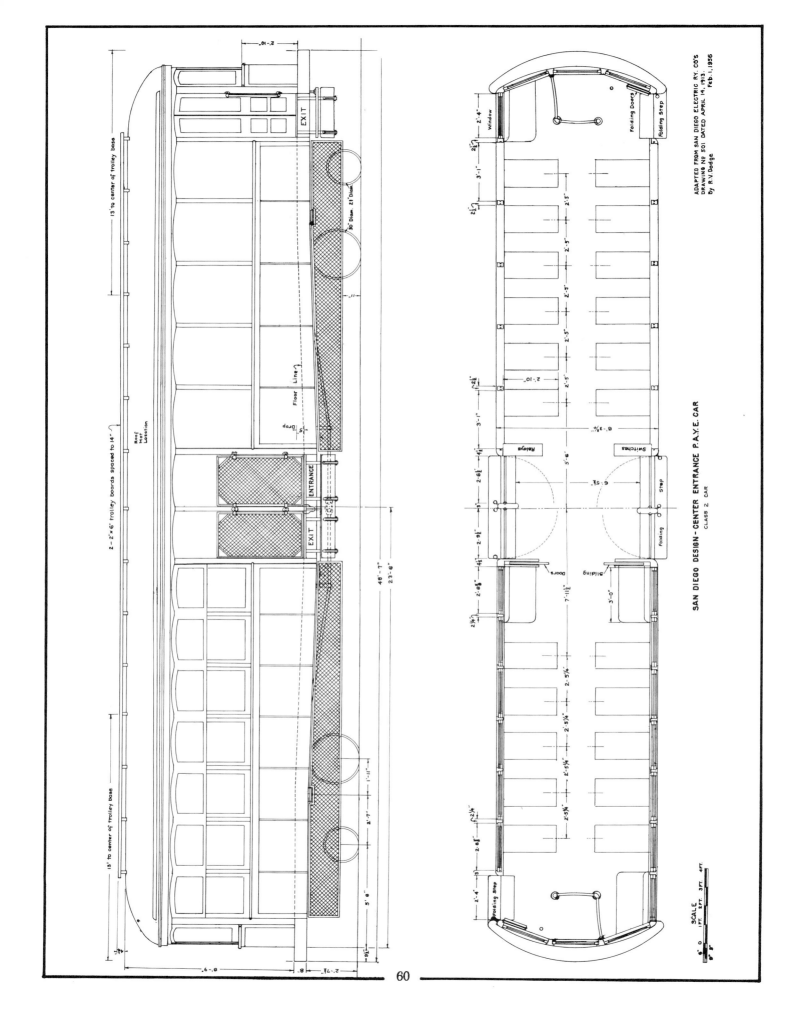

SAN DIEGO DESIGN - CENTER ENTRANCE P.A.Y.E. CAR
CLASS 2 CAR

ADAPTED FROM SAN DIEGO ELECTRIC RY. CO'S
DRAWING № 501 DATED APRIL 14, 1913.
By R.V. Dodge   Feb. 1, 1956

SCALE
1 FT.   2 FT.   3 FT.   4 FT.

more of the lovable California-type cars, a large order was placed for up-to-date cars for delivery in 1914.

The try-out of the San Diego type Center Entrance Pay As You Enter car No. 149 had been found to be highly successful. 35 additional cars were ordered from the McGuire-Cummings Company and 40 of the same type were purchased from the St. Louis Car Company.

The new cars were numbered No. 150 to 184 inclusive and No. 185 to 224 inclusive respectively. All were equipped for Multiple Unit operation and the MU equipment was added to No. 149.

So advanced was the design considered that the St. Louis Car Company built an additional car in 1914 and entered it as an exhibit in the Panama-Pacific International Exposition in San Francisco. It was awarded a prize as being the finest street car in the United States.

At the end of the San Francisco Fair, the "Exposition" car was bought by the

California State Building with its landmarking tower. The effect was both striking and harmonious.

At the main intersection was created the charming "Plaza de Panama". There was a "Cristobal" restaurant. The fun zone, located on what it now Park Blvd., north of Laurel St., was named "The Isthmus".

For public transportation, the nearest street cars were on the Fifth Ave. Line. This was augmented by the laying of a track on Laurel St., from Fourth Ave. to Fifth Ave., so that extra cars could be operated up and down the Third Ave. Line.

But these lines could not provide convenient service, so, in 1914, the "Park Line" was built, double track using 75 pound rails in the Park and heavier in the streets, on Twelfth Ave., from F St. to Ash St. then through the Park to Laurel St. There a handsome multi-arched tile-roofed Terminal was constructed. Pedestrian traffic was separated by fences, making it necessary for those entering the Exposition to use a subway. Storage side tracks and switches were installed north of the Terminal.

The franchise also provided for an extension of the tracks to the north line of the Park at Upas St., but this construction would require the erection of three double track trestles over ravines. The structural steel was ordered for them.

Second tracks were laid on B St., from Second Ave. to Twelfth Avenue, and on F St., from Third Ave., to Twelfth Ave.

In 1915, a turn-around loop was installed in Broadway at the new Santa Fe depot. A 1918 statement reveals that a loop track was also constructed at the

Car No. 158 was one of 35 San Diego type center entrance cars built by McGuire-Cummings in 1914 for Exposition service. A total of 77 cars of this design were purchased. The photograph below shows the interior from the closed section.—R. V. Dodge

Exposition Terminal, resulting in a loss of $4,069.25.

Much track reconstruction was undertaken at this time, replacing 60 pound rail with 114 pound "Trilby" section in downtown streets and in others scheduled to be paved.

Class Two Cars

In preparation for the expected rush and to provide for the replacements of

San Diego Electric Railway and was assigned No. 225.

These 77 cars constituted Class No. 2. The San Diego Electric Railway Company was well equipped to transport the anticipated exposition traffic.

More old cars were vacated and retired in 1914, including all the remaining California-type 33 ft. series except No. 69. The latter was remodelled into a one-man P. A. Y. E. car in 1915.

Car No. 55 was transferred to Service

Trolley car leaving Hotel del Coronado for Tent City about 1920. (Below) Race fans returning from Tijuana and homeward bound during 1916 racing season. Cars are operated in two car trains. (Lower) The year 1914 saw most 40 foot California type cars altered to Pay-As-You-Enter end entrance.

had to be done about the 40 footers built in 1910 and 1911.

Plans were prepared to convert them into 2-men PAYE type. 22 cars, No. 87 to 99 inclusive and No. 102 to 110 inclusive, were remodelled in 1914 and 1915. The improvements were: to install single wire mesh gates and folding steps at the forward end on the right hand side, according to the direction of motion, and double ones at the rear. The remaining openings were panelled to the window sill height. The seats were reversed against the sides, to face in and frames with iron bars prevented you from sticking your head or arms out. Wooden skirts were hooked onto the side sills between the steps, to prevent persons from rolling under the wheels.

The symmetrical beauty of the cars was destroyed as well as the feeling of freedom, but they were much safer. Now they were called "cattle cars".

Cars No. 100 and 101 had been assigned to the Coronado Division and were not altered.

Cars numbers 87 to 92 inclusive were retired in 1916.

The remaining ones were again rebuilt in 1917, changing from two to one-man operation. All were retired from passenger service in 1920 except numbers 103, 104 and 106. The latter were kept on the roster for several years more.

Mighty Organ Rolls

'Twas the night before the New Year, the final hours of 1914!

A large crowd had assembled in the south end of the now indescribably beautiful Plaza de Panama in Balboa Park.

J. D. was there. So overcome was he by the ovation he received that he could scarcely speak. With great difficulty, he said to John F. Forward, President of the Park Commission, simply: "I beg you to accept this gift on behalf of the people

Equipment and was converted into Wrecker No. 55. The others were stored for several years.

Cars No. 81 and 82 were remodelled for one-man operation and were sold to the Bay Shore Railway Company.

No. 80 and 83 to 86 were sold complete, as was, to the Phoenix Railway Company, Phoenix, Arizona, in 1918, No. 70 to 76 following in 1919. The remaining cars were dismantled.

"Box Car" No. 44, originally No. 11, was disposed of in 1916.

Car Rebuilds

The retirements from passenger car service of the 33 ft. California-type cars and the rebuilding of No. 69 solved the accident prevention program as far as they were concerned but something

The great outdoor pipe organ in Balboa Park.
—Union Title

Since these lines now provided service from downtown to the San Diego High School, the B St. Line was discontinued.

When it was decided to run the Exposition for a second full year, 1916, J. D. chipped in another $100,000. As he used to remark: It's "damn Spreckels, except when the hat is being passed around".

Jitney Busses

"The number of privately owned automobiles has increased to such an extent that we have one automobile to each 50 persons and *the end is not yet*." This was the ominous observation in 1915.

Already the automobile was working great injury to the street railway companies throughout the country. Not only was there the loss of the driver and his family as customers but accommodating car owners would happen by, stop at street corners and pick up their "friends"

of the City of San Diego". And the unique, the great, the magnificent *outdoor pipe organ* and its beautiful pavilion were dedicated. It was a noble gift from him and his loyal brother, A. B., to the people of the city he loved.

Then, an old friend of J. D's., the distinguished organist and composer, Dr. J. Humphrey Stewart, had the honor of playing the superb instrument that memorable first night (and continued to give daily concerts for years afterwards).

At the stroke of midnight, Pacific Time, Woodrow Wilson, the President of the United States of America, pressed a button in Washington, D. C. and the Panama-California Exposition was formally opened.

Getting back to the materialistic, the gift of the four manual Austin organ and the artistic pavilion, which had been designed by Harrison Albright, had cost almost $125,000. In addition J. D. provided for its upkeep and furnished the services of the organist.

The Panama–California and the Panama-Pacific International Expositions became a double attraction, the one complementing the other. More visitors came to San Diego in 1915 than in any previous year. The railroads helped by advertising "Two Fairs for One Fare". The Santa Fe operated through trains from San Diego via Los Angeles and Barstow to Richmond (ferry to San Francisco) and to Oakland. They were named "The Saint" and "The Angel".

To handle the large crowds, the San Diego Electric Railway was prepared to operate Class 2 cars in two car trains on one minute headway over the Park

For safety and economy, car No. 69 was remodeled into a front entrance car.—F. W. Reif

Line, whenever traffic demanded.

Route No. 7 cars ran from the Exposition Terminal via Twelfth Ave., F St., Third Ave., B St., Twelfth Ave. to the Terminal.

Route No. 11 cars operated around the downtown loop in the reverse direction, namely: from the Exposition Terminal via Twelfth Ave., B St., Thrid Ave., F St., Twelfth Ave. to the Terminal.

when there was room for just one or two more.

Soon enterprising but irresponsible drivers were making a business of picking up the potential patrons of the street cars and carrying them downtown or bringing them back for the usual five cent fare. Some just had touring cars, others vehicles fitted with crude contraptions for passenger carryalls, sort of fore runners of the station wagons.

Jitney bus on the left had little appeal to the race fans boarding the Race Specials.— R. C. Brandt

Up to 1914, the **San Diego Electric** Railway's business had been increasing steadily year after year. It was thought that the Exposition would greatly add to the revenues. The Company had spent more than $1,600,000 for additions and betterments.

The Park Line had cost	$215,000
Second Tracks on B St. and F St.,	125,000
75 new cars	495,000
Increased Power	105,000
Adams Ave. Car House	145,000
Track Reconstruction	245,000

Plus paving and other facilities.

As of January 1, 1915, the Company had 38.9 miles of Single Track, 22.4 miles of Double Track, making a total of 83.7 miles to Equivalent Single Track.

It did not receive enough income from the Exposition to pay the operating expenses.

The unregulated jitneys were permitted to operate in direct violation of the exclusive franchise granted by the City of San Diego. It was estimated that the Company lost more than 8,000,000 nickel fares to the jitneys during the years 1914 and 1915. The failure to produce favorable operating figures caused large decreases in the values of the corporate securities.

"Municipal public utility and State authorities looked upon the jitneys as a joke — Comedy. It turned out to be a Tragedy." It was impossible to sell bond issues, which had been authorized, in the open market.

Belatedly the "jits" were ruled off the streets.

Too Much Water!

All over town — the mud!
The failure of the Lower Otay Dam during the floods which occurred in January 1916 has been mentioned. It so happened that the City of San Diego had employed a professional rainmaker, named Hatfield. A storm on the 17th brought a record rainfall, for which he was given credit. All the railroads were washed out. Then another storm followed and the Dam collapsed on Thursday, the 27th. Poor Hatfield! He never got the money due him, since the City could not pay him without assuming the liability for all the havoc.

The losses and the damages to the railroad companies were terrific.

There was no through train service to Los Angeles on the Santa Fe until February 19th. The branch line from the junction north of Oceanside, up the Temecula Canyon, to Fallbrook Station was badly washed out, marooning engine No. 721, 3 coaches and several freight cars. As the result, the easterly half of the branch was abandoned and the present line to the City of Fallbrook was built in the following year. Then the engine and the serviceable cars were laboriously dragged from the canyon, up the steep grade on a County Road, on short track sections, and down the main street to the new track.

So great was the damage done to the San Diego & Southeastern's lines by the floods that it seemed utterly impractical to rebuild. All of its divisions were wrecked.

The electric line used the former National City & Otay's tracks, which crossed the Sweetwater River Valley about a mile and a half east of the Cleveland Ave. and 24th St. station in National City. The crossing in the river bottom was completely obliterated. Express Car No. 111 was caught in the maelstrom, was carried downstream and nearly buried in mud and sand. It had to be

Sweetwater Dam during the floods of January 1916.—Union Title

abandoned. As soon as the track from San Diego to National City, across Chollas Valley and other bad places was repaired, interurban service was resumed from San Diego, out 24th St., to the north bank of the Sweetwater River.

The remainder of the National City & Otay's system was abandoned, except for a portion on Third Ave., in Chula Vista. These retirements included the lines to Sweetwater Dam, to La Presa and to Tijuana.

The Coronado Belt Line's bridges and tracks across the Sweetwater Valley could be repaired and it was decided to do this.

The operation of the Electric Division was then turned over to the San Diego Electric Railway, under a lease arrangement. From 24th St., in National City, the Coronado line was electrified as far as F St., in Chula Vista. New electric

tracks were laid from a connecting switch, named Marmarosa Junction, on F St. and cross lots to join with the old line on Third Ave. Service was then established from San Diego to Chula Vista as far as Third Ave. and K St. The line on 24th St. in National City was discontinued.

On the Southern Division, trains using steam power were operated over the Coronado Belt Line only, in freight service.

The Eastern Division had suffered severe damage. There was little track left between Santee, north of El Cajon, to the end of the line at Foster. Time Table No. 8, effective February 22, 1916, shows operations cut back to Santee. By November, the road had been rebuilt as far as Lakeside. The trackage from that point to Foster was abandoned.

The San Diego & Arizona did not

escape severe damage, but particularly in the Otay River Valley. Engine No. 50, when operating on temporary track laid in the bed of Sweetwater River, toppled over into the mud and laid there for a month before it could be lifted out.

To improve the operating conditions on the interurban line, the San Diego Electric Railway fitted up a portable sub-station in 1917. 500 Kilowatt Motor-Generator Set, Unit No. 4, was removed from the Power Plant and was mounted on a San Diego & Southeastern's flat car, to-gether with the Alternating and the Direct Current Switchboards. A wooden housing was built to protect the equipment. This served as a booster station.

Balboa Park Line

After the elimination of the jitneys and the close of the Exposition at the end of 1916, the extra tracks at the Laurel St. Terminal were removed.

Then the three steel trestles were constructed over the canyons north of Laurel St. When completed, double tracks were laid from the ends at Laurel St., to the north line of the Park and were extended up Indiana Ave. and Park Blvd. to University Ave. all in 1917.

A rough breakdown of the cost of building the extension is:

3 Bridges	$96,000
75 pound Rail inside the Park, 114 pound in the remainder	15,000
Ties	4,000
Crossings	5,000
Ballasting	11,000
Labor and Incidentals	6,000

A new Route No. 7 was formed from Third Avenue and Broadway to Twelfth Avenue, through the Park to Indiana St., to Park Blvd., to University Ave., to Euclid Ave., the University Ave. Line having been extended from Fairmount Ave., to Euclid Ave. in 1916.

This new line eliminated the University Ave shuttle, and Route No. 2 was cut back to 30th St. and University Ave.

Some service was started to Adams Ave. and Kensington Park through Balboa Park as Route No. 11 but, as late as 1919, this was operated only during the morning and the afternoon rush hours.

Progress on S.D.&A. Ry.

J. D. remarked: ". . . if being a one-man town is bad for the town, it's hell for the one-man." And being a one-man railroad did not quench the tortures any.

Ground–breaking ceremonies for the new railroad were held near 28th St. and Main St. in San Diego on September

7, 1907. Thereafter construction work was started.

But 1907 was a depression year. Silver and gold, the real money used in California at that time, became so scarce that the use of fiat money or scrip was threatened. Therefore not much was accomplished.

In mid-summer of 1909, the contractors were working on the fill across Sweetwater River Valley and in the cut in the South bank to reach Chula Vista.

A large excursion was run on August 13, 1910 to Hot Springs (Agua Caliente), Baja California, and the railway's first passengers entered Mexico. There were two sections. A locomotive leased from the Santa Fe, number 490, pulled the first section and Number 1, the San Diego & Arizona's only engine at the time, brought up the second.

Tunnels numbers 1 and 2, near the present Rodriguez Dam, were completed in that year and, at the same time, construction was begun west from Seeley, the terminus of the Holton Interurban Railroad in Imperial Valley. And it had been decided to terminate the new road at El Centro.

But E. H. Harriman had died in September 1909 and R. S. Lovett succeeded him. The Southern Pacific then reneged on Harriman's agreement. Not only did the Southern Pacific refuse to contribute any more money but it started suit to recover the amounts already advanced. This was a staggering blow to J. D. Harriman had been furnishing the money and J. D. was spending it. The litigation ended with the Southern Pacific's final demurrer being thrown out of Court. The Southern Pacific was forced to remain part owner, but J. D. would have to raise the money to complete the road or

quit. J. D. didn't know what the word "quit" meant.

In 1911, a series of revolutions broke out in Mexico. The Mexican laborers left their jobs on the railroad. At one stage, war between the United States and Mexico seemed imminent and all United States' citizens were ordered out of Baja California.

Mid-January of 1914 found the end of the track near La Puerta, about 8 miles west of Tecate.

William Sproule had been elected President of Southern Pacific Company in 1911 and Julius Kruttschnit succeeded Lovett as Chairman of the Executive Committee on January 13, 1913. With this change of "Top Brass", cordial relations were again restored.

The European War had started in 1914. Money became tight. Word from the rail front was most discouraging. The line was going to cost much more than had been estimated.

Carriso Gorge was government property. J. D. had filed only homesteader's claims for the right-of-way. It was discovered that these had become void by default, due to the failure to perform the required work within the specified time. To avoid the risk of someone fil-

The first passenger train into Mexico on the San Diego & Arizona Railway on July 29, 1910. The train on the bridge is headed by leased Santa Fe 490, while the second section sports SD&A Number 1. (Below) Tijuana Race Specials with consolidations Nos. 50 and 101, pause at the Mexican Border about 1916.—R. V. Dodge

A view of the rugged right-of-way through the Carriso Gorge section of the line.—
R. V. Dodge

San Diego & Southeastern Dissolved

In a determined but futile effort to regain the loss of patronage to the private automobiles and the buses on the Eastern Division, William Clayton announced in August 1916 that radical reductions in fares would be made, that a new service would be on trial between San Diego, La Mesa, El Cajon and Santee. He expected to put on some gasoline Motor Cars and Trailers, making nine round trips a day.

Two General Electric - Schenectady Gasoline-Electric Motor Cars were purchased, second hand, from the "Dan Patch Lines", the Minneapolis, Northfield & Southern Railway. They had a rated seating capacity of 90 and were lettered and numbered San Diego & South Eastern Ry. No. 41 and No. 42. Both had express compartments and open rear platform entrances. At the same time, a Gasoline Automobile Car was purchased from Hewitt-Ludlow Auto Company and was fitted up locally, as number 31. A third General Electric-Schenectady Gasoline-Electric Motor Car, GE No. 3707, which had operated on the Buffalo, Rochester & Pacific Railway, was acquired as number 43.

This service would be handicapped by having the terminus at the 13th and Commercial Sts. station. Clayton stated that the Gas Cars will terminate at "Union Station".

To accomplish this, a franchise was asked to permit the building of a line parallel with the San Diego & Arizona Railway's track from Eighth Ave. to First Ave., to Market St., connecting there with the San Diego Electric Railway's track on First Ave. Before the franchise could be granted, a logical change took place.

The San Diego & Southeastern had lost much of its trackage in the flood, it was operating Motor Cars, thereby releasing steam power, it proposed to duplicate San Diego & Arizona trackage and the San Diego & Arizona needed locomotives.

The *San Diego & Arizona Railway Company* absorbed the San Diego & Southeastern Railway Company in 1917, taking over the operation of the steam divisions and the motor cars, while the San Diego Electric Railway continued to operate under lease the interurban line to Chula Vista. The motors retained their numbers but were relettered San Diego & Arizona.

Now the motor cars could be operated

ing on the right-of way claims, J. D. bought the whole mountain range.

Tunnels numbers 3 and 4 were finished and the rails were back in the United States in 1916, completing the 44 miles in Mexico. The international boundary line is crossed in tunnel No. 4 between Lindero, Baja California, and Division, California. That was the year of the big flood damage.

The United States entered the European War on April 6, 1917. The United States Railroad Administration took over the control of all the nation's railroads on December 28th. All railroad construction was stopped — except J. D's. J. D. went to Washington and obtained an exemption, the only one issued.

In that year work was begun in the difficult, almost impossible, Carriso Gorge. The track hangs on to a bench cut in the steep side of the mountain, high above the bottom of the Gorge. There are many twenty degree curves and there were seventeen tunnels. Many spindly wooden trestles, wood being necessary on account of the heat, had to be constructed. In addition, there are fourteen "side-hill" trestles, where the inside rail is on the ground and the outside one out on the trestle, so steep are the slopes.

Doggedly, construction was carried on.

Leaving for Ocean Beach and Point Loma. Note marker flags and air whistle.—R. V. Dodge

After the flood of 1916, the San Diego Electric took over operations of the San Diego & South Eastern interurban line. Here we see car No. 211 at the National City terminal about 1925. (Below) This San Diego & Arizona gasoline-electric motor car carried a unique open observation platform.

One Man Completes Railroad

Instead of building its own depot, as had been planned originally, the San Diego & Arizona had made arrangements with the Santa Fe for joint use of its station, forming "Union Station".

Difficulties in the awful Carriso Gorge delayed the opening and the cost of the stretch through the Gorge was over $4,000,000. The total cost of the road exceeded $18,000,000.

The "Gold Spike" was driven by J. D. in the Gorge on November 15, 1919. And he had "finished one of the biggest things one man ever did single-handed and against overwhelming odds".

In J. D's. own words: — "Well! In spite of hell (and it was hell, believe me) a direct train slid into our Union Station on December first and San Diego got what I had promised."

J. D. brought the first train in at 3:40 P.M. The Mayor, Louis J. Wilde, shouted; "Here comes San Diego's first real smokestack."

A big parade followed, terminating at the Organ Pavilion in Balboa Park.

In the evening, a banquet was held in Hotel del Coronado. As the appointed representative of the people, Carl H. Heilbron presented a watch, fob and charm to J. D. The charm was composed of leaves which opened like a book. On the outside one, was an etching of a San Diego & Arizona locomotive with a diamond set in the headlight and inscribed with the words: Presented to John D. Spreckels by San Diego Citizens December 1, 1919 — A tribute to greatness. The second leaf showed a street car system with a relief picture of the business blocks on Broadway and the inscription: To the City Builder. The Spreckels Organ Pavilion appeared on

over the San Diego & Arizona's tracks to First Ave. and a connecting track was laid in First Ave., to Market St., including a crossing. For the time the motors terminated at First Ave. and Broadway.

But this was not satisfactory since the cars could not be turned around. So, arrangements were made with the San Diego Electric Railway to make further use of its tracks from Broadway on First Ave., to B St., to Kettner Blvd. A curve was installed in the Southwest quadrant at First Ave. and B St. Then to avoid interference with the First Ave. electric cars, Route No. 6, another curve was put in, in the Northeast quadrant. The First Ave. cars were then routed via B St., First Ave. to Laurel St., and the crossing was taken out. A Wye was built at the foot of B St. and a siding

was installed on the San Diego & Arizona right-of-way property, opposite the Santa Fe Station. Effective February 10, 1918, the motors continued up First Ave., to B St., to Kettner Blvd., where they were turned.

The San Diego Electric Railway had found that its Class 2 cars were more satisfactory and economical to operate than the interurbans. In 1915, the three Niles Cars, numbers 401, 402 and 400, which had been assigned to Point Loma Railroad operation, were vacated. All ten of the interurbans were sold to Pacific Electric Railway in 1918.

Air whistles were installed on the Class 2 Cars regularly assigned to interurban operation. Route Indicating Boxes displayed: NC for National City, CV for Chula Vista and OB for Ocean Beach.

NORTH ISL[...]
land and the[...]
army and navy; [...]
improvements and [...]
hundreds of planes. [...]
Two hundred and s[...]
the City of San Dieg[...]
the air."

PASSPORTS AN[...]

Passports are not require[...]
over the San Diego and [...]
Arrangements have been m[...]
Mexican Customs authorities [...]
venienced in any manner wha[...]
Baggage agents will check b[...]
tination, and it is not necessary [...]
not required to look after baggag[...]
not opened by Custom Officials.

AMERICAN RAILWAY [...]
Is maintained on this railroad, furnish[...]
rapid transportation of express matter. [...]
car routes between principal points.

SAN DIEGO AND ARIZONA [...]
All freight handled promptly and efficiently. [...]
Shortest line between San Diego and Chicag[...]
Memphis and New Orleans.
Through package cars from Chicago, St. Louis [...]

DIRECT LINE ROUTING
From New York and New England:
Morgan Line—Sunset Route, Southern Pacific [...]
Arizona Railway at El Centro.
From Chicago, St. Louis, Minneapolis, Kansas City, an[...]
Direct lines to Southern Pacific care San Diego an[...]
at El Centro.
From Southern and Southeastern Points:
Direct lines to New Orleans, Southern Pacific care Sa[...]
zona Railway at El Centro.
From Texas, Oklahoma, and Southwestern Points:
Direct lines to El Paso, Southern Pacific care San Die[...]
Railway at El Centro.
Full information as to rates, service, etc., may be obtained by [...]

SAN DIEGO AND ARIZONA RAILWAY
SAN DIEGO, CALIFORNIA
A. T. MERCIER
General Manager
F. B. DORSEY
Assistant Traffic Ma[...]
A. D. HAGAMAN, Assistant General Freight and Passenger A[...]
SOUTHERN PACIFIC LINES
G. W. LUCE, Freight Traffic Manager
Southern Pacific Co., San Francisco, Cal.
E. W. CLAPP, Asst. Freight Traffic Manager
Southern Pacific Co., San Francisco, Cal.
C. S. FAY, Traffic Manager
Morgan's Louisiana & Texas R. R. and Steamship Co., New Orleans
C. K. DUNLAP, Traffic Manager
Galveston, Harrisburg & San Antonio Ry. Co., Houston, Texas
J. T. SAUNDERS, General Freight Agent
Southern Pacific Co., Los Angeles, Cal.
E. J. FENCHURCH, Asst. General Freight Agent
Southern Pacific Co., Tucson, Arizona
S. C. CHILES, General Agent Freight Department
Southern Pacific Co., New York City
WM. SIMMONS, General Freight and Passenger Agent
Southern Pacific—Atlantic S. S. Lines, New York City

ENTRANCE BALBOA PARK, SAN DIEGO, CALIFORNIA

THE SAN DIEGO AND ARIZONA RAILWAY, completed December 1st, 1919, forms, in connection with the Southern Pacific and its eastern connections, a new transcontinental route between San Diego and the East. Through Pullman cars are operated between San Diego and Chicago on Golden State Limited in connection with the Southern Pacific, El Paso and Southwestern and Rock Island lines, and connecting Pullman service with Southern Pacific between San Diego and New Orleans. It is the terminal railroad of the shortest line between Kansas City and the Pacific Tidewater and between New Orleans and the Pacific Tidewater.

Points of Interest Along the Line

MEXICO—The San Diego and Arizona, operated in connection with the Southern Pacific, passes across the border four times between San Diego and Yuma, through that peaceful portion of Mexico—Lower California. This delightful trip through scenic Mexican Territory is a novel experience not to be had on any other trans-continental journey.

YUMA, Arizona (on the Southern Pacific)—Near Yuma is located the Laguna Dam for diverting waters from the Colorado River for irrigating purposes. There are 50,000 acres in Arizona irrigated at this time, and project under way that will eventually irrigate 120,000 acres in the vicinity of Yuma.

Climatic conditions provide for the growing of some of the most delicious fruits that are grown anywhere in America.

MEXICALI, Mexico. CALEXICO, California—Interesting adjoining border towns where trains stop and passengers have opportunity to acquaint themselves with the customs of the people.

IMPERIAL VALLEY—That remarkable land below sea level as fertile as the Valley of the Nile. Annual soil production measured at approximately $65,000,000. Trimmed with the jewel-colored mountains of the desert; set below sea level at the delta of the greatest of western rivers; watered with the rains and snows of the Rocky Mountains running swiftly through the Grand Canyon of the Colorado to the miracle valley of the desert, a great semi-tropic garden; wide fields of cotton, mile after mile; cantaloupes covering thousands of acres; alfalfa knee deep in February, waist high in June, as far as the eye can see; date palms, lemons, grapefruit; cities shiningly new, strung along the railroad—all this a transformation from the unwatered, uninhabited, iridescent "bottom of the bowl" of the Colorado desert in twenty years, to a home place of 60,000 people.

EL CENTRO—County Seat of Imperial Valley. Excellent hotel accommodations, and is a mecca for tourists and settlers. Located 49 feet below sea level.

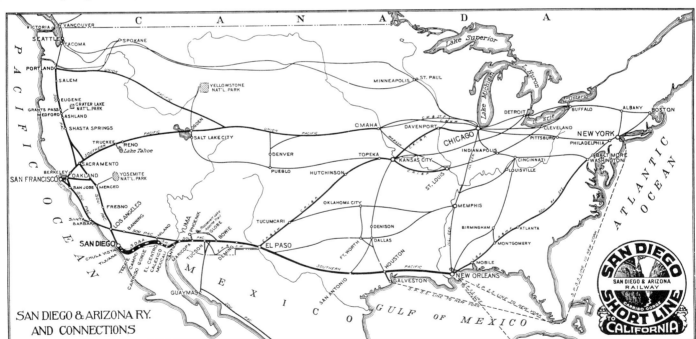

SAN DIEGO & ARIZONA RY. AND CONNECTIONS

SCENE IN CARRISO GORGE

CARRISO GORGE—Eleven miles long, and takes its name from a grass in its depths which is used by Indians in basket-work.

Across its precipices, its gulfs and crags, and its mountain pinnacles, are spread gorgeous blanket-patterns of color, measured in miles and woven from fluid rocks when the world was made. The reds and oranges of the sunset, splashed upon the walls of the chasms, are broken by lozenges of Navajo black, as big as a house, or edged with a border of white crystal, ten or twenty feet wide and half a mile long. The knots in this mighty tapestry are tied with outcroppings of marble; its foundation is of granite and hard rock, amethyst in the dawn, gray-black or burnt-umber under the brilliant noon-day sky, and toning to purples and violets in the haze of the distant peaks. To build a railroad along the ragged canyons of Carriso Gorge, an enterprise long considered impossible, finally was accomplished by blasting from solid rock a broad and secure avenue, on an easy gradient, for the rails of the San Diego and Arizona Railway.

There are seventeen tunnels in Carriso Gorge. The longest is 2604 feet, and the shortest 287 feet. When passing through the tunnels you are not bothered with objectionable fumes and smoke from locomotives as is usual when trains are operated through tunnels. This is due to the large bore of tunnels, especially light atmosphere, and a slight draft continually passing through Carriso Gorge. Depth of gorge from railroad 900 feet.

JACUMBA HOT SPRINGS—Summer and Winter resort, 92 miles from San Diego. Altitude 2835 feet; hot and cold artesian mineral water; large outdoor swimming pool; hotel, tent houses, cottages and auditorium.

CAMPO CREEK VIADUCT—Length 600 feet, height 185 feet, cost, $151,700.

REDONDO—When approaching Redondo Westbound, or leaving Redondo Eastbound, notice the horse shoe curve where the track can be seen on the mountain side, three different locations at one time.

LINDERO—Here the railroad passes across the international boundary line in Tunnel No. 4.

TECATE—Is an interesting Mexican town where Mexican Customs Officers are located.

TIJUANA—Is noted as a Mexican sightseeing place for tourists. A one hundred day racing meet is held at Tijuana once each year, with a large attendance from all over the world. Race track can be seen from train.

CHULA VISTA—Between Tijuana and San Diego line passes through the Chula Vista lemon groves.

SAN DIEGO—Eighty thousand people, has doubled its population within the last ten years, and will double it again within the next five.

Of all American cities its climate is the most even and desirable. Winters are mild and summers are cool.

It is a city of charming homes, set in semi-tropical verdure, built upon terraced slopes and table lands that face the sunset sea, with a background of granite-walled mountains.

The hotels, first-class and of modern pretentions. are excellent and in variety. Apartment houses care for thousands of winter visitors. Coronado Tent City, at Coronado Beach, cares for thousands more in the summer; there are daily band concerts.

Commercially, San Diego is rapidly becoming one of the great manufacturing and distributing seaports of the Pacific.

BALBOA PARK—1400 acres of trees, lawns and flowers in the heart of the city, and where remains permanent palaces which formed a part of the Panama-California International Exposition held in 1915-16. Immense out-door pipe organ in concrete ampi-theatre where free organ recitals are given every day in the year.

SAN DIEGO HARBOR—The land-locked home of 103 battleships and destroyers, the great Pacific fleet of the United States. The greatest haven of our navy; millions are now being spent by the government on additions to marine facilities. Nearest American harbor on the Pacific to the Panama Canal; admits the vessels of greatest draught; free from storms; room for all the commerce of the Pacific; miles of available waterfront.

MAIN LINE

From San Diego EASTBOUND No. 52 Mixed Daily	No. 4 Daily	Miles	Corrected to June 1 1922	Elev	To San Diego WESTB'ND No. 3 Daily	No. 51 Mixed Daily
10 00	10 00	------	Lv San Diego____S.D.&A. Ar	10	2 45	7 20
s10 28	s10 16	5.0	Lv National City____ " Lv	--	s 2 27	s 6 44
s10 37	s10 22	7.4	Lv Chula Vista____ " Lv	--	s 2 21	s 6 36
f10 45	f10 28	11.1	Lv Palm City____ " Lv	--	f 2 15	f 6 25
s10 55	s10 35	15.5	Ar Tia Juana (U.S.) " Lv	100	s 2 07	s 6 15
s11 10	s10 40	16.2	Lv Tijuana (Mex.)_T.&T. " Lv	---	s 2 02	s 6 04
f11 29	f10 54	24.0	Lv Garcia " ___ " Lv	210	f 1 51	f 5 44
s12 11	s11 20	36.6	Lv Redondo " __ " Lv	765	f 1 32	f 5 13
s 1 08	s12 00	52.8	Lv Tecate " __ " Lv	1690	s 1 02	s 4 35
f 1 30	f12 17	59.6	Lv Lindero " __ " Lv	2120	f12 48	f 4 12
s 1 57	s12 34	65.8	Lv Campo(U.S.)_S.D.&A. " Lv	2590	s12 34	s 3 55
s 3 02	f 1 20	84.5	Lv Hipass____ " Lv	3660	f11 58	s 3 02
s 3 32	s 1 40	92.9	Lv Jacumba Hot Spg " Lv	2830	s11 28	s 2 07
f 4 00	f 2 04	100.7	Lv Carriso Gorge____ " Lv	2380	f10 59	f 1 20
f 4 31	f 2 34	109.7	Lv Dos Cabezas____ " Lv	1670	f10 28	
s 5 00	------	117.7	Lv Sugar Loaf____ " Lv	790		f11 40
s 5 20	s 3 01	122.5	Lv Coyote Wells____ " Lv	290	s 9 45	s11 15
f 5 56	f 3 20	134.4	Lv Dixieland____ " Lv	-10	s 9 23	f10 45
s 6 12	s 3 29	139.8	Lv Seeley_____ " Lv	-44	s 9 15	s10 31
s 6 40	s 3 45	148.1	Ar El Centro____ " Lv	-49	9 00	10 05
7 05	3 50	148.1	Lv El Centro____So.Pac Ar	--	s 9 00	s 9 45
†s7 30	s 4 15	157.2	Lv Calexico (U.S.) " Lv	.2	8 35	†9 15
† 9 30	4 25	157.2	Lv Calexico (U.S.)____ Ar	.2	s 8 13	s†5 30
s 9 45	s 4 30	157.5	Lv Mexicali (Mex) " Lv	----	s 8 08	s 5 20
------	------	208.9	Lv Cantu (U.S.) " Lv	----		
s12 40	s 6 28	218.5	Ar Yuma (P.T.)____ " Lv	137	6 10	2 00
3 45	7 05	218.5	Lv Yuma (P.T.)____So.Pac. Lv	----	5 50	10 34
5 00	8 20	219.5	Lv Patio (M.T.)____ " Lv	----	6 30	11 15
9 30	12 55	383.6	Ar Maricopa_____ " Lv	----	1 55	6 35
------	7 35	------	Lv Maricopa_____A E. Ar	----	12 10	6 00
------	8 50	419.0	Ar Phoenix _____A.E. Lv	----	11 00	5 00
*Tues.	12 55	------	Lv Maricopa_____So. Pac. Ar	----	1 55	Thur.
Tues.	3 35	469.7	Lv Tucson_____S.P. Lv	2390	11 35	Wed.
------	------	593.0	Ar Douglas __E.P.S.W. Lv	----	735	Wed.
------	------	781.6	Ar El Paso(M.T.)E.P.S.W. Lv	---	125	Wed.
Tues.	12 50	781.6	LvEl Paso(M.T.)E.P.S.W. Ar	3713	105	Wed.
Wed.	5 40	1733	Ar Kansas CityC.R.I.&P. Lv	766	9 05	Tues.
Wed.	9 00	----	Lv Kansas City C.R.I.&P. Ar	766	7 50	Tues.
Thur.	7 40	2029.	Ar St. Louis ___ " Lv	600	9 03	Mon.
Wed.	11 30	----	Lv Kansas City C.R.I.&P. Ar	766	7 20	Tues.
Thur.	7 05	1963.	Ar Des Moines ___ " Lv	----	11 40	Mon.
Thur.	3 40	2223.	Ar St. Paul " Lv	----	2 55	Mon.
Thur.	4 20	2233.	Ar Minneapolis " Lv	----	2 15	Mon.
Wed.	6 40	----	Lv Kansas City C.R.I.&P. Ar	766	8 15	Tues.
Thur.	9 15	2249.	Ar Chicago____ " Lv	603	6 30	*Mon
No. 102	No. 110	148.1	Lv El Centro ____So.Pac Ar		No. 109	No. 101
	8 40				1 08	
3 45	11 20	218.5	Lv Yuma (P.T.) ____ " Lv	137	10 34	1 45
5 00	12 50	219.5	Lv Patio (M.T.)____ " Lv		11 15	2 25
9 30	6 05	383.6	Lv Maricopa____ " Lv	1172	6 05	9 38
11 59	9 50	469.7	Lv Tucson____ " Lv	2390	3 15	7 25
8 30	8 45	781.6	Ar El Paso(M.T.)__ " Lv	3713	4 30	10 00
9 50	11 30	781.6	Lv El Paso (C.T.)__ " Ar	3713	5 00	10 45
3 20	11 30	1401.6	Lv San Antonio____ " Lv	661	7 50	5 00
9 25	7 15	1612.6	Lv Houston_____ " Lv	64	11 50	10 50
7 35	6 25	1975.6	Ar New Orleans____ " Lv	7	11 30	12 10

Black type denotes p. m. Light type a. m.

f—Indicates trains stop on flag to receive and discharge passengers.
s—Indicates regular stop. Where no time is shown train does not stop.
*—Example by days. Service daily. †—Stops for Meals.

NOS. 3 AND 4

Through Pullman, Drawing-room, Compartment Car between San Diego and Chicago daily. (S-D-C). Through Pullman Yuma to St. Louis, St. Paul and Minneapolis.

Through Coaches and Baggage Car between San Diego and Yuma.

Observation and Dining service operated on trains 3 and 4 between San Diego and Chicago.

Westbound between El Paso and Tucson train is operated via E. P. & S. W., Eastbound via Southern Pacific.

Nos. 51 and 52—IMPERIAL VALLEY LOCAL.

Pullman Sleeper, Coach and Baggage Car Between San Diego, El Centro, Calexico & Yuma.

LAKESIDE LINE

EASTWARD	‡ AM	† AM	PM	† PM	PM	PM	B PM	C PM
San Diego (Foot of B St.) _	7 20	10 30	12 25	2 35	5 15	6 05	9 20	11 00
San Diego (1st and Bdwy) _	7 25	10 35	12 30	2 40	5 20	6 10	9 25	11 05
San Diego (13th and N Sts.) _	7 34	10 44	12 39	2 49	5 29	6 19	9 34	11 14
Encanto_____	7 52	11 02	12 57	3 07	5 47	6 37	9 52	11 32
Lemon Grove_____	8 02	11 12	1 07	3 17	5 57	6 47	10 02	11 42
La Mesa_____	8 10	11 20	1 15	3 25	6 05	6 55	10 10	11 50
Grossmont_____	8 18					▲6 13	7 03	
El Cajon_____	8 22					▲6 17	7 07	
Santee_____	8 31					▲6 26	7 16	
Riverview_____	8 35						7 21	
Lakeside_____	8 40					▲6 35	7 25	

WESTWARD	‡ AM	† AM	‡ AM	† PM	PM	PM	B PM	C PM
Lakeside_____	6 35	8 55						
Riverview_____								
Santee_____	6 42	9 05						
El Cajon_____	6 51	9 14						
Grossmont_____	6 58	9 21						
La Mesa_____	7 04	9 30	11 30	1 30	4 30	6 20	10 15	11 55
Lemon Grove_____	7 11	9 37	11 37	1 37	4 37	6 29	10 22	12 02
Encanto_____	7 18	9 45	11 45	1 45	4 44	6 37	10 30	12 09
San Diego (13th andN Sts.) _	7 34	10 03	12 03	2 03	5 00	6 51	10 48	12 24
San Diego (1st and Bdwy.)	7 40	10 10	12 10	2 10	5 07	6 57	10 55	12 31
San Diego (Foot of B St.) _	7 45	10 15	12 15	2 15	5 10	7 00	11 00	12 35

† Daily   ‡ Daily except Sunday.   ▲ Sunday Only.
B Daily except Wednesday and Saturday.   c Wednesday and Saturday only.

For information regarding freight rates, passenger fares, tickets, baggage and Pullman reservation, call upon or address the following representatives:

SAN DIEGO AND ARIZONA RAILWAY

324 Broadway or 602 Spreckels Building, San Diego

A. T. MERCIER_____General Manager
F. B. DORSEY_____Assistant Traffic Manager
A. D. HAGAMAN....Assistant General Freight and Passenger Agent

SOUTHERN PACIFIC LINES

SAN FRANCISCO, CAL., Southern Pacific Bldg., 65 Market St._____
_____{ Chas. S. Fee, Passenger Traffic Manager
_____{ F. E. Batturs, Asst. Passenger Traffic Manager
LOS ANGELES, CAL., Pacific Electric Bldg., 6th and Main Sts._____
_____F. S. McGinnis, General Passenger Agent
PORTLAND, ORE._____John M. Scott, General Passenger Agent
HOUSTON, TEX._____Jos. Hellen, General Passenger Agent
NEW ORLEANS, LA._____J. T. Monroe, General Passenger Agent
TUCSON, ARIZ.____E. J. Fenchurch, Asst. General Freight and Passenger Agent

GENERAL AND DISTRICT AGENTS

ATLANTA, GA., Healey Bldg., Walton and Forsyth Sts.....D. Ashbury, General Agent
BALTIMORE, MD., Hartman Bldg., Light and Redwood Streets._____
_____W. B. Johnston, General Agent
BIRMINGHAM, ALA., Woodward Bldg., 20th St. and First Ave._____
_____S. J. Brown, General Agent
BOSTON, MASS., 294 Washington Street_____J. H. Glynn, General Agent
CHICAGO, ILL., Southern Pacific Bldg., 35-37 W. Jackson Boulevard._____
_____C. L. McFaul, General Agent
CINCINNATI, O., Wiggins Bldg., 5th and Vine Sts.____H. F. Kern, General Agent
CLEVELAND, O., Hippodrome Bldg., Euclid Ave.____Robert McDowell, General Agent
DENVER, COLO., 315-316 Denham Bldg., 18th and California Sts._____
_____F. W. Sedgwick, General Agent
DETROIT, MICH., Majestic Bldg., Woodward and Michigan Aves._____
_____W. W. Hale, General Agent
EL CENTRO, CAL._____C. W. Runge, District Freight and Passenger Agent
EL PASO, TEX., 206 North Oregon St._____
_____W. C. McCormick, District Freight and Passenger Agent
KANSAS CITY, MO., Railway Exchange Bldg., 7th and Walnut Sts._____
_____L. B. Banks, General Agent
MEMPHIS, TENN., Exchange Bldg., 130 Madison Ave._____
_____L. C. Bouchard, General Agent
NEW YORK, N. Y., 165 Broadway.____
_____A. J. Poston, General Agent, Passenger Department
OKLAHOMA CITY, OKLA., Colcord Bldg._____J. A. Eads, Traveling Agent
PHILADELPHIA, PA., 1602 Chestnut St._____F. T. Brooks, General Agent
PHOENIX, ARIZ., Adams and Central Ave._____
_____P. Bancroft, Dist. Freight and Passenger Agent
PITTSBURGH, PA., Chamber of Commerce Bldg., 7th Ave. and Smithfield St._____
_____G. G. Herring, General Agent
SAN ANTONIO, TEX., 613 Navarro St.....E. McClannahan, Division Passenger Agent
SAN DIEGO, CAL._____A. D. Hagaman, Dist. Freight and Passenger Agent
ST. LOUIS, MO., Southern Pacific Bldg., 312-314 North Sixth Street._____
_____C. T. Collett, General Agent
MEXICALI, MEXICO, Inter-California Railway (Southern Pacific)._____
_____E. G. Burdick, General Manager

FOREIGN AGENCIES

GENOA, ITALY, 10 Piazza San Siro.......Brizzolesi, Kimsley & Millbourn, Agent
HAMBURG, GERMANY, 25-27 Ferdinand Strasse____R. Falck, General Agent
HAVANA, CUBA, 106 Cuba St._____W. E. Ridgeway, General Agent
LIVERPOOL, ENGLAND, 21 Water St._____Thomas Cooper, General Agent
LONDON, ENGLAND, 49 Leadenhall St._____R. G. Bonsor, Agent
MEXICO CITY, Avenida Cinco de Mayo, Num. 32._____
_____George F. Jackson, General Agent
PARIS, FRANCE, 3 Rue Tronchet_____H. Desmidt, General Agent

San Diego & Arizona Railway No. 25 heading a passenger train through the rugged awe-inspiring Carriso Gorge in the early 1920's.

the third and on the back was a sketch of Morena Dam.

A parchment album, containing water color sketches of the Spreckels' Institutions was also given to him.

J. D. said: "This is the happiest day of my life."

Other Ten-Year Developments

In 1910, J. D. had purchased the palatial steam yacht, Venetia, having a length of 226 ft., a displacement of 1,000 tons, with an engine which developed 1,000 Horse Power. Not only did this finest of yachts enable J. D. to go on long voyages for relaxation and entertainment but it permitted him to commute between his offices in San Francisco and in San Diego, in a joyful manner. World War I interrupted these trips, when the Venetia was commandeered by the Government as a naval auxiliary vessel. She performed admirably and was officially credited with having destroyed two submarines.

During the War, potash became of short supply. In 1916, the Hercules Powder Company established a large plant on the bay shore near the north boundary line of Chula Vista, to manufacture potash and byproducts from sea weed. The kelp was cut under water

off Point Loma and was brought in by barge-like self-propelled boats, called harvesters. It was digested, sterilized, evaporated and crystallized. For the transportation of the workmen, a track was laid from 31 St. on National Ave., to 32nd St., to Newton Ave., connecting with the electric interurban line. At change of shift hours, "Potash Specials" using Class 2 cars, in two or three car trains, were operated from B St., on Third Ave., to Market St., to 16th St., and out Route No. 1 through Logan Heights to the connecting track, over the interurban line to Chula Vista and

into the plant on a private spur.

Merchant shipping suffered tremendous losses all during the war and steel supply became critical. In 1918, a ship yard was built at the foot of 32nd St., to construct two vessels with reinforced concrete hulls. The Government agreed to pay, on a five year refund basis, the cost of extending the street car tracks down 32nd St., from Newton Ave. to the San Diego & Arizona Right-of Way. Transportation of workmen was supplied by special cars running through at shift change hours and by shuttle service in the interim. The ships were not completed until 1919, after the Armistice was signed.

In 1914, the bridge at 28th and B Sts., on Route No. 2, was filled in and the tracks were reconstructed.

A line change was made on No. 1 Route in 1916. Tracks were laid on Park Blvd., from University Ave. to El Cajon Ave. Then Number 1 cars continued on University Ave., to Park Blvd. to Mission Cliff Gardens and the trackage on Normal St. was abandoned.

Route No. 1 was split in 1918 and the Logan Heights end became Route No. 12.

In 1918, a double track connection was made from Fifth Ave. and University Ave. to Washington St. and First Ave. Route No. 3 cars were taken off Third Ave. and ran out Fifth Ave. to Washington St. to Hawk St., to Mission Hills. The Third Ave. line was cut back to First Ave. and Washington St. and was assigned Route No. 13.

A double track was laid in 1919 on Spruce St., from Fourth Ave. to Fifth Ave. and on the January 10, 1920 Time Card, Route No. 13 became the "First and Fifth Avenue Line", operating from L St., on Fifth Ave., to Spruce St., to

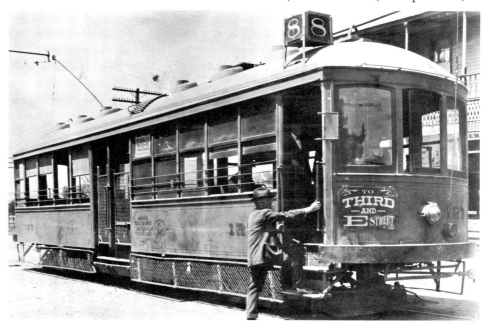

Car No. 127 pictured at the end of Route 8
—Old Town Line—F. W. Reif

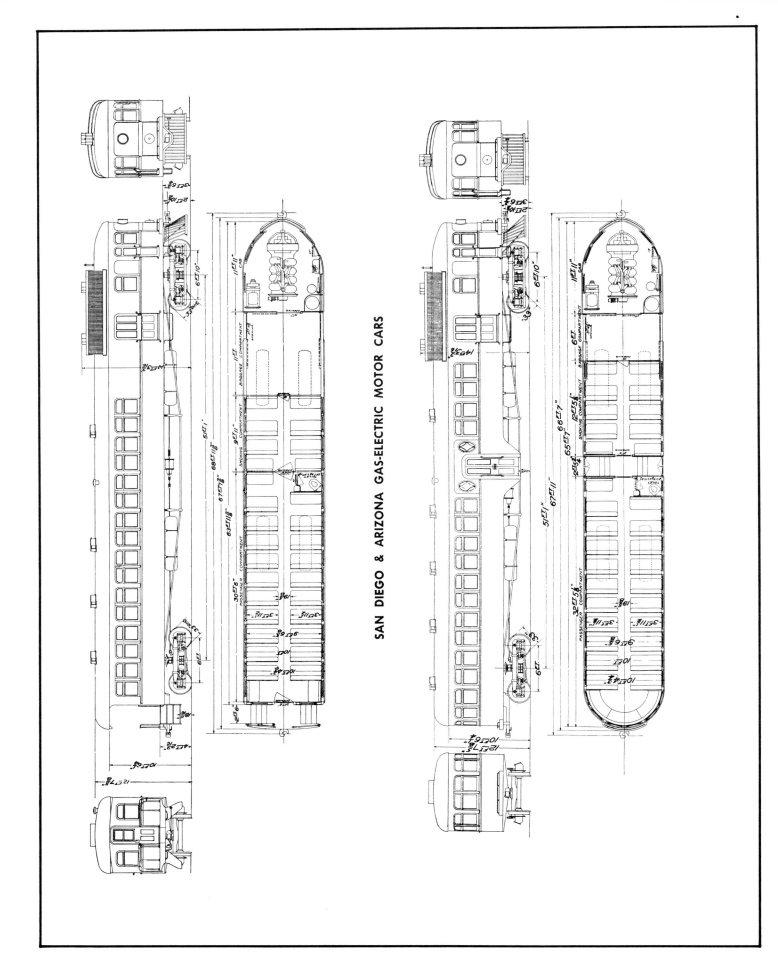

SAN DIEGO & ARIZONA GAS-ELECTRIC MOTOR CARS

Locomotive No. 12 was a beautiful 4-6-0 built by Pittsburgh in 1912 for the San Diego & Southeastern Railway. This locomotive later became San Diego & Arizona No. 23 in 1917. (Below) Locomotive No. 25, a Baldwin 4-6-0 built in 1907 for the Las Vegas & Tonopah ready to leave San Diego with train No. 3.—Dave Myrick collection.

Locomotive No. 27, former Las Vegas & Tonopah No. 11, switches the afternoon passenger at the Santa Fe depot. (Below) No. 101, a hefty 2-8-0 built by Schenectady in 1914 at the San Diego & Arizona roundhouse. Dave Myrick collection (Opposite page—Top) Eastbound San Diego & Arizona passenger hugging the canyon walls of Carriso Gorge.—John Ferris collection. Locomotive No. 26, former Las Vegas & Tonopah No. 10.—Dave Myrick collection.

First Ave. to Washington St. Tracks on Third Ave., north of B St., Fir St. and Fourth Ave. were then abandoned. The First and Fifth Ave. line lasted for a few months, then Route No. 13 was vacated and the tracks from Fifth Ave. and Spruce St. to First Ave. and Washington St. were torn up.

The lengths of the city blocks are unusually short. Most of the downtown blocks are only 200 ft. by 300 ft. Stopping at every corner consumed much time. The schedules were speeded up by inaugurating the Skip-Stop system in 1917 and 1918. Car Stop signs were put up in 1918.

PAYE-PAUL. To reduce the loading time in the downtown section, some of the One-Man Cars were tried out, marked: INBOUND — PAY AS YOU ENTER, OUTBOUND — PAY AS YOU LEAVE.

The changing conditions were reflected in a newspaper article in 1917. "The people are continually demanding longer rides and more expensive equipment. The cost of materials has advanced 50 to 150%. Wages are up 35%. A 5¼% gross tax on revenues goes to the State of California and 2% to the City of San Diego." Wages of motormen and conductors had been increased in 1914. The new rates varied from 27 cents an hour the first year up to 33 cents an hour for five or more years of service.

The growth of the San Diego Electric Railway is shown by the "car-miles" operated: 1906 — 798, 152 and 1916 — 3,521, 571. That of the City is reflected by the 1920 Census figure — 74,361.

The financial woes of the San Diego Electric Railway Company kept going from bad to worse.

There were: the irreparable loss to the jitneys in 1915, the flood damages in 1916, the Declaration of War in 1917 with its attendant inflation, increasing the cost of everything.

The City of San Diego had embarked upon a vast program of street paving. This entailed huge reconstruction costs, relaying the tracks with girder type rails, three to four times as heavy as the original installations, setting the tracks in concrete and paying the assessments for surface paving. The company was required to pave between the rails and two feet outside of them. This was a cost inherited from horse car days to provide a footing for the horses.

All these ever increasing costs had to be absorbed with no increase in fares.

Finally, on November 1, 1918, the San Diego Electric Railway filed an unusual application for relief, with the Railroad Commission of the State of California. In this case, all the facts were set forth in voluminous detail and the company requested that the Commission recommend solutions to the problems.

The Commission made a thorough investigation but dilly-dallied in rendering a decision.

The Point Loma Railroad, facing the prospects of expending large sums of money to pave streets, had applied to the Railroad Commission for authority to discontinue service and take up the tracks.

The City Attorney stated that the City would require the street railway to live up to the provisions of the franchises to the fullest extent.

Then came the bomb shell. J. D. wrote a letter on September 26th, 1919 to the City Council filing a petition for the abandonment of franchises, not only on the Point Loma Line, but several city lines. These included: Adams Avenue from Alabama St. to the City Limits; trackage from Fourth Ave. and Spruce St., to First Ave., to Washington St.; on Imperial Ave. from 32nd St. to Greenwood Cemetery; on K St. from 16th St. to 25th St., to Ocean View Blvd., to 30th St., on F St. from 16th St. to 25th St., to Broadway; and all the Logan Heights Line.

He set forth that without increase in revenue and in face of having to meet franchise obligations, it will be impossible to operate the Point Loma Railroad or the trackage mentioned.

City officials greeted with a broad smile J. D's. announcement that he intended to abandon a part of his street railway. They believed that it was just a bluff. But notices were posted that services on car routes numbers 6 — First Ave. and Market St. Line; 8 — F St. Line, 13 — Third Ave. Line and on the 5th St. Line in Coronado would be discontinued on October first.

Then the Council got busy. Invitations were issued to "responsible" persons to apply for franchises for jitney lines. A hurried message was sent to the Railroad Commission. On October first, the Council hoped that early resumption of service would result.

It was effective. The Commission issued a directive to the San Diego Electric Railway on October second: "You are hereby ordered to resume and continue service as it existed on September 30th pending further order of the Railroad Commission. Your applications . . . have been set for adjourned hearing Tuesday, October 7th, at 2 P.M.

The company printed notices to the public that, effective October 3rd, reduced services on the Adams Ave. Line and the Point Loma Railroad, with minimum services on Routes numbers 6, 8 and 13, would be rendered.

After the hearing, the Commission issued some unusual orders.

First, the 5 cent fare area was divided into two 5 cent zones, known as the "Inner Zone" and the "Outer Zone". Ticket strips were sold, good for four two zone rides for 30 cents. Later metal tokens replaced the tickets.

The Commission recommended that the City fo San Diego relax its severe requirements for the paving of the center portion of streets occupied by car tracks.

One-man car operation was recommended.

The South "Scenic" Loop of the Point Loma Railroad was ordered to be abandoned.

Service on the 5th St. Line in Coronado was to be discontinued but the tracks were to be left in order to handle special movements.

A general program of rehabilitation was to be inaugurated.

The "Zone" system was established on January 1, 1920.

CHAPTER VI

1920's - General Prosperity & Line to the Beaches

Following the Railroad Commission's orders and working on the theory that smaller, safer one-man cars operating on shorter headways would render the public more satisfactory service than the larger cars with less frequent ones, 25 One-Man Birney Safeties were purchased in 1920; 10 more were acquired in 1922. They were assigned numbers 301 to 335 inclusive.

These cars were equipped with such modern features as: improved air brake valves, door openers and step operators, "dead man" control with automatic operation of the emergency valve if the operator removed his hand from the controller in running position. The entire elimination of step accidents was anticipated as the doors could not open while the car is in motion. Slack adjusters were added to all 35 cars in 1923.

In 1920, the Birneys were assigned to Routes No. 2 — Broadway and Brooklyn Heights; No. 4 — Imperial Ave. Line; No. 5 — K St. and Ocean View Blvd.; No. 6 — First Ave. and Market St. and No. 8 — Old Town Line.

But they were single truck and "Transportation suffered a set-back." They became decidedly unpopular and were

quickly dubbed: "grass hoppers", "dinkies", "puddle jumpers" and, since they followed the European or World War I, "cootie cars".

Quite a number became involved in traffic accidents.

So disposals of the Birneys began in 1923, as follows:

No. 301 to 304 and 309 to 311 retired in 1923-1925 and sold to Sacramento Northern Railway. Renumbered 62 to 68 respectively (per records of Addison Laflin).

No. 326 to 329 and 335 retired in 1924 and traded in on the purchase of an electric locomotive.

No. 305 to 308, 312, 313 retired in 1924 and sold to Stockton Electric Railroad. Delivered in 1925 and renumbered 61 to 66 (per The Western Railroader).

All the remaining cars except No. 316 and 318 were retired in 1925. Some sold to Wichita Falls, Texas, railway. Others dismantled and bodies sold.

No. 316 and 318 retired and dismantled in 1934. Body of one was set up as a "change room" at the Company's Garage, 15th and K Sts.

Subsequent to the purchase of the Birneys, more of the older cars were re-

moved from service in 1920, including: 2nd No. 11; Coronado cars No. 41, 42, 43 and the four trailers.

"Claus Spreckels' Play Toy"

William Clayton, who had been General Manager or Vice-President and Managing Director down through the years, retired in 1922. J. D. had been grooming his only surviving son, Claus, as his successor.

Claus Spreckels was appointed to the position of Vice-President and General Manager of the San Diego Electric Railway Company and the San Diego & Coronado Ferry Company in that year. The same progressive policy was to be continued. E. J. Burns was selected as Assistant General Manager.

In a humorous but opportune article in the AERA magazine published by the American Electric Railway Association, issue of October 1924, Claus referred to the prevalent statements to the effect that "His father put Claus at the head of the street railway that he might have something to play with and to keep him out of mischief." It turned out to be the biggest and the best "play toy" he ever had. The real enjoyment he de-

Auto traffic comes to a complete halt on Broadway, while car No. 125 turns south on 16th Street. Note birney car No. 308 at the extreme left.
—Union Title

rived out of it was "in knowing that I am accomplishing something for the benefit of the public of San Diego — the joy of being able to serve and serve well".

He made an inspection tour of the system and afterwards remarked: "Oh, boy, but this was a broken up playtoy that they handed to me." He rode one of his 98 "minimum traction truck" cars in which the seats in the open section were of hardwood construction — "to improve the riding qualities". Pounding over the rough tracks, he quipped: "I soon noticed that I had developed corns — but not on my feet . . . No wonder the public cursed the street railway." He then and there resolved to try "to give the public what it likes: beautiful terminals, substations, smooth tracks and easy riding cars."

At the memorable banquet for San Diego business men in 1923, J. D. besought their support for his son "on whose shoulders must soon rest the heavy burden of my responsibilities and the carrying-out of my future plans . . . All I ask for him who is to follow me is your support and sympathy in his efforts to realize, after I am gone, the dream and hope I cherished for San Diego."

Up Come the Rails

Despite the recommendation of the Railroad Commission, a dispute with the City arose, in 1922, over the paving of

Birney No. 328 at 30th and Ivy during 1923.
—Union Title

a section of Adams Avenue.

Manager Spreckels, according to an article in The San Diego Union of May 13th, "said yesterday if the Company is required to pay for the paving of Adams Avenue, the Adams Avenue line will be abandoned and the track torn up".

As an amicable settlement of the problem was not reached, some buses were rented. These were put into service on August 27th on Adams Avenue from

the Car House at Florida St. to the end of the route in Kensington Park. During the night, under the guise that the track was in such poor condition that it was not safe to operate over it, the rails had been torn up from the Car House to the City Limits at Boundary St.

The tracks were reconstructed in December, street car service was resumed and the buses were discontinued.

Mission Beach Precursor

Extending south from Pacific Beach, there is a narrow peninsula which separates the Pacific Ocean from Mission Bay, then more commonly known as False Bay. At the southerly tip was the entrance to the bay with Ocean Beach laying along the south shore. The strip was nothing but barren sand dunes. But it had great possibilities, as some foresaw, especially if comfortable transportation could be provided.

About 1914, the *Bay Shore Railroad Company* was formed by a group of promoters, Messrs. Fox, Barney, Rife and McKie. When the bridge (now removed) was built to span the channel, an electric rail line was constructed, in 1916, from a junction with the Point Loma Railroad at Wonderland Station, near Voltaire and Bacon Sts., in Ocean Beach, running to and over the bridge and continuing about two miles up the peninsula. The development of a new resort, Mission Bay Beach, including a Tent City, was then undertaken, in a small way.

Two of the retired California type cars, numbers 81 and 82, were acquired from the San Diego Electric Railway and shuttle service was started.

The Tent City enjoyed an auspicious first season in that year.

When J. D. decided to build a fast interurban line to the beaches, the Bay Shore Railroad was taken over.

Interurban to the Beaches

J. D. had purchased a large number of those sand dunes along the Bay Shore Railroad. Coronado Tent City had

passed its hey-day. So the decision was made to develop a new sea and bayside resort at Mission Beach, on an elaborate scale.

An area was selected to be the amusement center. Plans were drawn for the construction of a large dancing casino, a fine bath house with a plunge and access provisions for surf bathing, public facilities, concessions including a roller coaster and a miniature San Diego & Arizona railway.

The question of furnishing adequate transportation for large crowds was a serious one. The Point Loma Railroad was a roundabout route, slow, with

hills to climb and, by this time, the cars had to pass through the rapidly growing residential areas on Point Loma. In preparing the layout, since J. D. owned and operated an electric railway system, little consideration was given to the automobile traffic and parking.

The thing to do was to build a fast interurban line to Mission Beach, with provision for the replacing of the Point Loma line, in part, for better service to Ocean Beach.

Surveys were made and plans were developed for the building of a new electric railroad from Kettner Blvd. and Broadway in San Diego to Mission Beach. There was the abandoned route of the defunct Los Angeles & San Diego Beach Railway on Kettner Blvd. But right at the start, difficulties developed on account of the position of the Santa Fe Station. These were solved by deciding to locate the outbound track on the San Diego & Arizona right-of-way property on the easterly side of Kettner Boulevard from Broadway to Date St. and the inbound track in the sidewalk area on the east side of the street from B St. to Broadway. The Los Angeles & San Diego Beach route was followed out Kettner Blvd. as far as Winder St., from which point the tracks of the Point Loma Railroad on Hancock St. could be utilized.

At Witherby St., there was a complicated situation. Barnett Ave., at that time (before Pacific Highway was construct-

Waiting for the Point Loma connection at Ocean Beach about 1923. (Opposite) Traversing the sand dunes of Mission Beach during the 1920's.—R. C. Brandt

Kettner Blvd. after the removal of the Los Angeles & San Diego Beach tracks in 1919. (Below) To improve the grade, a cut was required at Bird Rock south of La Jolla.— Union Title

ed), was an active highway and the Point Loma Railroad's crossing in it at grade with the tracks of the Santa Fe Railway would not do. The solution was to relocate the highway to dip under the tracks at Witherby St. and to build an elaborate viaduct for the new line to pass over both the railroad and the highway. Five pile timber bents and stringers made up the approaches. Concrete abutments were poured, first to carry the track on a long-span "through" steel plate girder bridge over the Santa Fe, then, on a "deck" plate girder bridge over Witherby St. On the overpass, the line was to be single track. At the north end the track dropped down to the flats, where a connection was made with the Point Loma Railroad's line on Barnett Ave., to provide service to Loma Portal, Roseville, La Playa and Fort Rosecrans.

The route then continued on what is now Frontier St., nothing but mud flats at the time, following north of Point Loma Blvd., to the Mission Bay Bridge. The bridge had to be rebuilt, then the Bay Shore Railroad's track was reconstructed as far north as the amusement center, where a fine terminal was built. Through Mission Beach, the tracks were slightly elevated and automobile traffic was divided with barely enough room for one lane and parallel parking on either side of the tracks.

Before the bridge was reached, a junction was formed and a branch track was constructed, taking off to the left into the Bacon St. line and connecting with the Point Loma Railroad at Voltaire St. Thus service for Ocean Beach would be provided on Bacon St., to Santa Cruz St., to Sunset Cliffs Blvd.

The new line was designed for freight as well as passenger and express services.

On March 17, 1923, General Manager Claus Spreckels had announced that a $2,500,000 construction and reconstruction program, including the purchase of 50 new cars, would be undertaken.

Then the people of La Jolla, without rail transportation since the folding up of the Los Angeles & San Diego Beach Railway, began clamoring for electric transit, too. Petitions were filed with the City Council urging that body to induce the San Diego Electric Railway to extend the new beach line to La Jolla. Manager Claus went before the Council and agreed to build the line to La Jolla provided the City would extend the General Franchise, which was due to expire in 1952. It was also agreed that the Railway would pay the 2% tax

Construction of the La Jolla line viaduct over the Santa Fe tracks in December 1924 — Union Title

Substation and passenger shelter at La Jolla
Hermosa.—Union Title

turn around track, looping the building,
was constructed.

Another attractive building was erected at La Jolla Hermosa for San Carlos
Substation and a passenger platform. At
Ocean Beach a substation building of
Egyptian design was erected.

The catenary type of suspension had
been adopted for the overhead trolley
wires for the new tracks and most of the
city lines were to be converted to that
type of construction. It was the plan to
use pantographs on all the cars, eventually.

The physical properties of the Bay
Shore Railroad and its franchises were
taken over. Cars numbers 81 and 82
were scrapped in 1928.

on gross revenues even though the new
line was considered to be a commercial
project.

The Council, on September 8, 1923,
accepted the bid of the San Diego Electric Railway for the new General Franchise covering various lines and for the
new line to the beaches.

Construction work was started on October 21st.

The extension to La Jolla meant continuing the tracks through Mission
Beach to Grand Ave. in Pacific Beach.
From that point the old grade of the
Los Angeles & San Diego Beach Railway would be utilized to Fay and Prospect Sts., in La Jolla. There a fine terminal was built on private property. A

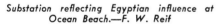

*Substation reflecting Egyptian influence at
Ocean Beach.—F. W. Reif*

*The terminal at La Jolla was most attractively appointed. Car No. 435 has just completed running around the loop circumscribing the terminal.—
Union Title*

San Diego Electric Railway Company

TIME TABLE 1

INTERURBAN DIVISION

To Take Effect Tuesday, July 1, 1924
at 12:01 A.M.

Pacific Standard Time (120 Meridian)

For the Government and Information of Employees Only.

CLAUS SPRECKELS
Vice-President and General Manager

E. J. BURNS
Assistant General Manager

S. E. MASON
General Superintendent

W. A. NICKERSON
Superintendent

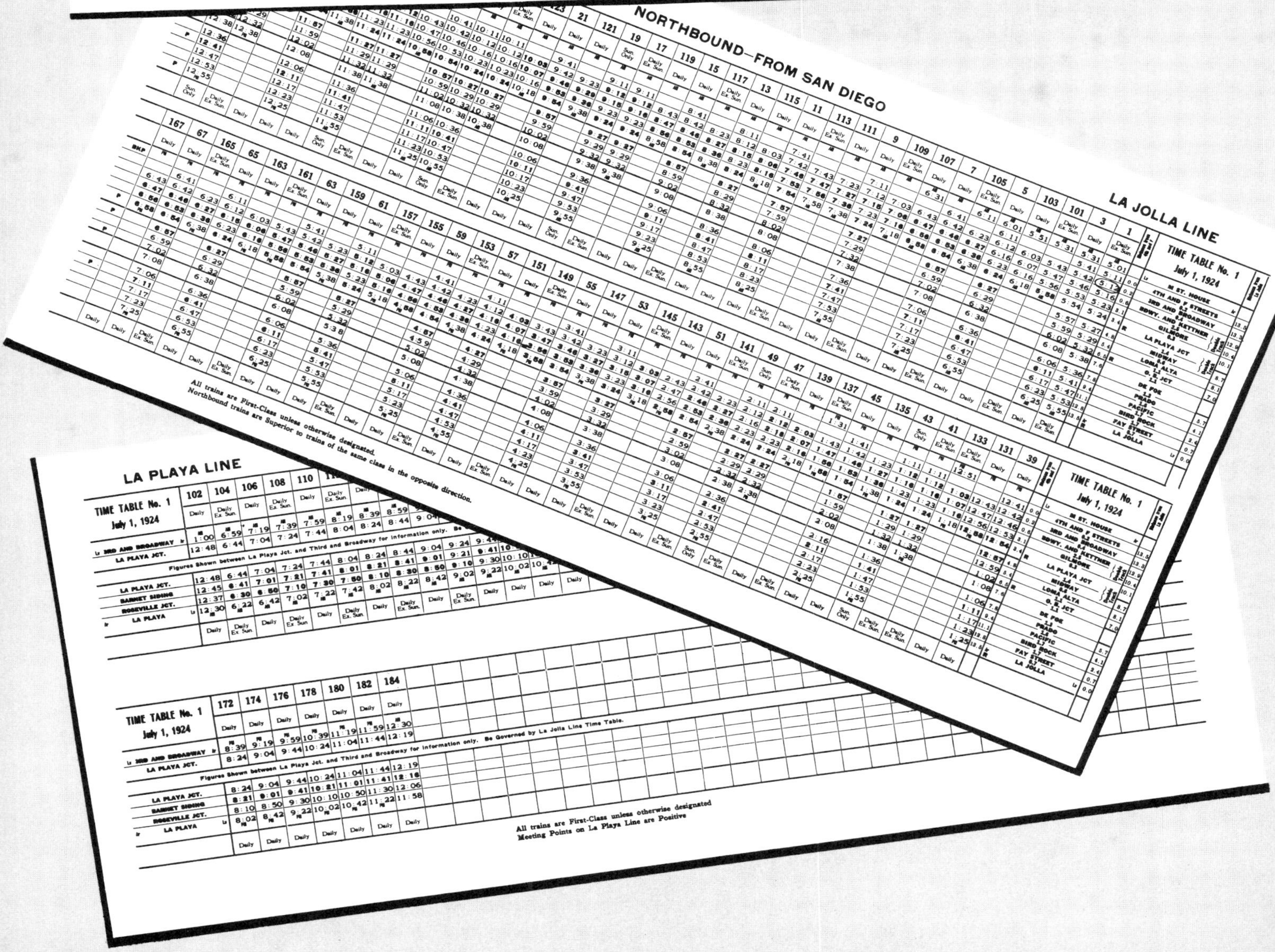

NORTHBOUND—FROM SAN DIEGO

LA JOLLA LINE

TIME TABLE No. 1
July 1, 1924

4TH AND E STREETS
4TH ST. HOUSE
BDWY. AND KETTNER
3RD AND KETTNER
GILLERS
LA PLAYA JCT.
MISSION
LOMA ALTA
D. ST. JCT.
DE FOE
PESO
PACIFIC
BIRD ROCK
FAY STREET
LA JOLLA

LA PLAYA LINE

TIME TABLE No. 1
July 1, 1924

	102	104	106	108	110	
	Daily	Daily Ex. Sun	Daily	Daily Ex. Sun	Daily	Daily
Lv 3RD AND BROADWAY	12:48	6:44	7:04	7:24	7:44	8:59 9:04
LA PLAYA JCT.						
LA PLAYA JCT.	12:48	6:44	7:04	7:31	7:51	
BARNEY SIDING	12:45	6:41	7:01	7:16	7:36	
ROSEVILLE JCT.	12:37	6:30	6:50			
Ar LA PLAYA	12:30	6:22	6:42	7:02	7:44	

Figures Shown between La Playa Jct. and Third and Broadway for information only.

	172	174	176	178	180	182	184
	Daily	Daily	Daily	Daily	Daily	Daily	Daily
Lv 3RD AND BROADWAY		8:39	9:19	7:39	9:59	11:59	12:30
LA PLAYA JCT.		8:24	9:04	9:44	10:24	11:44	12:19
LA PLAYA JCT.		8:24	9:04	9:44	10:24	11:01 11:44	12:19
BARNEY SIDING		8:31	9:01	9:41	10:31	11:01	12:06
ROSEVILLE JCT.		8:31	8:50	9:30	10:50	11:30	12:06
Ar LA PLAYA		8:02	8:42	9:22	10:42	11:22	11:58

Figures Shown between La Playa Jct. and Third and Broadway for information only. Be Governed by La Jolla Line Time Table.

All trains are First-Class unless otherwise designated
Meeting Points on La Playa Line are Positive

All trains are First-Class unless otherwise designated.
Northbound trains are Superior to trains of the same class in the opposite direction.

Mission Beach terminal where patrons entered a subway to reach the amusement grounds.— F. W. Reif

and went to Ocean Beach. The other cars, Routes No. 15 and 16, continued to Mission Beach and La Jolla. La Jolla celebrated the inauguration of interurban rapid transit with its Jollafication on The Fourth. The station facilities there, however, were not ready until 1925.

A bulletin of the Ohio Brass Company described the details of operation, in essence, as follows:

Trains of 3 to 6 cars leave the Plaza at Third Ave. and Broadway, at San Diego. Route numbers are: No. 14 for Ocean Beach, No. 15 for Mission Beach and No. 16 for La Jolla. The train runs as a unit under the control of a single motorman to Ocean Beach Junction, 6 miles, running time 18 minutes.

There the rear car (or cars) No. 14 is detached, while the train is in motion, and it then runs separately to Ocean Beach.

The front sections then proceed to Mission Beach Amusement Center, one mile.

There the leading car normally is uncoupled and proceeds 6 miles farther to La Jolla. The running time from San Diego to Mission Beach is 21 minutes and to La Jolla 35 minutes.

The return trip is a reversal of the evolutions.

The couplers require many safeguards. The arrangement of circuit connections renders them ineffective until the mechanical coupling between cars has been completed. Emergency brake applications

Onward Roll the 400's

It was Manager Spreckels' determination to make the San Diego Electric Railway the best street railway system in the United States. $800,000 was provided for the purchase of the 50 new cars, the finest ever constructed.

Traffic on all beach lines is highly fluctuating. Therefore it was necessary to select cars which would be peculiarly elastic in operation. The type chosen was one equipped for Multiple Unit control but also designed for individual operation as either one or two man units. In multiple unit running, connecting arrangements were such that a car or a section of the train could be coupled or uncoupled quickly en route.

Car No. 400, the first one, was delivered on December 18, 1923. A total of 35 new cars was ready for service in January 1924. They were of steel construction with closed type bodies and each was fitted with a pantograph for collecting the current. The remaining 15 followed in February and March. They were numbered consecutively to No. 449 inclusive.

A special two car train made a trial run over the new line to the end of the track at Turquoise St. in Pacific Beach on February 22nd, carrying railway company officials and city and county dignitaries.

The building of the overpass at Witherby St. was a complex undertaking and it was not completed until 1925. Until then, the beach cars had to use the crossing at grade of the Point Loma Railroad with the Santa Fe and a temporary connecting track was put in from the Point Loma line to the new track near Barnett Ave.

With a four day celebration, Ocean Beach welcomed the opening of the new line, Route No. 14, providing fast service on a 20 minute headway, on May 1, 1924. Temporary shuttle service to Mission Beach was established at that time.

On the morning of July first, a three car train left the Plaza in San Diego. The last car, marked No. 14, cut off

La Jolla line viaduct crossing over the Santa Fe Railway main line to Los Angeles about 1925.—Union Title

Car No. 438 headed for Ocean Beach using Point Loma tracks to the temporary junction with the new beach line. (Opposite) Interior of the 400 class car. (Lower) View of the cars as they rolled out of the American Car Company plant in St. Louis.—F. W. Reif

are thus prevented. The push buttons are interlocked.

The motorman approaches the car to which a coupling is to be made, at a safe speed, engages the couplers, then presses the coupling button. This energizes the electro-pneumatic valves, admitting air to the disconnecting switch engine, which completes the coupling operations by closing the switches and simultaneously opening the valves in the air brake pipes. End of details.

With the opening of the new line to the beaches, service via the Point Loma Railroad, out State St., through Wabaska canyon, and over Voltaire St. in Ocean Beach, was abandoned.

A new route, No. 13, was established from Third Ave. and Broadway, via the new tracks to Barnett Ave., to Lytton St., to Rosecrans St. to the Military Reservation, providing through service to Roseville and La Playa.

Operations with pantograph require further explanations. As previously pointed out, work was in progress converting the trolley wire suspension to catenary type with the ultimate aim being to standardize on pantograph type current collectors. These jobs continued into 1925.

Since only a few lines had been changed over when the 400 series, Class 5, cars were put into service, it was evidently the desire to use some of the new cars on lines with orthodox suspensions.

Pantographs and trolley poles cross in front of the U. S. Grant Hotel on Broadway.—
Union Title

The pantographs were removed from several cars and 2 pole trolleys were installed, as evidenced by the photograph of the four cars at La Jolla on July 4, 1924.

Unfortunately the performance of the pantographs was not satisfactory. They were of light construction and the sobriquet "Hay stacks" was soon applied to them. Many collapsed, stranding the cars. Soon a pole trolley was put on each car at the opposite end of the panta-graph. The "pans" tore down the overhead, particularly at switches, in so many instances that a General Manager's Order was issued late in 1924 to make a thorough investigation. As a result all the remaining pans were removed and were replaced with second pole trolleys.

When it was proposed to establish express service on the Line to the Beaches, former California type passenger car No. 106 was converted for that purpose, being renumbered 1000. Before the alterations

When the Ocean Beach line (Route 14) opened, a birney car was used to shuttle passengers to Mission Beach. Photo was taken at Ocean Beach Junction on May 1, 1924.—*Union Title*

were completed, ex-passenger car No. 99 was equipped temporarily and express service to Mission Beach began on April 29, 1924 and was extended shortly thereafter to La Jolla. The operation was short lived and No. 1000 was altered and outfitted as "Wrecker-Service Car" No. 010 in 1926.

Freight Trains

The franchise for the electric road to the beaches was of a commercial type. At the same time the interurban tracks were constructed, industry spur tracks and interchange tracks were built.

These included, in 1923 and 1924:

An interchange track with the Santa Fe from the yard tracks on the west side of Hancock St., between Wright and Witherby Sts.

A transfer track from Broadway to Market St., over the San Diego & Arizona Railway's Right-of-way property, east of Kettner Blvd., and an interchange connection south of Market St. at India St.

The formation of a double track wye at Kettner Blvd. and Market St.

A 320-ft. siding for the San Diego & Arizona.

A spur track from Market St. and Pacific Highway over the Tide Lands to the Spreckels Brothers Coal Bunker Wharf.

Connecting tracks to Gilmore Oil Company's spurs on Hancock St. and to the Vitrified Products Company's spur at Old Town, forming a wye at the latter location.

Later, a spur track from Reed St. to Pacific St., for the Griffith Company, at Pacific Beach.

A spur to the Spreckels Brothers Lumber Company in La Jolla.

Others were added, including one

Car No. 404 descends from the viaduct. It turned off to the left and used the former Point Loma tracks to La Playa.—R. C. Brandt

near the High School at La Jolla, and some team track facilities were provided.

For motive power, negotiations had been carried on to trade in five Birney cars on the acquisition of a second-hand electric locomotive. Early in 1925 a Baldwin-Westinghouse 50-ton Electric Locomotive, built in 1923, was purchased. It bore number 35, but was entered in the "Locomotives" account and re-numbered No. 1025. Motored Work Flat Cars were used until it ar-

rived.

Flat cars had been purchased for Work Equipment and were transferred for freight service as soon as they were no longer needed for construction. All were second hand.

4 were purchased from the San Diego & Arizona Railway, in 1923, 40,000 pounds capacity, and were numbered 32 to 35. No. 32 was fitted out as a "rail laying" car. The others, when transferred, were renumbered No. 1051, 1052 and 1053.

12 were purchased from Southwest Sales and Equipment Company, in 1924, 60,000 pounds capacity and were numbered 28, 29, 36 to 39 inclusive and 48 to 53 inclusive. They were renumbered No. 1101 to 1112 inclusive.

16 more were purchased from United Commercial Company in 1924, 80,000 pound capacity. These were charged directly to the "Freight and Express Cars" account and were numbered No. 1151 to 1166 inclusive.

Many carloads of cement were delivered to the Vitrified Products Company. Merchandise from ships was haul-

San Diego Electric's door to door express service only lasted two years.—Union Title

— 88 —

Baldwin-Westinghouse 50-ton electric freight motor used for switching and freight service on the La Jolla line—Al Haij

ed from dock to La Jolla and way points, in addition to the car loads from the regular carrier interchanges.

East San Diego, North Park and the surrounding territory were building up rapidly. A spur track was constructed from the San Diego Electric Railway's track in 30th St., north of University Ave., swinging to the east, to serve the Klicka (Dixie) Lumber Company's yards, in 1924, and a permit was obtained to operate freight trains over certain city streets and through Balboa Park. Many train loads of lumber and building materials rumbled over the Park Line and out University Ave.

The brake rigging on the flat cars had to be revamped to enable them to make the sharp curves in the city tracks. The Klicka Spur was removed in 1929 and freight train service was discontinued to that part of the city.

Busses Intrude

Entry: 1922: Purchase 2 Fageol Buses No. 1 and No. 2 and 1 Reo Bus No. 4.

"For a Greater San Diego, Motor Coach Service of San Diego Electric Railway"!

So read the banner of gasoline bus No. 1, after which it went into service, November 8, 1922, between National City and Chula Vista. This run supplemented the functions of the interurban electric cars, but it was the opening wedge.

When the portion of the Point Loma Railroad was abandoned on Voltaire St., in Ocean Beach, on account of the inauguration of new Route No. 14 in 1924, bus service was provided on Voltaire St., from Bacon St. to Wells St.

The first motor bus on the San Diego Electric.—F. W. Reif

Then came the first street car line displacement in that year. This was a portion of Route No. 8, the State St. — Old Town Line. It was abandoned from State and Ivy Sts. to the end of the line at Ramona's Home in May.

Bus Route No. 8 was established from the Plaza, Third Ave., and Broadway, to Ramona's Home.

Route No. 4, the Imperial Ave. Line, was changed to run up State St. from Broadway to Ivy St.

The remainder of the State St. Line was abandoned in June 1925. Then the No. 4 cars were changed to start at State St. on B St., to Fifth Ave., to K St., etc. Previously the east end of the route had been cut back from the Cemeteries to 34th St., on Imperial Ave. and a bus shuttled from 34th St. to 40th St.

The next casualty was the First Ave. end of Route No. 5, the First Ave. — Ocean View Blvd. Line, in September 1928, from Laurel St. on First Ave., to B St., to Third Ave. No. 5 cars then

looped downtown via Fifth Ave., to B St., to Third Ave., to F St., to Fifth Ave. No. 4 cars were changed to make the same loop at that time.

Bus Route "B" replaced the street cars on First Ave. The designation for the Bus Route, State St. to Old Town, was changed from No. 8 to "A".

If anyone is interested, the three original buses were traded in in 1924. From hereon, no attempt will be made to record the additions to, changes in or vagaries of the bus system, except as motor vehicles displaced street car lines.

Last Big Undertaking

Heretofore, J. D. has confined his investments on Broadway to the area west of Third Avenue.

For his first venture in building east of Fifth Ave., he purchased the 200 ft. frontage on the South Side of Broadway, from Sixth Ave. to Seventh Ave. and plans were drawn for the stately 13 story office structure, the *J. D. Spreckels Building.*

On December 11, 1925, the building permit was taken out, indicating an expenditure of $1,750,000.

It was proposed to house his First Trust and Savings Bank, then located in the Electric Building at Sixth Ave. and E St., on the ground floor.

J. D. did not live to see the culmination of this dream nor the great structural growth of the city during the years of prosperity prior to the Stock Market crash in 1929. But he had seen his city grow in population from less than 17,000 to over 100,000.

J. D. Passes On

It was sad news, on June 7, 1926, that John D. Spreckels had paid his fare in full and had reached the end of the

*The J. D. Spreckels Building. (Opposite)
Right-of-way by the San Diego High School.
—Union Title*

line from which no passenger returns. The people of San Diego had lost their "One-Man", the big, simple, great man, whose chief aim in life had been the building up of the City of San Diego.

The value of the holdings in San Diego County was estimated at 25 millions.

Sweeping changes were in the offing. From this point on the "Spreckels Interests" began to wane.

Liquidation

How vast were the properties of the J. D. and A. B. Spreckels Estates in San Diego County probably only Donald E. Hanson, who supervised the disposal process, knows. Only a limited number of the enterprises have been discussed here.

Many holdings had been sold or given away by J. D. during his life time.

The Southern California Mountain Water Company, as has been mentioned, was transferred to the City of San Diego at cost.

North Island was sold to the United States Government for five and one-half million dollars during the first World War.

The fabulous, multi-million dollar Mission Beach Amusement Center was donated to the State of California in 1934, which, in turn, transferred it to the City of San Diego.

Gradual disposures of the other holdings began soon after J. D's. death. However, up until 1948, only the heirs held stock in the J. D. & A. B. Spreckels Company.

In 1928, the two newspapers, The

San Diego Union and The Evening Tribune, were sold to the late Col. Ira C. Copley.

The towering office structure, which bore a plaque designating it the J. D. Spreckels Building, now carries the big roof sign reading: "Bank of America".

In 1933, the shares in the biggest project, the San Diego & Arizona Railway Company, were sold to Southern Pacific Company. "Eastern" was then tacked on to the corporate name.

Claus Spreckels had already been forced out as General Manager. It was a squeeze play. On June 26, 1925, President Hannam issued a Bulletin reading: "Effective this date, Mr. S. E. Mason is appointed Assistant General Manager of the San Diego Electric Railway Company and the San Diego & Coronado Ferry Company, and will have full charge of these companies, reporting direct to the President."

And the elimination process goes on and on.

Msc. in Roaring Twenties

In Coronado, a new car house, 73 ft x 160 ft., was built on First St., the old one was razed and the loop track at the Ferry Building was put in in 1920. In that year the track on 5th St., which had been reconstructed with 60 pound rails in 1912, was retired. A new ferry boat, the *Morena*, was placed on the run in June.

Coronado Ferry Landing and Terminal loop track about 1924.—Union Title

The impact of the two cars knocked the trolley of car No. 211 off the wire by about two inches where it was held in place by the retriever just enough so that, to all appearances, it was on the wire. The motorman failed to test the air, released the brakes and started down the hill. When he attempted to apply his brakes and found that he had no air, he then wracked up the emergency brake wheel. By this time, of course the car had gained considerable momentum so that the hand brakes were ineffective in stopping it. Panic ensued and Conductor Abrahams had to fight the passengers to keep them from jumping off. At terrific speed, estimated between 40 and 50 miles per hour, the car hit

No. 146 was the first class 1 cars remodeled for one man operation. Interior view shows the hard wooden seats retained in what had been the open section.—F. W. Reif

Fire damaged the ferry slip on the Coronado side in 1921. It was caused by oil on the water becoming ignited.

The tracks on Third and Fourth Aves. in San Diego, which had been abandoned in 1920, were removed the next year.

The "Ship Yard Line" now served the Destroyer Repair Base of the U.S. Navy at the foot of 32nd St., until abandonment to buses in 1929.

There was much ado over the application for a franchise on 16th St., from Broadway to Market St. A charter amendment was required. Before election, a car was fitted up as an illuminated traveling billboard. It carried the message "BOOST FOR A GREATER SAN DIEGO, Let's get together. Vote for the 16th St. franchise. Vote 'Yes' on the Charter Amendment. Election to-morrow, October 10, 1922." Carried. The tracks and connections were installed. The No. 12 and the National City and Chula Vista cars from Union Station used Broadway to 16th St., to Logan Heights. Route No. 5 cars continued to operate

on Market St. but the south track was removed. This made very bad conditions, operating against the flow of traffic in one direction. Red flashers were added to the cars.

The Weekly Pass system was inaugurated in 1923. 537 were sold the first week.

The worst street car accident in years, according to The San Diego Sun, occurred on April 29, 1923. Car No. 168, on Route No. 11, had stopped in Balboa Park at the High School to take on a baseball crowd from the Stadium about 4:30 P.M. Car No. 211 on Route No. 7, following collided with No. 168. Inspector Jack Wilson decided that the latter car was too badly damaged, so the passengers were transferred to No. 211 and he piloted No. 168 to the car house.

The new ferry Morena paddling toward Coronado.—F. W. Reif

the switch at Twelfth Ave. and Broadway and derailed in the asphalt pavement, continuing toward the southwest corner. Half way across it struck a Buick Sedan, hurling the auto against the sides of a wooden building, occupied by a shoe repair shop. The walls were demolished and the machine landed inside, injuring its two occupants. The car sped on, jumped the curb, sheared off an electric pole, uprooted an acacia tree and came to a stop at another pole. No one was killed but 38 persons were injured.

The buses forced the suspension of the electric interurban service from 24th St., in National City, to Chula Vista in June 1925. The overhead was taken down but all the tracks were retained by the San Diego & Arizona Railway for freight movements.

A single track was laid on 30th St., from University Ave. to Adams Ave., including catenary overhead, in 1923.

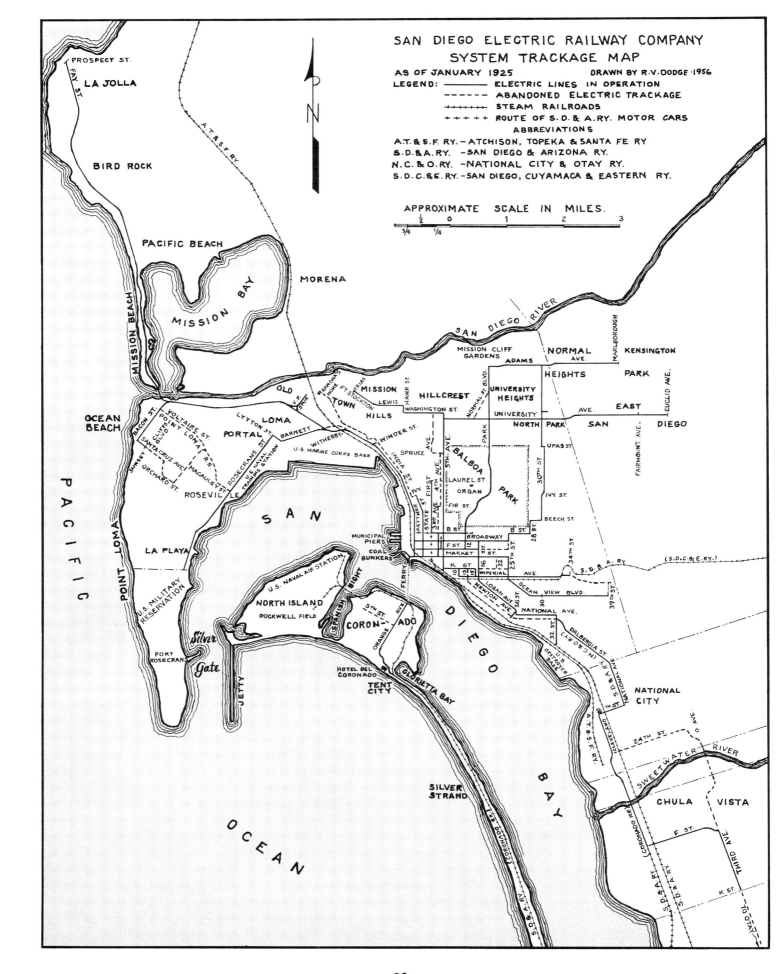

motors or trucks. The rebuilt cars were assigned to Class 6, later being returned to number One classification.

Other experiments were made on Class 2 cars but it was decided merely to secure the center gates, relocate the controls, remove the multiple unit equipment and to install air foot valves. The changed-over cars were known as Class 3. The conversions were made, a small number at a time, over a period of several years.

The northerly one-third of the block where the power plant is located, including the car Paint Shop and Los Banos Baths, was sold to San Diego Consolidated Gas & Electric Company in 1923. A new Auto Repair Shop and a

PEP UP!!! A Package deal in 1924 for six-bits.—R. V. Dodge. (Below) The first Coronado ferry was a paddle wheeler, while the second Coronado was diesel powered. — San Diego Transit System

Block signals were installed on the Balboa Park Line and to control the single track on F St., from State St. to Kettner Blvd. in 1923.

A Work Order for an extension to Route No. 5 was issued in 1924. Tracks were to be laid on Ocean View Blvd., from 30th St. to 39th St. and on 39th St., from Ocean View Blvd. to Imperial Ave. and the Cemeteries, catenary suspended trolley wire being erected. A franchise for a connection on 25th St., from Market St. to K St. was obtained and tracks were laid. The No. 5 line was then taken off K St. and Imperial Ave. and the route became on Market St., from Fifth Ave. to 25th St. to Ocean View Blvd., to 39th St., K St. tracks from 16th St. to 25th St. were taken up. In 1927 the City Council authorized the abandonment of the 39th St. franchise and the track, if any, was removed.

In 1923, investigations were made of the feasibility of remodelling Class 1 and Class 2 cars for one-man operation. As an experiment, the running gear of Class 2 car No. 192 was changed to Brill 77 E-1 trucks with small wheels and 4 Westinghouse 514 A-3 motors with K 14 controllers. These did not work out satisfactorily and the electric energy consumed was greatly increased.

So, in 1924, the four motor equipment was transferred to Class 1 car No. 141 and car No. 192 was placed in storage on temporary trucks.

Class 1 car No. 146 was rebuilt, closing the center entrances and moving the controls. All the other Class 1 cars were similarly remodeled, without change of

Paint Shop were erected at 15th and K Sts.

A package deal was offered in 1924 to popularize Mission Beach. For the entire cost of 75 cents, you got round trip transportation, use of a bathing suit, a towel and a locker, a swim and a good lunch.

Due to the heavy load concentrations in the northeastern sections of the city, a substation was constructed in the block bounded by 30th St., University Ave., Kansas St. and Lincoln Ave. It was known as the 30th St. Substation and was placed in service about 1924.

In 1927, it was determined that additional booster facilities were desirable. A building was erected on Tenth Avenue, north of University Ave., and equipment not needed at the San Carlos Substation was transferred to it.

The peak track mileage occurred in 1924, after the Line to the Beaches was completed. The total mileage as of December 31, 1925 was 106.97 equivalent single track.

The Brown Hoist self propelled crane—F. W. Reif

Plymouth 7-ton locomotive called the Spark Plug coupled to a rubbish car. (Below) The side dump cars played an important part in beach lines construction.

The steam engine driven paddle wheel ferry "Coronado" was retired in 1922 and was purchased by a moving picture producer. Disguised as a galleon, she was doomed and sunk in the epic battle of the Spanish Armada. A new Diesel-electric powered, propeller driven ferry, also named *Coronado,* was built in 1929.

San Diego's population was 147,995 in 1930.

A grand array of work equipment was assembled in the years prior to the construction of the Beach Line. Of particular interest were the Brown Hoist 10 ton self-propelling Crane, equipped with a lifting magnet, and the Plymouth 7 ton gasoline locomotive, known as "Spark Plug".

Two work flat cars, one with a side dump body, were built in the Company's shops and an additional one was purchased. Each had two cabs.

Several 40 ft. California type passenger cars, which had been retired, were withdrawn from storage, remodeled and fitted up for trash hauling, rail bonding, track sanding and for a "line tower". Three others, non-electric, were adapted for use as a field office and flat cars called "dollies".

16 second-hand flat cars were acquired. Rail laying equipment was installed on one of them. 6 center dump "ballast" cars and 7 air-operated side dump cars were purchased.

40 ft. California type passenger cars numbers 103 and 104 and Class 2 cars numbers 182 and 202 were transferred and were used for the transportation of workmen and other assignments.

Welding Car
Mission Beach line
May 5th - 24

Old passenger car No. 108 equipped for rail
bonding.—F. W. Reif

Work flat No. 025 had quite a career (see
roster). In the later years it looked like this.
—R. P. Middlebrook

Work flat No. 23 picking up the scrap from
the Point Loma Railroad in 1923.—F. W. Reif

A Train load of old track
from Voltaire on May 17 24

Work flat car No. 21 purchased new from American Car Co. in 1912.—F. W. Reif

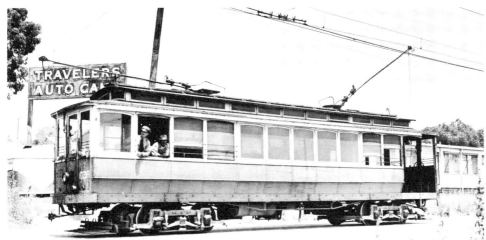

Service car No. 28 was old passenger car No. 99. Car hauled sand and was fitted with a trolley greasing appliance.—R. P. Middle-brook

Line tower car No. 26 and crew out on the line.—R. C. Brandt

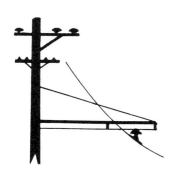

CHAPTER VII
1930's - Depression and Recovery

Too Heavy! Too Slow! Too Complicated! And Too Noisy, Too! Thus was the conventional street car condemned.

In an effort to stem the tide of motor bus encroachments, the presidents of representative street railway companies got together and worked out the design features for a light weight car which would excel the rubber-tired competitors in many ways. There is a certain field of city operation where modern street cars will give the public the most attractive service. The result was the Presidents Conference Committee's Car with its streamlined appearance, its fast acceleration and deceleration, automobile type controls, its progressive triple braking system — dynamic, air and magnetic, rubber insulated wheels and riggings which were extremely quiet when properly maintained.

First with P.C.C. Car

The San Diego Electric Railway quickly responded in 1936 with a contract with the St. Louis Car Company to furnish 25 single end cars of the new specifications. An order was placed for three additional cars in 1937. 25 were delivered during the period — February

Almost noiseless, one of the PCC cars glides across Balboa Park trestle No. 2 on its way downtown. (Below) PCC No. 518 pauses at the end of Route 2.—Both Donald Duke

through June, 1937 and the other three, with minor improvements, came in January 1938. These were called "Class 6" cars and were numbered 501 to 528 inclusive.

To stimulate public interest, one car was placed on exhibition on the Broadway side of the Plaza, headed east, before going into service.

Since the cars were designed for single end operation, it was necessary to make provisions for turning them at the ends of the runs. There was the loop at the Union Station on Broadway which would serve the purpose there. Other lines made loops around blocks in the downtown district. Orders were issued for the installations of turning wyes for:

Route No. 1 — at Park Boulevard and Lincoln St. So much opposition arose that the plans for the wye were abandoned and the needed curve was installed in the southwesterly quadrant at the intersection of University Ave. and Park Blvd. The cars could then turn

Depressing Thirties

The first thing in January 1930, buses took over the transportation of passengers between San Diego and National City, thus ending the electric interurban service which had been begun by the National City & Otay Railway in 1907. The track from 32nd St. and Newton Ave., Dalbergia St., National Ave. in National City, 12th St. to Cleveland Ave. was taken up.

In that year, considerable correspondence was exchanged with the General Electric and Westinghouse Companies regarding trackless trolleys. A Work Order was issued to prepare an estimate of the cost of installing the 2 wire, positive and negative, overhead on First Ave. The figures were submitted and that ended the trolley coach idea.

The decade was marred by three bad wrecks. The first one happened at 7

The new and the old pass on the Balboa Park trackage.—Donald Duke. (Below) San Diego & Coronado ferries North Island and San Diego.—San Diego Transit System

from University Ave. south into Park Blvd. and cross-over. Then they ran north on Park to clear the cross-over north of University Ave. Heading through the latter, the car was ready for the inbound run.

Route No. 2 — at Adams Ave. and 30th St. The turning movements interfered with vehicular traffic in Adams Ave., so a loop was formed around the block bounded by Madison Ave., Kansas St., Adams Ave. and 30th St. in 1942.

Route No. 3 — at Trias St. and Fort Stockton Drive.

Route No. 7 — at Euclid and University Aves.

Route No. 11 (later) at Edgeware Road and Adams Ave., including track extension.

And one was formed at the Adams Avenue Car House.

Service with the PCC cars started on July 12, 1937, with 100% operation on Routes numbers 1, 2, and 3 and night service and all day Sundays and Holidays on Route No. 7.

While the PCC's did expedite traffic, increase revenues substantially and perform splendidly, they did not accomplish the primary objective — of stopping the abandonment of street car lines to buses. And many patrons still preferred the heavier and roomier Class 5 cars, the faithful 400's.

The purchase of the PCC's turned out to have been a most timely investment a few years later.

An outbound train for the beaches on the private right-of-way section along Kettner Blvd. (Below) A night view on Route 2 at University Avenue.
—F. W. Reif

P.M. on January 9, 1930, when Operator Sisson lost control of his car, No. 223, westbound, down hill, on Broadway at 18th St. The runaway struck the rear end of car No. 212, operated by E. H. Schroeder, which was turning from Broadway south into 16th St., The impact derailed No. 212 and inflicted severe damage. The runaway shot fan-wise off the track with the rear end describa half circle. It struck one automobile, hurling it into another. General Manager's Order No. 2833 was issued to retire and scrap cars No. 212 and 223.

Bulletin No. 96, July 25, 1930: "Sliding Trolley Shoes are being installed on all street cars instead of trolley wheels, on a regular program as cars go through shops. These shoes provide better contact with the trolley wire, less arcing, less radio interference and less noise in cars."

Due to the loss of patronage on account of automobile travel, as well as to the Depression, a wage reduction of 8% was put into effect in September 1931. Motormen were cut from $5.25 to $4.83 a day.

With the falling off of traffic, there was not the need for much multiple unit operation. A Work Order, authorized in 1932, instructed to "Reduce weight on 5 Class 5 cars." This meant the removal of all the MU equipment and the converting of the cars to strictly one-man operation. Others followed.

The old exposition buildings in Balboa Park must come down! Such was the ultimatum of the City Council in 1933. Of temporary construction, they had been patched up after the close of the Panama California Exposition. During World War I they were taken over for military purposes. Now they presented a sorry appearance and had been condemned. A mighty furore arose. Destroy all those graceful, colorful examples of Spanish-Colonial architecture! Never! So right in the midst of the worst depression ever experienced, the people of San Diego decided to hold another great world's fair. The California-Pacific International Exposition opened in 1935 and continued through 1936. The San Diego Electric Railway did not have to make much preparation for this one, except to purchase a fleet of 6 Ford Tractors with passenger carrying semi-trailers. These were operated from the Laurel St. entrance, east of Sixth Ave., through the Exposition grounds.

Mission Cliff Gardens was transferred to "Physical Non-Operating Property" in 1930, indicating that it was closed as a park for street car patrons.

Another diesel-electric ferry boat, named San Diego, was built in 1931. Then the ferry Ramona was dismantled in 1932. Her hull was towed to the foot of Market St. and fitted up as a floating restaurant until one day it didn't float. In 1938 the Southern Pacific — Golden Gate's Diesel-Electric ferry boat "Golden West" was purchased, rebuilt and renamed North Island. The paddle wheel ferry Morena was taken out of service.

The operation of the gasoline-electric

Brown-and-ivory No. 351, ex Glendale & Montrose car, outbound by Hotel del Coronado.
- Collection of Al Haij

(LEFT) One of the famous big trolley bridges in Balboa Park. - Donald Duke

tacular collision took place near Loma Alta station, close to West Point Loma Blvd., soon after 8 A.M. on November 22, 1937. An outbound Ocean Beach car, Route No. 14, operated by Edward W. Weiss, and an inbound car from La Jolla, Route No. 16, with Helge E. Erickson at the controls and carrying over 40 commuters, met head-on, seriously injuring nine persons, including Erickson, and causing minor injuries to twenty two others. So terrific was the impact that the police regard it miraculous that neither the motormen nor many of the passengers were not killed outright. This is a tribute to the sturdy construction of cars No. 401 and 405.

Snow fell in San Diego! This was in 1937 and it was the first of record since 1882.

Two double truck cars with closed bodies were purchased from the Glendale & Montrose Railway in 1938. They had been built in 1923 and bore numbers 10 and 13. They were reconditioned, repainted to cream and green, renumbered 351 and 352 and were hauled on semi-trailers to Coronado. They continued in operation there until the end of street car service in that city.

Two street cars and the car barns at 15th St. and Imperial Ave. were struck by lightning in September 1939.

Most of Class 1, Class 2 and Class 3 cars were retired during this decade. Several "bungalow" courts were constructed using the car bodies at various locations including San Diego, Old Town,

motor cars was discontinued by the San Diego & Arizona Eastern Railway Company about 1934. The tracks and connections on B St. and First Ave. were torn up in 1937.

Another runaway occurred on the Balboa Park Line on December 20, 1934. A Class 5 car on No. 11 Route plowed into the rear of a Class 3 car on No. 7 line, which was unloading passengers at the main entrance to the High School at 7:35 A.M. Motorman G. A. Johnson began blowing warning whistles before the crash. Fred Cameron, operator of the standing car, said that he heard the whistling but was unable to move his car forward on account of pedestrians. Mischievous students were suspected for releasing the compressed air at the rear end of the runaway car but tampering could not be proved. Johnson stated that the brakes did not seem to take complete hold but he succeeded in greatly reducing the speed prior to the collision.

There was a "pea soup" fog enshrouding the shores of Mission Bay and there was a sickening crash. The San Diego Electric Railway's most spec-

Car No. 352 running the shuttle on the Coronado Beach line.—Al Haij

Coronado shuttle car No. 352 at the Coronado Barn. This car was acquired from the Glendale & Montrose Railway—Al Haij

ended dismally on September 16, 1940. So rapid had been the development of the territory traversed that the cars had been slowed to local street railway pace most of the way.

The San Diego Electric Railway had acquired the bus lines of Fred H. Sutherland and took over operation in January 1930. These included one route between San Diego and La Jolla and two to Encanto, Lemon Grove and Spring Valley. Thus the Company's buses competed with the La Jolla electric line. The complaints that the tracks obstructed automobile traffic were many and forceful, particularly in Mission Beach where they were elevated above the street level. The Company agreed to tear out the tracks and the City of San Diego received permission to use gasoline tax money to remove the roadbed and to pave the street.

With the abandonment of Routes No. 15 and 16, the beautiful terminal in La Jolla was razed, the elaborate overcrossing trestles were torn down and all the rails were removed except those in paved streets.

Following these abandonments, Car Route Numbers 1, 2, 3, 4, 7, 9, 11, 12 and 20 (Coronado) were left, still operating in the '40's.

tion of the Line to the Beaches, went from street cars to buses on December 19, 1938, becoming Route "O".

At the same time, Route No. 5, the Ocean View Blvd. Line, was discontinued, the street cars being replaced by buses as Route "H".

Then came the tragedy! What had started as a high speed interurban line in 1924 to Mission Beach and La Jolla

El Cajon and Morena Lake. A few were retained either on the roster or non-operative.

The population of the City of San Diego in 1940 had increased to 203,341, according to the official count.

One by One They Fall

Previously, the abandonments of the electric lines to National City, Chula Vista and Otay, parts of the Point Loma Railroad, the State St. — Old Town Line, the First Ave. Line and the Third Ave. Line have been reported.

Route numbers 6, 8 and 10 had been vacated.

In 1937, Route No. 13, the line to Loma Portal, Roseville, La Playa and the U.S. Military Reservation succumbed, being replaced by a bus route on February 18th.

Route No. 14, the Ocean Beach sec-

La Jolla car passing through Mission Beach in 1929. (Below) The last car to run on the line to the beaches on September 16, 1940.

CHAPTER VIII
1940's - War - Inflation - The End

In August 1939, war had been declared in Europe. It started out as a "phoney" war but soon got too hot to handle. The United States had to hurry to re-arm and to furnish materials to assist England and France.

Then came Pearl Harbor on December 7, 1941 and we were at war with Japan and the "axis" countries.

War Emergency

Vast expansions in strategic industries in and around San Diego took place, particularly in the airplane manufacturing facilities. The Government built the immense Plant No. 2 for Consolidated Aircraft Corporation, extending from the site of the former Witherby St. over-crossing to Rosecrans St. in Old Town. Soon three large shifts were working.

Gasoline had been rationed. The workmen had to have transportation, both to Plant No. 1 and Parts Plant No. 2.

Fortunately, on the abandonment of the Line to the Beaches, the tracks had not been removed in the paved streets. So, in 1942, the route from B St., on Kettner Blvd. and Hancock St. to Bandini St., near Witherby St., was rehabilitated.

But the out-bound track of the Beach Line had been located on the San Diego & Arizona Right-of-Way and parcels of

The World War II babies (Above) acquired from the Wilkesbarre Railway. (Below) A former Utah Light & Traction car on the San Diego Electric.—Al Haij

this property had been sold. This made it necessary to lay a second track in Kettner Blvd., from B St. to Date St. New double tracks were built on B St., from Kettner Blvd. to Third Ave. Anything available was used. For ties, pieces of angle iron cut from old bed rails were welded to the track rails and all were set in concrete.

With this accomplished, a double track line was established from 12th Ave. and B St. to near Plant No. 2, except for the single curve with turnouts at Kettner Blvd. and B St.

All the buses that could be obtained had been purchased and pressed into service, but they were insufficient to handle the loads. Most of Class 1, Class 2 or Class 3 cars had been dismantled. Several had been kept in Coronado and these were brought around the bay and reconditioned to help move the war traffic. Not enough!

So there was a hunt to find second hand street cars.

The first to arrive were 14 large

Park Terminal in the former pedestrian subway under the tracks and in the basement of the Spreckels' Theater Building. The latter was electronic type, using Ignitron Rectifiers.

Even some decrepit antiques from a New York City Bus Line were imported. The transportation task during the emergency was immense.

But, with Victory Japanese Day in August 1945, the grand rush was over.

Several axles had broken on the Salt Lake cars and they were generally unsuited to the conditions. They were soon dismantled and their large bodies were sold for houses and shops, several being hauled out to El Cajon. Some of the New York cars and some of the San Diego Electric Railway's old cars were scrapped in 1946.

But most of the Pennsylvania and the New York cars were kept in service on the Logan Heights, Imperial Ave., Coronado Ferry and Mission Hills Lines.

Third Avenue Railway (TARS) cars. The view above shows the larger type car with 12 windows on Broadway. (Below) Car No. 1051, one of the small cars with only 10 windows.

heavyweights from the Utah Traction Company in Salt Lake City. They were worked over, hastily painted cream and green, and were numbered No. 1001 to 1014. These were called Class 8 Cars.

Then 16 more were purchased in Wilkesbarre, Pennsylvania. These were steel cars which had been built in 1922 and were in fairly good condition. They were cleaned up, repainted and numbered 1015 to 1030 inclusive. They became Class 7.

Lastly came two lots of ancient wooden cars from the Third Avenue Railway System of New York City. They were in dilapidated condition, some so flexible that they seemed to bend around the curves. The first bunch was 20 TARS 400 series cars with 12 windows on a side. Originally they had been built for the Metropolitan Street Railway about 1905. That company sold them to the New York & Harlem Railway which, in turn, transferred them to the Third Avenue Railway. There they had been remodelled to one-man operation and the typical Third Ave. fronts were installed. These were patched up in San Diego, repainted and renumbered 1031 to 1050 inclusive.

Six smaller ones, with 10 windows on a side, were also acquired. All in 1942. These were TARS 800 series, originally designed for "conduit" (underground trolley) operation and were built for TARS in 1907 or 1908. All had been converted to pole cars. These received similar face liftings and were numbered 1051 to 1056. All 26 cars were designated Class 9.

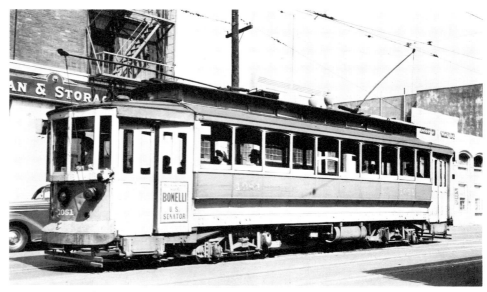

All these old cars were put in service on the war runs. Processions of these cosmopolitan vehicles would come in from Kensington, Route No. 11 East San Diego, Route No. 7 via the Park Line, Broadway, Route No. 2 and the East End line Route No. 12 and parade down B St. and out Kettner Blvd. at shift change hours.

To meet the greatly increased demand for electric current, additional substation facilities were a necessity. In 1940, the 30th Street Substation had been expanded and the equipment from the no longer needed Ocean Beach Substation was transferred and installed there. Two years later, substations were established in the Adams Ave. Car House; at the Balboa

An advertisement in February 1947 read: Progress in your Transportation Since the War. Despite declining revenues and increased costs, 5 new routes added, 31 miles of new and extended service, 29 new buses in service (more are still on order), 41 old street cars retired.

The ferry boat "Morena" was commandeered by the U.S. Navy during the War and was used to transport service men from the 28th Street Landing in San Diego to the Amphibious Base on the Coronado Strand. Then it lay moored at the Case Construction Company's plant, partially dismantled. The hull was sold in 1947 to a Mexican fishing concern and was towed to San Quintin, Baja

San Diego Electric car No. 410 streaks along the heavy duty right-of-way located in Balboa Park. This scene is on the eastern edge of the park between two of the large steel trestles. This trolley is bound for downtown San Diego and the turn around at Union Depot.—Donald Duke

California. Paddle wheel days in San Diego were gone.

Another former Golden Gate ferry was added to the fleet. The "Golden Shore" had been sold to a Seattle company and had been renamed "Elwha". It was acquired in 1944 and, again, the name was changed, this time to *Silver Strand*.

Transit Survey

Transportation equipment and facilities had been badly strained during the War. Arrangements were made for a complete survey, to determine what steps should be taken to meet normal needs.

Representatives of the Westinghouse and General Electric Companies and engineering consultants were called in. The setup was examined and reports were rendered for modernizing San Diego's street car and bus system.

Trackless trolley coaches were being considered for some or all the street car lines, but this was only a gesture.

General Manager Sam. E. Mason, said that "a complete postwar improvement program, aimed at removing some of the ancient trolley cars and buses from the streets will get underway as soon as the reports are fully digested." "Meanwhile, the Company is awaiting promised delivery of 12 new gasoline buses from the American Car & Foundry Company and 17 diesel buses from General Motors.

The war's end brought a 16 to 18% decrease in passenger loads, from the all-time peak which had been reached in July 1945. Passenger traffic had increased 600% during the emergency.

It wasn't long until the truth came out, when R. F. MacNally, Assistant General Manager, stated that "the San Diego Electric Railway hopes to cease operations on about a third of its present trackage." A decision as to the remainder was deferred. "The gasoline and Diesel buses fit our needs pretty well . . . It is very expensive to dig up old track and replace it . . . With buses, we do not have to go to that expense. Then, too, the buses are more flexible. In a city where population is growing and shifting as fast as it is in San Diego, we can shift our routes to meet changing needs faster than with street cars."

However, MacNally admitted that "cars are being kept on the heavily travelled lines because of the great number of persons they are able to move in rush

The above view shows the Silver Strand. Other photographs were taken along Orange Avenue on the Coronado Line during 1947.

Trolleys and motor traffic in East San Diego just before abandonment. (Below) Inbound car on the Balboa Park private right-of-way.
Al Haij

hours. It takes three of the Company's biggest buses to seat as many as two big street cars and, for rush hour work, the street cars will accommodate more standees."

The car lines already doomed were routes numbers 1, 3, 4, 9, 12 and 20 (Coronado)

Last Rites

As the next step in the transition, an application was filed with the State Public Utilities Commission (formerly known as the Railroad Commission), in July 1946, for permission to substitute buses for the "junk" street cars which have been used during the war emergency on six lines, numbers 1, 3, 4, 9, 12 and 20.

About this time Sam. E. Mason, formerly Vice President and General Manager, was elected President of the San Diego Electric Railway Company and the San Diego & Coronado Ferry Company.

Operation of Route No. 1, which had previously been cut back to Park Blvd. on University Ave., was entirely discontinued on June 30, 1946, on account of bridge construction for the Cabrillo Freeway. The "F" bus line was extended to Fifth and University Aves. to pick up passengers from Route No. 3 cars.

When 14 new buses were available, plans were made to continue the junking. Then came the demise of the royal 4 and 12, with their decrepit TARS Cars. For some unknown reason it had been found expedient to retain these old trams in active service.

But their last runs did not pass out peacefully. Ardent mourners came down from Los Angeles on Saturday night, December 7th, 1946. They were joined by some local "juice fans" and, as the cars made their last runs, fitting "wakes" were held over them.

At 34th St. and Imperial Ave., all automobile traffic was halted with red fusees while some pictures were taken of the No. 4 line car.

The car was stopped at 25th St. by city police to inquire the meaning of the red fire on its rear end.

At 16th St. and Imperial Ave., the group got off and gathered on the northwest corner, waiting for the car to run to the barn. Some miscreant had placed a couple of torpedoes on the track. Hardly had the car cleared the intersection when there was a bang — bang and one of the boys fell over backwards just as a taxicab passed by on 16th St., Within minutes, three prowl cars were on the scene to investigate a shooting.

The car went into the barn minus certain articles suitable for retention as cherished mementos, and the operator breathed a prayer of thanksgiving.

All the wartime cars released by the change-over were dismantled and the bodies were advertised for sale as suitable for country homes, mountain cabins, offices, etc. The bodies from Class 3 cars, numbers 218, 219, 221, 222 and 225 had been sold and were hauled out to Lexington Park. No. 225, the handsome Exposition car, had been converted into a home at 3218 Van Dyke St. A storm of protests arose from residents of the neighborhood. Zoning restrictions pro-

Route 7 trolley on bridge No. 1 in Balboa Park. (Below) Car No. 501 pauses after completing the loop at the end of Route 2.—Both Donald Duke

hibited such construction.

Co-operation with the City was pledged by President Mason in a letter to the Council as reported May 14, 1947: "We will not hereafter sell any of these old street cars and run the risk of their misuse. The additional old street cars will be burned with the exception of a possible sale to a distant community which desires to continue to operate them as street cars."

So, all bodies from the ancient New York cars, not retained for further service, were hauled to the waterfront and burned.

Two bays of the Imperial Ave. Car House had been demolished by that date.

More Follow

At a public hearing held in February 1947, a spokesman for the San Diego Electric Railway told the examiners of the Public Utilities Commission how it could better San Diego's public transportation facilities by replacing worn-out tracks and street cars with buses on three more local routes.

The change-over would include a new "through" service to Coronado as far as the Amphibious Training Base on the Silver Strand where Tent City used to be. The buses would "ride" the ferry, eliminating the two transfers of passengers. The request also provided for the elimination of street cars to Mission Hills.

Dale Harlan, Superintendent of Traffic, put into the record that no fare changes are planned, other than some adjustments previously asked for.

The Tenth Ave. Substation would be abandoned.

The authority was granted but the switch-over on Routes numbers 3, 9 and 20 could not be made until more buses were received. The celebration of the delivery of 39 buses from Consolidated Vultee Aircraft Corporation took place on May 28th. His honor, the late Harley E. Knox, the Mayor of San Diego, nicknamed the new conveyances "Liberators". The last day of operation on the three lines was Saturday, May 31st, and street car service in Coronado came to an end.

As the last No. 3 car from Mission Hills turned off the Fifth Avenue tracks early Sunday morning, an era ended in San Diego. Public rail transportation on Fifth Street, which began with the opening of the horse car line on July 3, 1886, was now just a memory.

This change-over displaced all the Wilkesbarre cars and the remaining New Yorkers. Car number 1043, ex. TARS No. 436, was acquired by the Bay Area Electric Railroad Association and was shipped to Oakland, California, for preservation. All the others were dismantled and the bodies or the combustible portions of them were burned. The cars in Coronado were also retired.

At the same time, all remaining Service Equipment was disposed of, except work cars number 010, 026 and 028.

Brown Hoist 10 ton Crane, No. 022, had been sold to Southern Pacific Company in March.

The others were dismantled and the bodies were cremated alongside the passenger cars.

Only three car lines now remain, Routes numbers 2, 7 and 11, with the 50 Class 5 cars and the 28 Class 6 cars, the PCC's, more than meeting the passenger traffic demands.

Sold!!!

Came March 1, 1948 and the announcement that: "The Spreckels' interests have agreed to sell the San Diego Electric Railway Company and the San Diego & Coronado Ferry Company to an organization that operates transit lines in

On Broadway, passing the U. S. Grant Hotel in downtown San Diego. (Opposite) PCC on light steel trestle, note wig way to indicate trolley on bridge.—Al Haij

several other western cities . . ." Terms were agreed upon by R. L. Regal, President of the J. D. and A. B. Spreckels Company and Jesse L. Haugh, of Oakland, organizer of the City Transit Systems, subject to Public Utilities Commission approval.

Based upon a brief biography which appeared in the San Diego Union, Mr. Haugh had been employed in the Engineering Department of the Chicago & Northwestern Railroad. During the First World War he served as an engineering assistant to the Regional Director of the United States Railroad Administration.

After the War, he joined the Union Pacific Railroad Company as Assistant to the President and later became a Vice President.

In 1942, he left the Union Pacific and became Chairman of Pacific City Lines until that Company was acquired

by National City Lines in 1946. Mr. Haugh then became President of the Key System in Oakland and a Director of National City Lines. He resigned in January 1947 to organize and develop his own companies.

The local system was reported as having 78 street cars and 284 motor coaches. The Ferry Company had four ferries: the *North Island* and the *Silver Strand* with wooden hulls and the newer *San Diego* and *Coronado* with steel hulls.

According to the figures made public, over the 56-year history under the Spreckels' ownership, the San Diego Electric Railway Company suffered a net loss of more than $1,700,000.

The transfer was made to J. L. Haugh and the Western Transit Company. The gross consideration was revealed as involving some $5,500,000.

In a hearing, Mr. Haugh explained that the Western Transit Company and

he proposed to assign the purchase contract to a firm known as City Transit Systems and that the Railway Company and the Ferry Company would continue as the operating companies for a time.

On September 9, 1948, Mr. Haugh announced that *San Diego Transit System* will be the new name for the San Diego Electric Railway Company. That name would soon appear on the sides of the buses in an emblem described as a pair of wings with a shield carrying the slogan: *Safety, Courtesy, Service.*

End of the Empire

When the sale of the San Diego Electric Railway was concluded in 1948, the holdings of the J. D. and A. B. Spreckels Company were reduced to about 100 acres of land of little value.

Hotel del Coronado and some 470 acres of Coronado land had been sold to Robert A. Norblom for slightly more than $2,000,000 in January.

About the 10th of November of that year, Don E. Hanson, Disposal Supervisor, sent a laborer out to an 80-acre tract of unimproved land, 3 miles northwest of Camp Miramar, with the instructions to put up a sign. Little did that workman realize that he was the leading man in the last act of a 61-year historical drama.

Tap, tap, tap, went his hammer and the sign was set. It bore four letters, spelling S-O-L-D.

And the final curtain was rung down, marking the end of the colossal Spreckels' Empire in San Diego County. There was no applause.

Color Schemes

Up to 1931, the standard golden yellow, as originally adopted, was used on all the cars, except the "Sight Seeing" car. Various schemes were tested out then and a cream and green combination was selected, as part of a plan to encourage the public to patronize the cars.

Making a startling contrast, several PCC cars came out in varying arrangements of orange and lemon yellow, in 1944. Soon they were referred to as the "citrus colored" cars. None of these changes was adopted, and they were repainted cream and green.

In 1945, cars numbers 502 and 503 were painted red, white and blue to advertise the Red Cross Blood Donation Campaign.

In January 1948, R. F. McNalley, Vice President in charge of Operations announced that "in keeping with modern trends" the buses and street cars soon will be wearing that "new look". The old three-color-tone design will be abandoned in favor of "a brighter and neater two-color scheme of emerald green on a broad background of cream". "Aside from being more attractive, the new colors are brighter and the buses and street cars will stand out better in traffic and at night, thus representing a considerable safety factor, not only to the Company but to other vehicles and pedestrians." But all the street cars were soon scheduled for elimination.

Then, when the 13 new 45-passenger buses were placed in service in August 1948, "in keeping with the new Company's policy of furthering development of public transportation here", it was disclosed that the color scheme had again been changed, this time from cream and green to yellow and white. It was explained that "the new combination is a safety measure, being easier to see in traffic."

In 1954, a number of buses were painted as traveling advertisement media. When they came down the street, you would think that a circus was in town. Other special paint jobs have appeared.

Then, in 1955, a reversion to the two-shades of green plus white has taken place, similar to the Metropolitan Coach Lines' standard in Los Angeles. One smaller "wings and shield" emblem is now being applied on the front end of the bus under the windshield.

Rails to Rubber

The San Diego Transit System, armed with permission to borrow $720,000 for the purchase of 45 new buses, made the application on January 13, 1949 to end street car service.

Deliveries of the $20,000 buses began in March. On the 3rd, a State Public Utilities Commission hearing was started on the request to substitute the buses for street cars on the three remaining routes. The authority was granted.

Much publicity about the conversion followed.

On Sunday, March 27th, a "farewell to street cars" excursion, sponsored by Railroad Boosters, now organized as the Pacific Railroad Society, of Los Angeles, was operated over the remaining trackage. Adams Ave. Car House was visited and the trolley enthusiasts had a field day there operating passenger and service cars a few feet at a time. The 3 service cars were coupled and shuttled

At the end of the line in East San Diego. (Below) Trolley slows down as it prepares to stop at the Balboa Park terminal before proceeding downtown.—Both Donald Duke

The Crown City is the most recent addition to the San Diego & Coronado Ferry Company's fleet. Revolutionary in design, the Crown City was fully radar equipped when it left the shipyard in 1954.—Union Title

back and forth as a train.

In a long parade, the 45 buses were introduced to San Diegans on April 23rd, the last day of street car service. Free rides were offered during the procession.

Street railway fans were on hand for the last runs but the atmosphere was more gloomy and sedate than when Route No. 4 bowed out. This was a mournful occasion.

The "owl" cars on each line were the last.

On Route No. 11, the Adams Ave. Line, it was car No. 510 with Operator George L. Kemble in charge. It left Union Station at 1:35 A.M., Sunday, April 24, 1949.

Route No. 2, the Broadway and 30th St. Line, was next with car No. 503 being the final one, leaving Union Station at 4:20 A.M.

Quite a crowd waited for the ultimate. Route No. 7, the East San Diego Line, with car No. 446 and a second section, car No. 432.

The departure was made at 4:25 A.M., with many notables, juice fans and a few revenue passengers aboard. Included were: J. L. Haugh, the Transit System President; Harold Starkey, Chamber of Commerce President and Vice-Mayor Elmer Blase. Too bad that the Mayor, Harley Knox, wasn't there to witness the consummation of his efforts to get rid of the street cars.

J. N. Jacobs was the operator of car No. 446 at the start. At 30th St., on University Ave., he relinquished the controls to N. A. Holmquist, the oldest operator on the seniority list.

At 40th St., a pajama-clad figure rushed out to put a coin on the track and, as the car passed, retrieved his flattened souvenir.

Then a series of torpedoes exploded, causing alarmed residents to hurry to the door to see wha' hoppened.

The end of the line, at University and Euclid Aves., was reached at 5:15 A.M. Trolleys were changed and the second car left for the barn, with No. 446 following.

Arriving at Adams Ave. and Florida St., at 5:35 A.M., all the "dead-heads" got out and Operator Holmquist guided his car, displaying a banner reading: RETIRED WITH HONOR, into the Car House. President Haugh congratulated him and his 42-year career as a motorman had ended. He retired along with the 50 — 400's and the 28 P. C. C's.

And San Diego was an all-bus city.

Skeletons of the Wilkesbarre cars during scrapping. (Below) An outbound car pulling into the Balboa Park station. Fence at right kept passengers from crossing tracks.

Little time was lost before the wrecking crews took over. The City Council granted the Transit System two years in which to remove tracks, trolley wires and structures.

On May 23, 1949, workmen began taking down the trolley overhead on the loop at Union Station, "the first step in a program to obliterate all evidence of street cars in the city". The wires had to be taken down to make room for a crane to operate in removing the loop track. Curves on Broadway at Third, Fourth and Fifth Aves. followed.

The track removal operations involved covering the tracks where rails and steel ties were embedded in concrete with black top. Tracks with the rails laid on redwood ties had to be removed completely, then the excavated bed was filled with concrete and covered with a layer of asphalt. Considerable mileage consisted of wooden tie construction, including portions of those on B St., F St., K St., 30th St., Adams Ave. and many other locations.

The 30th St. Bridge had to be closed to traffic while the tracks were being removed.

Substations and other structures were dismantled, demolished or otherwise disposed of. The 10th Avenue Substation property was taken over by the San Diego Gas & Electric Company. Equipment from the Adams Avenue and the 30th St. Substations was purchased by a firm in Logan, West Virginia, in 1950. The Ignitron Rectifiers from the Speckels Theater Building Substation were sold to the Lighting Department of the City of Seattle, Washington, at the same time.

It had optimistically been expected that all Class 5 and Class 6 cars could be sold for further street car service.

In 1950, 17 P.C.C.'s cars were sold to El Paso City Lines, for service on the international loop, between El Paso and

Car No. 439 crossing Balboa Park bridge No. 3 on its inbound run. (Below) Inbound Route 11 car on the Balboa Park private right-of-way. Note signal on 2nd pole behind car.—Both Donald Duke

Ciudad Juarez, Mexico. Before shipment, the conventional seats were removed and longitudinal replacements were installed. These were required to facilitate inspections at the border crossings. 3 more of the streamlined cars followed in December 1952.

It had been hoped that a buyer would be found for the 50 — 400's but there was no market. As the Adams Ave. Car House was to be occupied as a box factory, the cars had to be moved. All the Class 5 cars and the 3 Service cars were sold to the Allied Salvage Company for scrapping in 1952.

The 8 Class 6 cars, the P. C. C's, were moved to the Bus Parking Lot on 15th St., between L St. and Imperial Ave. There they stood all faded and forlorn until August 1957 when they were sold to the San Diego Mill Supply Company. Car No. 508 was purchased by a group of electric railroad enthusiasts organized as the **Orange Empire Traction Company** for its museum at Perris, Calif. The

Railway Historical Society of San Diego, Inc., rescued car No. 528 for preservation and exhibition.

They have done a good job in the obliteration process. There are only a few traces left to indicate that street cars had been running here.

The Terminal in Balboa Park still remains. The building is used for the parking of automobiles and its appearance is disreputable. The platforms, subway, fences and roadbeds are there in evidence. Some parts of the ballasted roadbed can be traced through the Park.

The name Spreckels has been all but obliterated too. Only at the Spreckels Theatre and Building is it plainly displayed. Even the great outdoor organ in Balboa Park is generally designated as "The Organ Pavilion", though, now and then, "Spreckels" is added. There is a John D. Spreckels Lodge, F. & A. M.

The Railway Historical Society of San Diego, Inc., has been given the private car J. D. used when he was President

of the San Diego & Arizona Railway. It, with San Diego & Arizona Eastern steam locomotive No. 104, both donated by Southern Pacific Company, is now on exhibit at the San Diego County Fair Grounds at Del Mar. Let us hope that some way will be found there to perpetuate the name of the One Man who did so much for San Diego.

Occasionally, here and there, a rail raises its head through the asphalt and peers around until the maintenance crew comes along and tamps some "cold lay" over it.

AFTERTHOUGHTS

What of the future?

After the raise of the basic bus fare to 20 cents in Sept. 1955 Clarence Winder, Rate Consultant for the City of San Diego, issued a report recommending public acquisition of the San Diego Transit System. He said that a metropolitan transit authority could be established in San Diego County. As a public agency, it could not be obligated to pay taxes. Fares could first be reduced to "stem the tide of private cars and then *convert to a rail transit system* supplemented by buses."

During the street car era, San Diego lays claim to several "firsts". Some of these may be contested but, so far, no documentary proofs have been offered.

The first electric street railway on the Pacific Coast to use the ground return for the electric current was the Electric Rapid Transit's line to Old Town, opened November 19, 1887.

It had the first electrically operated double deckers in the West.

It had the first electrically operated track switch on the coast.

It was first in the West to adopt the Presidents Conference Committee's streamlined cars.

And it has the dubious distinction of being the first major city in the Southwest to abandon street cars and go all-bus.

Paraphrasing an article which appeared in the Tribune-Sun:

The San Diego Electric Railway, which J. D. had built up with the spirit and the determination of the pioneer days, is gone and almost forgotten. It will not be the memorial to San Diego's One Man.

The San Diego & Arizona Eastern Railway, the railroad that was completed by the One Man, the last of the great railroad builders, is known only as a branch of the Southern Pacific. It should but it will not be his memorial.

Neither will the outdoor Pipe Organ and Pavilion in Balboa Park nor the towering "Bank of America" building be J. D's. memorial.

The monument to John D. Spreckels is — the glorious City of San Diego to-day.

APPENDICES

Roster of Equipment

PASSENGER EQUIPMENT

Car Number	Date Built	Builder	Length	Weight	Trucks	Motors	Control	Seating	Remarks
1-6 7-12 13-18 20-31	1886 1886 1887 1888	Terre Haute Pullman Brill St. Louis						16 32	Single truck, wood, horse cars of various lengths. Some cars open, others closed. Acquired with purchase of San Diego Street Car Co. in 1892. Retired 1892-96. Body of #25 remodeled to electric car #11. Bodies of four cars used for electric #12-15.
1-12	1890		24'					24	Double truck, single end, wood cable cars, 36" gauge, 8 converted to electric by Citizens Traction Co. in 1896. Acquired from C.T.Co. 1898. Retired 1901.
1-2	1892	Brill	28'	19,000	1B-10	2WP-30	K-2*	48	Single truck, wood double deck. Changed to heavier Brill trucks and 2 GE-800 motors in 1896. Rebuilt 1904 when upper deck removed. Retired 1912.
3-8	1892	Brill	22'	12,000	1B-10	2WP-30	K-2*	22'	Single truck, wood California type. #3 rebuilt to double truck in 1903 as #55. #4-8 rebuilt 1904. Cars retired 1912. #7 sold Los Angeles & San Diego Beach Railway 1913. #3 was 2 ft. longer, seating 24.
2nd 3	1893		21'	12,000	1B-10	2WP-30	K-2*	32	Single truck, wood open car #14. Renumbered in 1909. Retired late 1909 and used by San Diego Southern in 1910.
9-10	1892	Brill	26'	16,000	1B-10	2WP-30	K-2*	24	Single truck, wood closed. Retired 1909. #10 leased to Los Angeles & San Diego Beach Railway.
11	1895	San Diego Electric	27'	16,000	PE	2WP-30	K-2*	26	Single truck, wood closed. Body from horse car #44 in 1906.
12-15	1893	San Diego Electric	21'	12,000	1B-10	2WP-30	K-2*	32	Single truck, wood open horse car bodies. #13 altered to wrecker.. #12-13, 15 transferred to service equipment. #14 renumbered 2nd #3 in 1909.
2nd 11 2nd 12			35'	31,000	McGuire	2GE-54	K-10	36	Double truck, wood California type cars acquired from South Park & East Side Railway in 1909. Trucks changed to B-27G1 and 2 GE-202 motors in 1909. #11 retired in 1920. #12 transferred to service car #54 in 1913.
2nd 13 2nd 14			28' 28'	18,000 18,000	McGuire 1B-27	2WH-12A· 2GE-54	K-10 K-10	40 40	Both single truck, wood open cars. Acquired from South Park & East Side Railway in 1909. #13 retired 1913. #14 became flat car in 1912.
16	1902	American	25'6"	16,500	PE	2GE-800	K-2	26	California type wood body, mounted on single truck by San Diego Electric. Rebuilt to double truck car #56 in 1903.
35-38			38'					80	Double truck, wood open car trailers. Acquired with purchase of Coronado Railroad in 1908. Retired 1920.
39			38'					80	Same as above. Retired 1910.
41	1893	Brill	38'	26,000	2B-MT	2GE-67	K-11	72	Double truck, wood double deck. Rebuilt 1908 with upper level removed and lengthened to 43'. Acquired with purchase of Coronado Railroad in 1908. Retired 1920.
42	1892	Brill	22'	15,000	1B-10	2GE-800	K-2	24	Single truck, California type. Acquired from Coronado Railroad in 1908. Rebuilt 1904. Retired 1920.
43	1886	St. Louis	16'					14	Single truck, wood horse car. Acquired from Coronado Railroad in 1908. Scrapped 1909.
43	1904	Brill	43'	24,000	2B-MT	2GE-67	K-11	44	Double truck, wood California type. Acquired from Coronado Railroad in 1908. Vacated 1920.
44	1895	San Diego Electric	27'	16,100	PE	2WP-30	K-2	26	Single truck, wood closed. Former #11. Sold to Coronado Railroad 1906. Reacquired with purchase Coronado Railroad in 1908. Retired 1916.
50	1902	American	34'	25,000	2B-27	2GE-800	K-2	36	California type wood body, mounted on double trucks from Sprinkler Car #103 by San Diego Electric. Sold to Coronado Railroad in 1902. Trucks changed to B-27G and 2 GE-52 motors in 1903. Repurchased and rebuilt 1904. Retired 1914.
51-54	1902	San Diego Electric	33'	24,000	2B-27G	2GE-67	K-10	36	Wood cable car bodies, acquired from Citizens Traction Co, rebuilt to double truck California type cars. #51, 53 retired 1913. #52, 54 retired 1914.
55	1903	San Diego Electric	33'	26,000	2B-27G	2GE-67	K-10	36	Former car #3. Rebuilt double truck California type. Became wrecker #55 in 1916.
56	1903	San Diego Electric	33'	26,000	2B-27G	2GE-67	K-10	36	Former Car #16. Rebuilt double truck California type. Retired 1914. Scrapped 1919.

Numbers	Year	Builder	Length	Weight	Truck	Motor	Control	Seats	Remarks
57-59 60-62 63-68 69-74 75-86	1904 1905 1906 1907 1908	All San Diego Electric	33'	26,500	2B-27G	2GE-67	K-10	36	Double truck, wood California type. All retired 1914 except #69. This car converted to P.A.Y.E. 1915. #81-82 sold to Bay Shore Railroad 1916. Reacquired with purchase of Bay Shore Railroad 1924. Scrapped 1928. #80, 83-86 sold to Phoenix Railway 1918. #70-76 sold same 1919. Others scrapped 1918. #69 retired 1928.
87-102 103-110	1910 1911	San Diego Electric	40'	34,100	2B-27G	2GE-202	K-11	44	Double truck, wood California type. Motors changed on #100, 101, 103, 104 to 2GE-219, KE controllers. #100, 101 equipped for handling trailers and used in Coronado Service. #87 converted to 2-man P.A.Y.E. 1914. Others except #100, 101, converted in 1915. #87-93 retired 1916. #97-99, 102-110 remodeled to 1-man 1917. #94-110, except #103, 104, 106 vacated 1920. #89, 90 sold to Douglas Light & Traction Co. 1916. #103, 104 to service equipment. #106 to Express car #1000 in 1924.
125-148	1912	St. Louis	43'7"	40,520	2B-39EI	2GE-203	K-36H	40	Double truck, wood, center entrance P.A.Y.E. #131 retired 1920. #130 retired 1923. #141 rebuilt to 1-man and equipment changed to 2B-77E2 trucks and 4 WH-514A3 motors 1924. Others rebuilt only 1924. All retired 1937-1940 but #145-148 retained "Non Operative." Used during War Emergency. Dismantled 1947.
149 150-184 185-224 225	1913 1914 1914 1914	American McGuire St. Louis St. Louis	48'7" 48'7" 48'7" 48'7"	43,850 43,850 43,850 43,850	2B-39EI 2B-39EI 2B-39EI 2B-39EI	2GE-201 2GE-201 2GE-201 2GE-201	GE-H GE-99B GE-99B GE-99B	52 52 52 52	Double truck, wood and steel, center entrance. #149 trial car. Multiple unit equipment added in 1914. #225 exhibited Panama-Pacific International Exposition and purchase 1915. Cars changed in groups to 1-man, multiple unit control removed 1923 et seq. #209 retired 1923. #182 destroyed 1924. #212, 223, retired 1930. Remaining cars except #159, 217-219, 221, 222, 225 retired and dismantled 1935-1940. #150 retired 1940 but retained "Non-Operative." #159 used for line tower Coronado. All restored to passenger service during War Emergency. #159 retired 1946. #150 dismantled and others retired in 1947.
301-325 326-335	1920 1922	American American	28'	18,200	1B-79E		K63BR	32	One-man, single truck, steel Birney safeties. Motors: GE-264 #301-313, 326-329, 335; WH-508A #314-325, 330-334. #301-304, 309-311 sold to Sacramento Northern Railway 1923-1925. #326-329, 335 traded in on purchase of electric locomotive, 305-308, 312, 313 sold to Stockton Electric in 1925. Others, except #316, 318 retired 1925. Some sold to Wichita Falls (Texas) Railroad. #316, 318 retired 1934.
351-352	1920	American	43'7"	35,750	2B-77	4WG-514A3	K-28K	46	Double truck, steel closed. Acquired 1938 from Glendale & Montrose Railway. Retired 1947.
400-402	1908	Niles	45'10"	58,000	2B-27E1½	4GE-202A	K-35C	52	California type interurban cars, wood, San Diego Southern Railway #110, 108, 109 purchased 1910, 1909. Renumbered #400-402 and assigned to Point Loma Railroad operation. #400 fitted up as "Sight Seeing" car. Vacated 1915. Sold to Pacific Electric Railway 1917 as #416-418.
400-449	1923	American	47'5"	48,000	2B-77E1	4WH514A3	K-28K	56	Double truck, closed steel cars. Multiple-unit equipped for one or two man operation. One pantograph. Trolley added. Pantographs replaced with trolley 1925. Multiple-unit control removed starting in 1933. All cars retired 1949 and sold for scrap.
501-525 526-528	1937 1938	St. Louis	46'	34,000	Clark	4WH-1432	WH-PCC	62	Double truck, single-end PCC type. All cars retired 1949. All cars sold to El Paso City Lines 1950-52 except #505, 508, 510, 515, 522, 526-28. These cars in storage in San Diego until Aug. 1957 when sold to an equipment dealer. #508 acquired by Orange Empire Traction Co. museum, Perris, Calif., and #528 by Railway Historical Society of San Diego.
1001-1014	1927	American	50'6"	46,000	2B-39	4WH-93A 4WH-101B	HL K-28B	56	Double truck, closed steel cars. Secured 1942 from the Utah Light & Traction Co. (Salt Lake). Motors: 4WH-93A #1001-1005; 4WH-101B #1009-1014. Controller: K-34 #1001, 1003-1005; HL #1002, 1006-1008; K-28B #1009-1014. #1011 scrapped in 1946, others 1947. Bodies sold. (Note) Bodies were built in 1927, however, trucks were from old Salt Lake City cars.
1015-1030	1922	American	45'	38,460	2B-77E1 2B-177E1	4WH-514A1	K-36	48	Double truck, steel closed. Secured 1942 from Wilkesbarre Railway. Trucks: 2B-77E1 #1015-1024; 2B-177E1 #1025-1030. All cars scrapped 1947.
1031-1050	1905	Brill	46'11"	45,000	2B-39EI	2WH-310	K-27	44	Double truck, closed, wood and steel. Secured 1942 from Third Avenue Railway (New York). #1043 sold to Bay Area Electric Railroad Association 1947. Others scrapped 1947.
1051-1056	1907-08	Brill	41'3"	45,000	2B-39EI	2WH-310C	K-27	36	Double truck, closed, wood and steel. Secured 1942 from Third Avenue Railway (New York). Scrapped 1947.

*Replacement of original equipment

LOCOMOTIVES, EXPRESS and WORK EQUIPMENT

Car Number	Date Built	Builder	Length	Weight	Trucks	Motors	Control	Remarks
15-17	1893	San Diego Electric	21'	12,000	1B-10	2WP-30	K-2	Former single truck, wood, open passenger cars #12, 13 & 15. Equipment of #13 changed to Tripp truck and 2GE-52 motors in 1908. Transferred to work equipment in 1909. #15 the wrecker retired in 1912. #16-17 general work cars retired 1911.
18	1898	Miller Knoblock	35'		B-27	4GE-52		Double truck flat car built for street sprinkler #103, center control, renumbered #18 in 1909. Motors changed to 4GE-67 in 1917. Renumbered #25 in 1923.
19		San Diego Electric			PE			Single truck, non-electric flat car Ex #104. Renumbered #19 in 1909. Retired 1919.
20	1922	San Diego Electric	41'11"	48,000	2B-27G1	4GE-202	K-12A	Double truck, wood with 2 cabs and 30 cu. yd. dump body. Additional air compressors installed in 1923. Car used in construction of beach lines. Scrapped 1939 as #020.
21	1912	American	46'	61,400	Standard	4GE-73	K-34F	Double truck, wood flat car with 2 cabs. Scrapped 1947 as #021.
22	1923	Brown-Hoist	26'4"	72,000	Baldwin-Westinghouse	4GE-2004C	K-35	10 ton self propelling crane (length exclusive of boom). Sold to Southern Pacific in 1947 as #022.
23	1923	San Diego Electric	47'	48,000	Standard	4GE-219	K-12	Double truck, wood flat car with 2 cabs. Scrapped 1947 as #023.
24	1910	San Diego Electric	41'8"	34,000	2B-27G	2GE-202	K-11	Double truck, wood retired passenger car #95. Remodeled for hauling trash in 1923. Scrapped 1947 as #024.
25	1898	San Diego Electric	35'	40,000	2B-27G	4GE-67	K-35C	Double truck, wood flat car with cab in center. Ex #103 and 18. Air brakes, MCB coupler added 1923. Scrapped 1947 as #025.
26	1910	San Diego Electric	42'	35,000	2B-27G	2GE-202	K-11	Double truck, wood retired passenger car #96, remodeled into tower car in 1923. Vacated 1949 as #026. Sold for scrap.
27	1911	San Diego Electric	42'	34,100	2B-27G	2GE-202	K-11	Double truck, wood retired passenger car #108. Remodeled for rail bonding car in 1923. Scrapped 1935 as #027.
28	1910	San Diego Electric	40'	32,000	2B-27G	2GE-202	K-11	Double truck, wood retired passenger car #99. Used temporarily as Express car #56. Converted to track sander and trolley greaser in 1923. Vacated 1949 as #028. Sold for scrap.
2nd 28 29			34'	24,000				60,000 lbs. capacity double truck flat cars secured from Southwest Sales & Equipment Co. in 1924. Renumbered #1101 and #1102 1924.
2nd 29	1911	San Diego Electric	40'	34,100	2B-27G			Double truck, wood retired passenger car #107. Remodeled to field office car in 1924. Scrapped 1935 as #029.
30-31	1911	San Diego Electric	38'	16,000	2B-27G			Double truck, wood retired passenger cars #109-110, converted to flat cars in 1922. Scrapped 1935 as #030-031.
32			36'	23,000				San Diego & Arizona Railway flat car #4104 purchased in 1923. Converted to Pioneer Rail Layer with 16 rollers. Scrapped 1935 as #032.
33-35			36'	22,000	Barber			San Diego & Arizona Railway flat car #4105, 4110-4111 purchased 1923. Renumbered 1924 to #1051-1053.
34-39			44'					100,000 lbs. capacity Hart convertible center dump cars, purchased from United Commercial Co. 1925. Retired 1926.

Car Number	Date Built	Builder	Length	Weight	Trucks	Motors	Control	Remarks
35								Baldwin-Westinghouse locomotive. Renumbered #1025.
36-39			34'	24,000				60,000 lbs. capacity flat cars purchased Southwest Sales & Equipment Co. 1924. Renumbered #1103-1106 in 1924.
40-46			27'6"					Side dump cars 12 cu. yds. capacity and air operated. Purchased Southwest Sales & Equipment Co. 1923. Scrapped 1935 as #040-046.
47	1924	Plymouth		14,000				0-4-0 gasoline locomotive purchased Fato-Root-Heath Co. Nicknamed "Spark Plug." Retired 1926.
48-53			34'					60,000 lbs. capacity flat cars purchased Southwest Sales & Equipment Co. 1924. Renumbered #1107-1112 in 1924.
54			35'	31,000	2B-27G1	2GE-202	K-10	Double truck retired passenger car #2/12 converted to Wrecker in 1913. Scrapped 1940 as #054.
55	1903	San Diego Electric	33'	26,000	2B-27G	2GE-67	K-10	Double truck passenger car #55. Converted to wrecker. Retired 1930 as #055.
56								See work car #28. Ex passenger car #99 used temporarily in Express service.
56								Single truck flat car, original horse car. Scrapped 1935 as #056.
57		Buda						Hand car. Sold 1942.
103	1898	Miller Knoblock	30'	20,000	B-27	2-27HP		Double truck street sprinkler car with 5,000 gallon tank. Replaced trucks and motors using 4GE52 equipment 1899. Converted to flat car, center controls about 1905. Renumbered #18 in 1909.
104								Single truck, flat car, renumbered #19 in 1909.
103-104	1911	San Diego Electric	40'		2B-27G	2GE-219		Double truck passenger cars used as work equipment during construction of beach lines in 1923. Retired 1928.
182 & 202	1914	St. Louis	47'8"		2B-39E1	2GE-201		Same as above. #182 retired 1924. #202 returned to passenger service.
1000	1911	San Diego Electric	40'	36,000	2B-27G1	2GE-219	K-11H	Double truck, wood passenger car #106 retired. Remodeled for Express service in 1924. Became service car-wrecker #010 1926.
1025	1923	Baldwin-Westinghouse	29'6"	100,000	Baldwin	4WH-552	WH-HLF	Baldwin-Westinghouse 50 ton locomotive (Baldwin #56642). Purchased 1925. Sold to Bamberger Railroad 1940.
1051-1053								See work equipment #33-35. Flat cars scrapped 1935.
1101-1112								See Work Equipment #28-29, 36-39, 48-53. Flat cars scrapped 1935.
1151-1166			40'	27,600				80,000 lbs. capacity flat cars of St. Charles type. Purchased 1925 from United Commercial Co. Former Los Angeles & Salt Lake cars. All cars scrapped 1935-36 except #1154, 1163-64 which were scrapped 1947.
010	1911	San Diego Electric	40'	41,000	2B-27G1	4GE-219	K-12A	Double truck Express car #1000 fitted up as service car-wrecker in 1926. Vacated 1949. Sold for scrap.

LOCOMOTIVE LIST
COURTESY OF CHARLES E. FISHER

National City & Otay

1	0-4-2T	Fulton Iron Wks., S. F.		5/1887	"Wm. G. Dickinson" Dummy type 22,000 Total Wt.
2	0-4-2T	Fulton Iron Wks., S. F.		5/1887	"A. B. Lawrie" **Dummy type**
3	0-4-2T	Porter	No. 876	10/1887	"National City" 28,000 On Driv. To San Diego Sou. No. 3 7/1908
4	0-4-2T	Porter	No. 884	10/1887	"Sweetwater" 28,000 On Driv. To San Diego Sou. No. 4 7/1908
5	0-4-2T	Porter	No. 905	10/1887	"Chula Vista" 28,000 On Driv. To San Diego Sou. No. 5 7/1908
6	2-4-2T	Porter	No. 943	1/1888	"Tia Juana" To San Diego Sou. No. 6 7/1908
7	0-6-2T	Porter	No. 945	1/1888	"San Miguel" 54,000 On Driv. To San Diego Sou. No. 7 7/1908

San Diego, Cuyamaca & Eastern
San Diego & Cuyamaca

1	4-4-0	Brooks	No. 1544	6/1889	62-17x24 Sold To Sou. Calif. RR No. 8—1892
1	2-6-0	Porter	No. 1375	7/1892	48-14x18 Rebuilt new boiler 1904. To S. D. & S. E. No. 11—1912
2	4-4-0	Altoona	No. 208	8/1873	Ex PRR 2158—Phila. & Erie 2020—PRR 652 Acquired 1894. Scrapped in 1914
3	4-4-0	Rhode Is.	No. 941	1881	Ex AT&SF 012—Sou. Cal. 3—Cal. Sou. 1. 58-16x24. Acq. 4/1902 To S. D. & S. E. No. 15—1912
4	4-4-0	Schenectady		1889	Ex Union Pacific. Acq. 1904 from F. M. Hicks. 62-18x26. To S. D. & S. E. No. 14—1912
1	Motor	McKeen Co.			Sold to U. S. Reclamation District, Yuma, Ariz. (Yuma Valley RR).

Coronado Railroad

1	0-4-2T	Baldwin	No. 8036	7/1886	Ex University Heights Motor Road No. 1 Dummy type. Sold 7/1903
2	0-4-2T			1887	**Scrapped 1902**
3	0-4-2T	Baldwin	No. 8734	8/1887	Ex Univ. Hgts. Motor Rd. No. 3 Sold to Jardine Machinery Co. 1/1903
4	0-4-2T			1887	**Sold to Jardine** Lumber Co. 9/1902.
5	0-4-0T	Rhode Is.	No. 719	1878	Ex N. Y. Elevated No. 34 38-10x14. Sold to S. D. P. B. & L. J. No. 2
6	0-4-0T	Rhode Is.		1878	Ex N. Y. Elevated 38-10x14. Sold to Albion Lumber Co. 5/1902.
7	0-4-0T	Rhode Is.		1878	Ex N. Y. Elevated 38-10x14. Scrapped prior 1902.

8	0-4-0T	Rhode Is.		1878	Ex N. Y. Elevated No. 39 38-10x14. Wrecked and rebuilt. 12/1904. Scrapped 12/1906.
9	4-4-0	Rogers			No data on previous owners.. Was first numbered Coronado No. 13. Scrapped
10	0-4-4T	Baldwin		1894	Ex Chicago & Sou. Side Elev. Vauclain Comp. Scrapped 1908.
1	2-4-2T	Porter	No. 3258	7/1905	Bought new. To San Diego Sou. No. 1 7/08.
2	0-4-2	Baldwin	No. 9043	1888	Ex S. D. O. T. & P. B. No. 2. Traded for Coronado No. 5. Reblt. to tender engine. Sold to L. A. & S. D. B. No. 2.

San Diego Southern

1	2-4-2T	Porter	No. 3258	7/1905	Ex Coronado 2nd No. 1. To SD&SE No. 1 — 1912.
2	2-4-2T	Porter	No. 4812	1911	Bought new. Numbered No. 100 by builder. Renumbered No. 2 on arrival. To SD&SE No. 2 — 1912.
3	0-4-2T	Porter	No. 876	10/1887	Ex NC&O No. 3 Sold prior 1912.
4	0-4-2T	Porter	No. 884	10/1887	Ex NC&O No. 4 To SD&SE No. 4—1912
5	0-4-2T	Porter	No. 905	10/1887	Ex NC&O No. 5 Sold prior 1912.
6	2-4-2T	Porter	No. 943	1/1888	Ex NC&O No. 6 To SD&SE No. 6—1912
7	0-6-2T	Porter	No. 945	1/1888	Ex NC&O No. 7 To SD&SE No. 7—1912
5	2-4-2T	Porter	No. 5111	1912	Bought new. To SD&SE No. 5—1912.

San Diego & Southeastern

1	2-4-2T	Porter	No. 3258	7/1905	Ex SDS No. 1—Cor. No. 1 Sold by 1916
2	2-4-2T	Porter	No. 4812	1911	Ex SDS No. 2—100. To SD&A No. 2—1917
3	No locomotive				
4	0-4-2T	Porter	No. 884	10/1887	Ex SDS No. 4—NC&O No. 4. scrapped by 1917
5	2-4-2T	Porter	No. 5111	1912	Ex SDS No. 5. To SD&A No. 5—1917
6	2-4-2T	Porter	No. 943	1/1888	Ex SDS No. 6—NC&O No. 6 Scrapped by 1917.
7	0-6-2T	Porter	No. 945	1/1888	Ex SDS No. 7—NC&O No. 7. Scrapped by 1917.
11	2-6-0	Porter	No. 1375	7/1892	Ex SD&C No. 1—SDC&E No. 1. Sold to City of Los Angeles, Terminal Island, 1918
14	4-4-0	Schenectady		1889	Ex SD&C No. 4—SDC&E No. 4 Scrapped 1916.
15	4-4-0	Rhode Is	No. 941	1881	Ex SD&C No. 3—SDC&E No. 3—AT&SF No. 012—SC No. 3—CS No. 1. Sold to LA&SDB No. 15—1915

20	4-6-0	Cooke	No. 1029	1876	Ex SP 2011-1578-CP 213. Acq. 1/1911. Ran as SD&C No. 2011, 1911 to 1912. Sold to Sharp & Fellows Co. 1917. 57-18x24-93200-71500-150-17390.
21	4-6-0	Schen	No. 2470	1887	Ex SP 2115-1685-227. Acq. 7/1911. Ran as SD&C No. 2115 for five months. To SD&A No. 21—1917.
22	4-6-0	Rogers	No. 2883	1881	Ex SP 2112-1674-196. Acq. 8/1912. To SD&A No. 22 — 1917.
23	4-6-0	Pitts.	No. 52884	1912	Bought new. To SD&A No. 23 — 1917.
31	Motor	Gasoline—Mech. Pass. Hewitt-Ludlow Auto Co., San Francisco.			Scrapped
41	Motor	G. E. — Schen.			To SD&A No. 41
42	Motor	G. E. — Schen.			To SD&A No. 42
43	Motor	G. E. — Schen.	No. 3707		To SD&A No. 43 Ex BR&P

Electric Equipment

101	Comb. Coaches	Sold to P. E. No. 410-1918
102 — 110	Coaches	Sold to P. E. No. 411-419
111	Comb. Coach.	Destroyed in 1916 flood.

Note; Coaches No. 108-110 were renumbered No. 400-402 on the Point Loma Ry. before sale to Pacific Electric in 1918.

San Diego & Arizona
San Diego & Arizona Eastern

1	S-23	0-6-0	Pittsburg	No. 46689	1909	First engine on road.
2		2-4-2T	Porter		1911	Ex SD&SE 2—SDS 2—100. Sold US Navy Destroyer Base, San Diego.
2	S-1	0-6-0	Schen.	No. 4138	1893	Ex SP 1046. Scr. 9/40
3	S-5	0-6-0	Baldwin	No. 20900	1902	Ex SP 1096. Returned to SP 10/40
5		2-4-2T	Porter	No. 5111	1912	Ex SD&SE 5—SDS 5. Sold to Mojave Northern No. 4. Scrapped 1940.
10	T-12	4-6-0	Schen.	No. 2470	1887	Ex SD&A 21—SD&SE 21—SP 2115-1685-227. Scrapped 11/15/1938
11	T-13	4-6-0	Rogers	No. 2883	1881	Ex SD&A 22—SD&SE 22—SP 2112-1674-196. Scrapped 12/1925
12	T-56	4-6-0	Pittsburg	No. 52884	1912	Ex SD&A 23-SD&SE 23. Scrapped 10-31-47
20	T-57	4-6-0	Baldwin	No. 29727	1906	Ex Bullfrog—Goldfield No. 12-14. Reboilered SP Co., L. A. 1919 Renumb. SP No. 2385 6/19/41. Returned to SD&AE 4/24/43.
24	T-58	4-6-0	Baldwin	No. 31093	1907	Ex L. V. & T. No. 7 Scrapped 9/1940
25	T-58	4-6-0	Baldwin	No. 32250	1907	Ex L. V. & T. No. 9. Scrapped 9/1940
26	T-58	4-6-0	Baldwin	No. 32251	1907	Ex L. V. & T. No. 10. Renumbered S. P. No. 2386 6/20/41.

27	T-58 4-6-0	Baldwin	No. 32360 1907	Ex L. V. & T. No. 11.
50	C-30 2-8-0	Baldwin	No. 35953 1911	
101	C-31 2-8-0	Schen.	No. 54664 1914	Renumbered S. P. No. 2837—1918. Returned in 1919.
102	C-31 2-8-0	Schen.	No. 54973 1914	Renumbered S. P. No. 2838—1918. Returned in 1919.
103	C-9 2-8-0	Baldwin	No. 31453 1907	Ex SP No. 2523. Returned to S. P. 5/1941.
104	C-8 2-8-0	Baldwin	No. 23899 1904	Ex SP No. 2720. Returned to S. P. 5/1941.
105	C-10 2-8-0	S.P. Co., L.A.	No. 1 1917	Ex SP No. 2843. Acq. 1918.
106	C-10 2-8-0	S.P. Co., L.A.	No. 3 1918	Ex SP No. 2844. Returned to S. P. 5/1941.
515	M-9 2-6-0	Baldwin	No. 33817 1909	Ex SPdeM 515—AE 575—CRY&P 515. Acq. 1918. Returned to SPdeM 1919.

Nos. 41-43, Motors ex SD&SE Nos. 41-43   Scrapped in 1939 and 1940.

Mechanical data of SD&AE Locomotives

S — 1	51 — 18x24 — 91800 — 91800 — 140 — 18150	Engine No.	2
S — 5	57 — 19x26 — 130000 — 130000 — 180 — 25190		3
S — 23	51 — 18x24 — 98500 — 98500 — 175 — 22700		1
T — 12	57 — 18x24 — 97600 — 73400 — 160 — 18550		10
T — 13	57 — 18x24 — 85800 — 65600 — 165 — 19050		11
T — 56	57 — 18x24 — 123400 — 87000 — 170 — 19700		12
T — 57	63 — 21x28 — 162000 — 135000 — 190 — 31650		20
T — 58	63 — 21x26 — 188300 — 140000 — 200 — 30940		24 — 27
C — 8	57 — 22x30 — 216700 — 191900 — 210 — 45470		104
C — 9	57 — 22x30 — 218000 — 193700 — 210 — 45470		103
C — 10	Same as C — 9		105 — 106
C — 30	50 — 20x24 — 137000 — 122000 — 180 — 29400		50
C — 31	57 — 22x30 — 224000 — 210000 — 210 — 45470		101 — 102
M — 9	63 — 21x28 — 189000 — 153000 — 200 — 33320		515

San Diego, Old Town & Pacific Beach
San Diego, Pacific Beach & La Jolla
Los Angeles & San Diego Beach

SDPB&LJ

1	0-4-0T Dummy	National Iron Wks, S. F. 9/1887.	Ex SDOT&PB No. 1. Disposal unknown.
2	0-4-2T Dummy	Baldwin No. 9043 1888	Bought new. Traded to Coronado RR for their No. 5.
3	0-4-2T Dummy	Baldwin No. 9160 1888	Bought new. Became LA&SDB No. 1.
2	0-4-0T	Rhode Is. No. 719 1878	Ex Coronado RR No. 5—NY El. No. 34. Scrapped.

LA&SDB

1	0-4-2	Baldwin	No. 9160	1888	Ex SDPB&LJ No. 3. Scrapped 1918.
2	0-4-2	Baldwin	No. 9043	1888	Ex Coronado No. 2—SDPB&LJ No. 2. Sold 1918.
3	0-4-0	Baldwin		1880	**NP?. Scrapped 1918**
4	2-4-4	Rhode Is.			Ex Holton I. T. Ry. No. 4 Scrapped in 1918.
15	4-4-0	Rhode Is.	No. 941	1881	Ex SD&SE 15—SD&C 3—SDC&E 3—AT&SF 012—SC 3—CS 1. Scrapped 1918.
1	Motor	McKeen Comb.			Scrapped prior 1918.
2	Motor	McKeen Comb.			Scrapped prior 1918.

1 Electric Combination

2 Electric Open coach

3 Electric California coach. Ex San Diego Electric No. 7

10 Electric closed coach Ex San Diego Electric No. 10

51 Gasoline Motor coach. Made from Mack Truck.

Roster of Ferries

FERRIES of the SAN DIEGO & CORONADO FERRY COMPANY

Ferry service began between San Diego and Coronado early in 1886, using the steam launch *Della*, owned by H. L. Story, to tow barges from the Pacific Coast Steamship Company's Wharf, at the foot of Fifth Avenue, to a landing on the Coronado side. There was a connecting omnibus transported workmen and passengers to the beach. The omnibus was soon replaced with a horse car, then by a steam motor.

The steam tugboat *Rover* was used to tow lighters loaded with materials and, when needed, extra barges.

The San Diego & Coronado Ferry Company was organized that year by E. S. Babcock and H. L. Story.

The Babcock & Story Wharf was built, having a slip for a ferry, on the San Diego side, from what is now the intersection of Pacific Highway and Market Street. It was leased to the Ferry Company. A slip was also built at the dock on the Coronado side, at the foot of Orange Avenue. The Babcock & Story Wharf was sold to the California Central Railway Company, a Santa Fe subsidiary, in June 1887, but ferry rights were reserved.

The ferries are listed in chronological order of entry in service:

CORONADO—steam engine powered, side paddle wheels, wooden hull.
Built in 1886 by A. C. Hayes   At San Francisco
Hull dimensions—100 ft. x 26 x 9.2   Gross Tons—308
Acquired in 1886
Disposition—Retired in 1922. Sold to a Hollywood moving picture company, was blown up and sunk.

SILVER GATE—steam engine powered, propeller drives (one of first), wooden hull.
Built in 1888 by Coronado Iron Works   At Coronado, Calif.
Hull dimensions—187 ft. x 30 x 11   Gross Tons—528
Acquired in 1888 (Was a complete failure as a ferry)
Disposition—Decommissioned in 1890. Hull was used as a "Floating Casino", at Coronado Tent City, after 1900. Later moved to the foot of Grape St., San Diego, as San Diego Yacht Club's quarters.

BENICIA—steam engine powered, walking beam drive, side paddle wheels, wooden hull.
Built in 1881
Hull dimension—92 ft. x 24 x 7   At Martinez, Calif.
Acquired—1888   Gross Tons—144
Disposition—Dismantled in 1903, hull abandoned.

RAMONA—steam engine powered, side paddle wheels, wooden hull.
Built in 1903 by Risdon Iron Works   At Oakland, Calif.
Hull dimensions—118 ft. x 29 x 12.3   Gross Tons—417
Acquired in 1903. — 2 cylinder engine, 700 Horse Power
Disposition—Dismantled in 1932.

MORENA—steam engine powered, side paddle wheels, wooden hull.
Built in 1920 by Rolph & Chandler   At Wilmington, Calif.
Hull dimensions—156 ft. x 58 x 11.8   Gross Tons—381
Acquired in 1920 — 2 cylinder engine, 500 Horse Power
Disposition—Removed from service in 1938. Commandeered by U. S. Navy in 1942. Sold to a Mexican fishing concern and towed to San Quintin, Baja California, in 1947.

Second CORONADO—Diesel-electric powered, propeller drives, steel hull.
Built in 1929 by Moore Drydock Co.   At Oakland, Calif.
Hull dimensions—178 ft. x 43.6 x 14.9   Gross Tons—502
Acquired in 1929 — 2 eight cylinder enginers, 550 Horse Power each.
Disposition—In service.

SAN DIEGO—Diesel-electric powered, propeller drives, steel hull.
Built in 1931 by Moore Drydock Co.   At Oakland, Calif.
Hull dimension—191.4 x 43.6 x 14.1   Gross Tons—556
Acquired in 1931 — 3 engines, 350 Horse Power each
Disposition—In service.

NORTH ISLAND—Diesel-electric powered, propeller drives, wooden hull. Original name— "Golden West"
Built in 1923 by James Robertson   At Alameda, Calif.
Hull dimensions—214.1 x 44.4 x 15.2   Gross Tons—594
Acquired in 1938—Rebuilt in 1938. Engines replaced in 1953 with two 400 Horse Power
Disposition—In service.

SILVER STRAND — Oil engine-electric powered, propeller drives, wooden hull. Original name— "Golden Shore"
Built in 1927 by General Engineering Co.   At Alameda, Calif.
Hull dimensions—214 x 44 x 17   Gross Tons—779
Acquired in 1939 by Puget Sound Navigation Company. Rebuilt and renamed "Elwha". 3 six cylinder engines, 400 Horse Power.
Acquired in 1944 and renamed "Silver Strand."
Disposition—In service.

CROWN CITY—Diesel-electric powered, propeller drives, steel hull designed for motor vehicle traffic only, radar equipped.
Built in 1954 by Moore Drydock Co.   At Oakland, Calif.
(The first ferry built on the Pacific Coast in 22 years).
Christened by Mrs. J. L. Haugh, January 22, 1954.
Length—242 ft.   Gross tons—678
Acquired in 1954—First trip June 7, 1954.
Disposition—In service

Car Route Changes

CAR ROUTE CHANGES -- As Shown By Public Time Cards

Basis: Car Routes as given under the heading "Numbering the Car Lines," effective December 1, 1910.

Jan. 15, 1912
No. 2—Broadway and Brooklyn Heights Line.
Extended on 30th St., from Upas St., to University Ave., to Fairmount Ave., in East San Diego.
Discontinued operating over the First Ave. line, continuing down Broadway to the Depots.
University Ave. shuttle cut back to 30th St.

No. 6—First Ave. and F St. Line.
First Ave. paired with F St., operating from Laurel St., on First Ave., to Broadway, to Third Ave., to F St., to 25th St.

Feb. 13, 1912
No. 4—Imperial Ave. Line.
Discontinued operating over the State St. - Old Town Line.
Continued down Broadway from State St. to the Depots.
"This car for Pacific Coast tSeamship Co.'s Wharf and San Diego & Southeastern Ry. Depot."

No. 8—State St. - Old Town Line.
From Fourth Ave., on Broadway, to State St., etc. to Old Town.

April, 1913
No. 4—Imperial Ave. Line.
Discontinued Depot terminus.
Ran on Broadway to State St., to Market St., to serve the new Post Office.

No. 10—Coronado Ferry Line.
Discontinued operating over State St.
Routed from Fifth Ave., on Broadway, to Kettner Blvd., to Market St., to Ferry.

Nov. 2, 1914
No. 7—B St. - Balboa Park Line.
Ran from Kettner Blvd., on B St., to Twelfth Ave., to Exposition Terminal.
Abandoned B St., from Twelfth Ave. to 14th St.

Dec. 27, 1914
No. 1—Fifth Ave. - Logan Heights Line.
"This route for San Diego & Arizona Ry. Depot" at 26th St.

No. 6—First Ave. and F St. Line.
Discontinued operation over Third Ave. Ran from Laurel St., on First Ave., to F St., to 25th St.

No. 7—Park Line.
Service discontinued on B St., from Third Ave. to Kettner Blvd.
Operated from Exposition Terminal, to Twelfth Ave., to F St., to Third Ave., to B St., to Twelfth Ave. to Exposition Terminal.

No. 8—State St. - Old Town Line.
Scheduled to loop downtown on Broadway, to Third Ave., to F St., to Fifth Ave., to Twelfth Ave. (Reported never put into effect).

No. 11—Park Line.
Ran from Exposition Terminal, to Twelfth Ave., to Third Ave., to F St., to Twelfth Ave., to Exposition Terminal.

Jan. 1, 1915
D Street changed to Broadway.

May 12, 1915
No. 8—State St. - Old Town Line.
Changed back to terminate at Fourth Ave and Broadway.

OB—Ocean Beach Line.
Effective Nov. 2, 1914, operated from Fourth Ave, on Broadway, to State St., etc. to Ocean Beach.

June 24, 1915
No. 3—Third and Fifth Avenues Line.
Operated from Trias St., Mission Hills, via First, Fourth and Third Aves., to Market St., to Fifth Ave., to L St. "This route for Pacific Coast Steamship Co.'s Wharf."

No. 4—Imperial Ave. and State St. Line.
Discontinued on State St. from Broadway to Market St. Again paired with State St. - Old Town Line.

No. 6—First Ave. - Market St. Line.
Discontinued pairing with F St. Line.
Operated from Laurel St., on First Ave., to Broadway, to Third Ave., to Market St., to 25th St. Alternate cars turned back at Fourth Ave. and Market St.

No. 8—F St. Line.
Routed from 25th St., on F St., to State St.

Nov. 15, 1915
No. 4—Imperial Ave. Line.
Discontinued the pairing with State St. Line.
Operated on Fifth Ave., to Broadway and turned back.

No. 12—State St. - Old Town Line.
From Fourth Ave., on Broadway, to State St. etc. to Old Town.

Clover Leaf Sight Seeing Trip—$1.00.
Leave Fourth Ave., on Broadway, to State St., etc. to Ocean Beach, Auto. to Sunset Cliffs, Theosophical Grounds, Point Loma to Roseville. Launch to Municipal Pier, foot of Broadway. Electric cars to any part of the City.

Jan. 24, 1916
No. 2—changed to Broadway - East San Diego Line.

Mar. 1, 1916
No. 3—Vacated

No. 4—Imperial Ave. and Third Ave. Line.
Paired with Mission Hills Line. Operated downtown from Fifth Ave., on Market St., to Third Ave., etc.

No. 5—K St. - Old Town Line.
Operated from 30th St., on Ocean View Blvd., to 25th St., to K St., to Fifth Ave., to Broadway, to State St., etc. to Old Town.

No. 12—Vacated
H Street changed to Market St.
Grant Ave. changed to Woolman Ave., and in 1921 to Ocean View Blvd.

June 1, 1916
San Diego Electric Railway began operating cars of the San Diego & Southeastern Ry. to 24th St., National City.

July 25, 1916
No. 9—Coronado Ferry Line.
Extra cars operated 4:10 to 6:10 P.M. via Market St., to Fifth Ave., to Broadway, to Kettner Blvd., to Market St., to Ferry.

No. 10—Vacated

No. 11—Park Line. Discontinued. Vacated.

OB—Ocean Beach Line.
"Connects with Bay Shore Railway for Mission Beach Tent City."

NC—National City Line.
Operated from B St., on Third Ave., to Market St., to Fifth Ave., to K St., to 13th St., to Newton Ave., etc. to National City.

July 25, 1916

No. 2—Broadway - East San Diego Line.
Dropped Mission Hills run.
Operated on Fifth Ave., from K St., to Broadway to Union Station.

No. 10—Coronado Ferry Line.
Changed to return from Ferry, to Market St., to Fifth Ave., to Broadway, to Kettner Blvd., to Market St., to Ferry.

No. 12—Logan Heights Line.
Operated from Union Station on Broadway, to Fifth Ave., to Market St., to 16th St., etc. to National Ave. and 31 St.

No. 13—Third Ave. Line.
Operated from Broadway, on Third Ave., to Fir St., to Fourth Ave., to Spruce St., to First Ave. to Washington St.

NC-CV—National City and Chula Vista Line.
Operated from Union Station, on Broadway, to Third Ave., to Market St., to Fifth Ave., to K St., etc.

July 10, 1918

No. 4—Imperial Ave. Line.
Terminus at Union Station discontinued.
Route on Broadway to First Ave., and turn back.

Jan. 1, 1919

No. 1—Fifth Ave., Mission Cliff and Adams Ave. Line.
Alternate cars operated from Mission Cliff, on Adams Ave. to Kensington Park after morning and evening rush hours.

No. 11—Adams Ave. Line via Park.
Operated from State St., on Broadway, to Twelfth Ave., and via Park etc. to Kensington Park morning and evening rush hours only.

No. 12—Logan Heights Line.
Alternate cars connect at 31st St. and National Ave., with car for Shipyard (foot of 32nd St.) 6:30 A.M. to 5:36 P.M. Special cars run direct.

Jan. 10, 1920

No. 4—Imperial Ave. Line.
Extended on Broadway to Union Station.

No. 5—K St. and Ocean View Blvd. Line.
Discontinued operating over State St. Line to Old Town. Operated from 30th St., on Ocean View Blvd., to 25th St., to K St., to Fifth Ave., to Market St., to Third Ave., to Broadway.

No. 7—East San Diego Line via Park.
Discontinued downtown loop.
Operated from Twelfth Ave., to Broadway to Union Station.

No. 8—Old Town Line.
Routed to loop downtown on Broadway to Fourth Ave., to F St., to Third Ave., to Broadway, to State St., to Ivy St., to India St., to Washington Freeway, to San Diego Ave. to Old Town.

No. 11—Adams Ave. Line via Park.
Changed downtown from Twelfth Ave., to Broadway to First Ave. and turn back, morning and evening rush hours only.

No. 13—First and Fifth Aves. Line.
Operated from Washington St., on First Ave., to Spruce St., to Fifth Ave., to L St.
Service discontinued on Fourth Ave., Fir St., and Third Ave. to B St.

Mar. 20, 1920

No. 5—K St., Ocean View Blvd. Line.
Changed downtown, on Fifth Ave., to B St., to Fourth Ave.

No. 6—First Ave. and Market St. Line.
Changed downtown on B St., to Fifth Ave., to Market St.
Metal tokens replaced ticket strips.

Oct. 1, 1920

No. 8 and OB—Old Town and Ocean Beach Lines.
Times changed to 21 minute service through to Old Town during rush hours and 42 minute service provided by OB cars to India and Winder Sts, and No. 8 shuttle from there to Old Town.

July 25, 1916

No. 2—Broadway - East San Diego Line.
"This route for San Diego & Arizona Ry. trains at Santa Fe Depot."

Oct. 1, 1916

CV—National City Line.
Extended to Third Ave. and K St., Chula Vista. (Restoration of serviec after the floods).

Nov. 22, 1916

NC-CV—National City and Chula Vista Line.
Third Ave. and B St. terminus discontinued.
Operated from Santa Fe Depot, on Broadway, to Fifth Ave., to K St., etc.

Feb. 25, 1917

OB—Ocean Beach Line.
"Transfer at Roseville Jct. for La Playa."

June 1, 1917

No. 1—Fifth Ave. - Logan Heights Line.
Route discontinued on Normal St.
Operated on University Ave., to Park Blvd., to Mission Cliff Gardens.

No. 2—Broadway - Brooklyn Heights Line.
Cut back from East San Diego to a terminus on 30th St. at University Ave., North Park.

No. 7—East San Diego Line via Park.
Extended from Exposition Terminal, Laurel St., to Indiana St., to Park Blvd., to University Ave., to Euclid Ave., East San Diego.

No. 11—Adams Ave. Line via Park.
From F St., on Third Ave., to B St., to Twelfth Ave., through Park, to Indiana St., to Park Blvd., to Adams Ave., to Kensington Park.

June 12, 1917

No. 7—East San Diego Line via Park.
Looped downtown from Twelfth Ave., to F St., to Third Ave., to B St., to Twelfth Ave.

No. 11—Adams Ave. Line via Park.
Changed to loop downtown from Twelfth Ave., to B St., to Third Ave., to F St., to Twelfth Ave.

Sept. 12, 1917

No. 10—Coronado Ferry Line.
Operated from 4:10 to 6:10 P.M. from Fifth Ave., on Broadway, to Kettner Blvd., to Market St., to Ferry.

Feb. 1, 1918

No. 6—First Ave. - Market St. Line
Route changed from First Ave., to Broadway to First Ave., to B St., to Third Ave., etc. (on account of San Diego & Arizona Railway's gas-electric cars operated on First Ave. to B St.)

No. 8—F St. Line.
Route changed to loop on F St., to Kettner Blvd., to Broadway, to State St., to F St.
M Street changed to Imperial Ave.

July 1, 1918

No. 1—Fifth Ave. - Mission Cliff Line.
Discontinued operating to Logan Heights.
Ran on Fifth Ave., to Broadway to Union Station.

No. 3—Fifth Ave. - Mission Hills Line.
Connecting track put in on Fifth Ave., from University Ave. to Washington St., to First Ave. Route changed to run from Union Station, on Broadway to Fifth Ave., to Washington St., to Hawk St., to Lewis St., to Fort Stockton Drive, to Trias St.

Dec. 22, 1920

No. 13—First and Fifth Aves. Line.
Service discontinued. Vacated.

April, 1921

No. 10—Coronado Ferry Line.
Discontinued. Vacated.

Nov., 1922

No. 1—Fifth Ave. and Mission Cliff Line.
Alternate cars to Kensington Park discontinued.
Alternate cars operated downtown on Fifth Ave. to K St.

No. 3—Fifth Ave. - Mission Hills Line.
Alternate cars operated downtown on Fifth Ave. to K St.

No. 11—Adams Ave. Line via Park.
Operated regularly from Kensington Park, on Adams Ave., to Park Blvd., through Park, to Twelfth Ave., to F St., to Third Ave., to Broadway, to Twelfth Ave. et seq.

April, 1923

No. 5—Ocean View Blvd. Line.
Discontinued on K St., from Tenth Ave. to 25th St.
Operated on K St., to Tenth Ave., to Imperial Ave. to 25th St., to Ocean View Blvd. to 30th St., Inbound operated on K St., to Fifth Ave., to Broadway to Union Station.

No. 8—Old Town Line.
Downtown loop discontinued. Operated to and from Third Ave. and Broadway.

No. 9—Coronado Ferry Line.
Route changed to Ferry on Fifth Ave. to F St., to Kettner Blvd. Arctic St. changed to Kettner Blvd.

May, 1923

No. 1—Fifth Ave. - Mission Cliff Line.
The alternate cars changed to loop downtown on Fifth Ave., to Third Ave., to Market St., to Fifth Ave.

No. 3—Fifth Ave. - Mission Hills Line.
Ditto.

No. 12, NC and CV—Logan Heights, National City and Chula Vista Lines.
Cars routed from Union Station, on Broadway, to 16th St., to Logan Ave., to 26th St., to National Ave., to 32nd St. to Newton Ave., etc. San Diego & Arizona Ry's line on Newton Ave. and 13th St., abandoned.

June, 1923

No. 11—Adams Ave. Line.
Day route unchanged.
After 6:15 P.M., operated from Union Station, on Broadway, to Fifth Ave., to University Ave., to Park Blvd., to Adams Ave., to Marlborough Dr., Kensington Park.

July 30, 1923

No. 11—Adams Ave. Line.
All cars operated from Union Station, via Fifth Ave. to Kensington Park.

No. 1—Fifth Ave. - Mission Cliff Line.
Route extended from Mission Cliff on Adams Ave., to Texas St.

March, 1924

No. 1 and No. 11 Lines combined.
Union Station to Kensington Park, with alternate cars looping downtown, Fifth Ave., to Broadway, to Third Ave., to Market St. to Fifth Ave.

No. 4—Imperial Ave. Line.
Cut back from 40th St., on Imperial Ave., to 34th St. After 10:02 P.M., operated to Third Ave. and E St. only.

May, 1924

Nos. 1, 3 and 11—All cars terminate at Union Station.

No. 4—Imperial Ave. Line.
Discontinued operation to Union Station.
Ran on Broadway to State St., to Ivy St. (end of the line).

No. 5—First Ave. and Ocean View Blvd. Line.
Operated from Laurel St., on First Ave., to B St., to Fifth Ave. to Market St., to 25th St., to Ocean View Blvd., to 30th St. Track was extended about this time from 30th St., on Ocean View Blvd., to 39th St., on Ocean View Blvd., to 39th St. to Imperial Ave. and Cemeteries.

No. 6—Vacated.

No. 8—Old Town Line.
Discontinued and abandoned from State and Ivy Sts. to Old Town. Vacated.

No. 7—East San Diego Line.
Express service via Third Ave., from Broadway, to B St., to Twelfth Ave., etc. to East San Diego during evening rush hours daily except Saturday and Sunday.

No. 10—F St. and Broadway Line.
Operated from Union Station, on Broadway, to State St., to F St., to 16th St., to Broadway, to 25th St., to B St., to 27th St. Returned on F St. to Kettner Blvd., to Broadway.

No. 13—La Playa Line.
Operated from Third Ave. on Broadway, to Kettner Blvd., to Hancock St., over the Point Loma Railroad route to Barnett Ave., to Lytton St., to Rosecrans St. to La Playa and the Military Reservation at Fort Rosecrans. Shuttle discontinued.

No. 14—Ocean Beach Line.
Operated from Fourth Ave., on Broadway, to Kettner Blvd., to Hancock St., over the new line to the Beaches to OB Jct., to Bacon St., to Santa Cruz St. to Sunset Blvd., Ocean Beach.

OB—Vacated.
Point Loma RR tracks through Wabaska Canyon and on Voltaire St. abandoned. Shuttle service to Mission Beach opened.

Oct. 1924

No. 1—Fifth Ave. and Mission Cliff Line.
Operated from Union Station, on Broadway, to Fifth Ave., to University Ave., to Park Blvd., to Adams Ave., to 30th St.

No. 10—F St. and Broadway Line.
Discontinued. Vacated.

No. 11—Adams Ave. Line.
Operated from Union Station, on Broadway, to Fifth Ave., to University Ave., to 30th St., to Adams Ave., to Kensington.

No. 15 and 16—Mission Beach and La Jolla Lines.
Operated from Fourth Ave., on Broadway, to Kettner Blvd., to Hancock St., over the new high speed interurban line #15 to Mission Beach and #16 to Pacific Beach and La Jolla. (Regular service inaugurated July 1, 1924).

June, 1925

No. 4—Imperial Ave. Line.
State St. Line abandoned from Broadway to Ivy St.
Operated from State St., on B St. to Fifth Ave., etc.

CV—Chula Vista.
Service National City to Chula Vista replaced by buses. "CV" Vacated.

Oct., 1925

No. 4—Imperial Ave. Line.
Terminated at Third Ave. and B St., instead of State St.

Jan. 1926

No. 10—Kensington Express Line.
Operated from Union Station, on Broadway, to Twelfth Ave., through Park, to Park Blvd., to Adams Ave., to Marlborough Dr., during evening rush hours, daily except Saturday and Sunday.

Sept. 16, 1940

Nos. 15 and 16—Mission Beach and La Jolla Lines.
Service discontinued. Tracks abandoned from Kettner Blvd. and Broadway to La Jolla.

1942

Specials
Double tracks installed on B St., from Third Ave. to Kettner Blvd., second track laid on Kettner Blvd., from B St., to Date St., tracks of Line to the Beaches restored on Kettner Blvd., to Hancock St. to Wright St. Yard. Shift change hours service operated to Consolidated Aircraft Corporation's Plant No. 2 at Witherby St. Discontinued in 1945.

May 12, 1942

Nos. 1 and 3—Fifth Ave. Lines.
Downtown loop changed. Operated on Fifth Ave., to Market St., to Third Ave., to F St., to Fifth Ave.

No. 9—Coronado Ferry Line.
Changed to loop—Broadway to Fourth Ave., to F St.

June 30, 1946

No. 1—Fifth Ave. Line.
Service discontinued. Track on University Ave. abandoned account bridge construction for Cabrillo Freeway.

Dec. 7, 1946

No. 4—Imperial Ave. Line.
Service discontinued. Tracks abandoned from 16th St. and Imperial Ave. to end.

No. 12—Logan Heights Line.
Service discontinued. Tracks abandoned from 16th St. and Imperial Ave. to end.

June 1, 1947

No. 3—Mission Hills Line.
Service discontinued. Tracks abandoned from Fifth Ave. and Broadway to end.

No. 9—Coronado Ferry Line.
Service discontinued.

No. 20—Orange Ave. Line in Coronado.
Service discontinued. Tracks abandoned.

April 24, 1949

No. 2—Broadway - Brooklyn Heights Line.
Service discontinued.

No. 7—East San Diego Line via Park.
Service discontinued.

No. 11—Adams Ave. Line via Park.
Service discontinued.
All remaining tracks abandoned.

July, 1926

No. 5—Ocean View Blvd. Line.
Operated to 39th St. and Ocean View Blvd. 39th St. franchise surrendered in 1927. No record found of passenger service on 39th St.

June, 1927

No. 10—Kensington Express Line.
Service discontinued. Vacated.

Sept., 1928

No. 4—Imperial Ave. Line.
Changed to loop downtown from Fifth Ave., to B St., to Third Ave., to F St., to Fifth Ave., etc.

No. 5—Ocean View Blvd. Line.
Discontinued operation on First Ave., from Laurel St., to B St., to Third Ave. Track abandoned on First Ave. Changed to loop downtown same as No. 4 above.

Dec., 1929

No. 12—Logan Heights Line.
"Shipyard" tracks on 32nd St. from Newton Ave. to San Diego & Arizona Railway's right-of-way abandoned.

Jan. 10, 1930

NC—National Ctiy Line.
Service discontinued. Trackage Agreement cancelled. "NC" vacated.

July, 1931

No. 1—Fifth Ave. and 30th St. Line.
Operated from Union Station, on Broadway, to Fifth Ave., to University Ave., to 30th St., to Adams Ave.

No. 11—Adams Ave. Line via Park.
Operated from Union Station, on Broadway, to Twelfth Ave., through Park, to Park Blvd., to Adams Ave. to Marlborough Dr.

Dec. 6, 1931

No. 1—Fifth Ave. and 30th St. Line.
Discontinued on Broadway to Union Station. Changed to loop downtown from Fifth Ave., to Market St., to Third Ave., to Broadway, to Fifth Ave.

No. 3—Fifth Ave. and Mission Hills Line.
Changed same as No. 1 above.

May, 1935

No. 1—Fifth Ave. Line.
Cut back to terminate at 30th St. and University Ave., then to Park Blvd. and University Ave.

No. 2—Broadway - Brooklyn Heights Line.
Extended on 30th St., from University Ave., to Adams Ave.

Feb. 18, 1937

No. 13—La Playa Line.
Service discontinued. Track abandoned from junction with the Line to the Beaches to Fort Rosecrans.

Dec. 19, 1938

No. 5—Ocean View Blvd. Line.
Service discontinued. Tracks abandoned from 16th and Market Sts. to end.

Dec. 19, 1938

No. 14—Ocean Beach Line.
Service discontinued. Track abandoned from OB Junction to end.

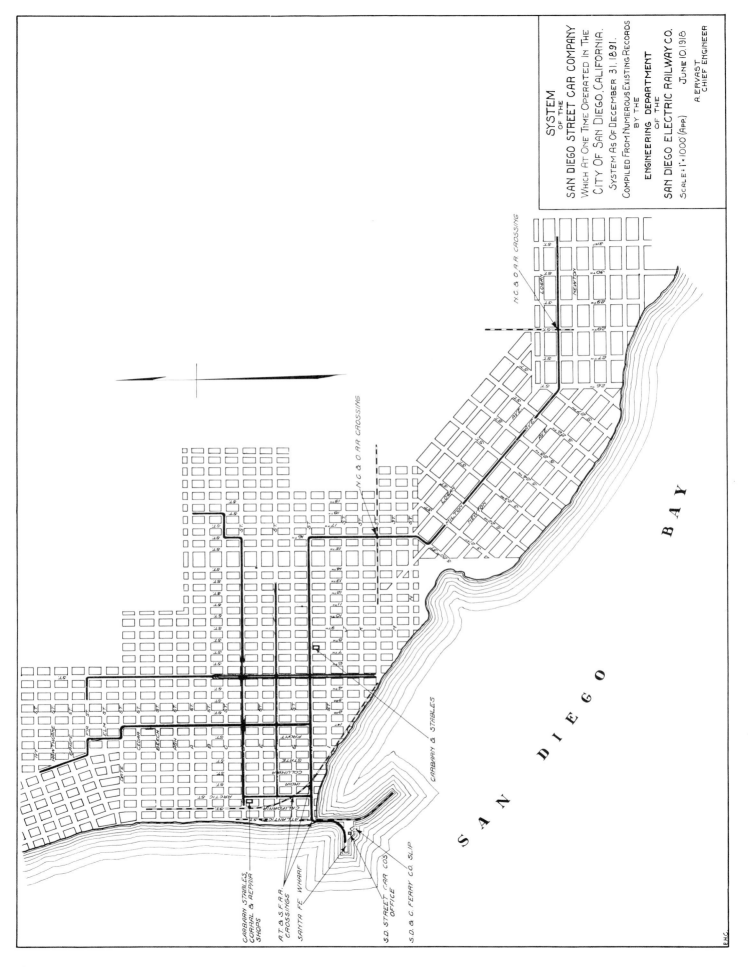

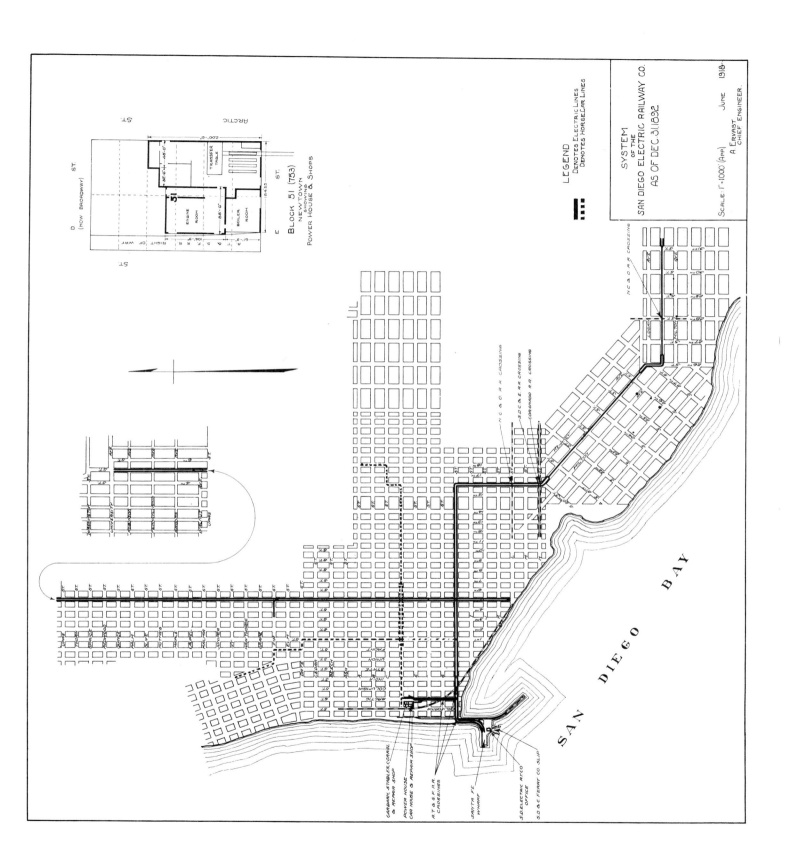

LEGEND
DENOTES ELECTRIC LINES
DENOTES HORSE CAR LINES

SYSTEM
OF THE
SAN DIEGO ELECTRIC RAILWAY CO.
AS OF DEC 31, 1892

SCALE 1" = 1000' (App)   JUNE   1918
A. ERVAST
CHIEF ENGINEER.

BLOCK 51 (753)
NEW TOWN
SHOWING
POWER HOUSE & SHOPS

SAN DIEGO BAY

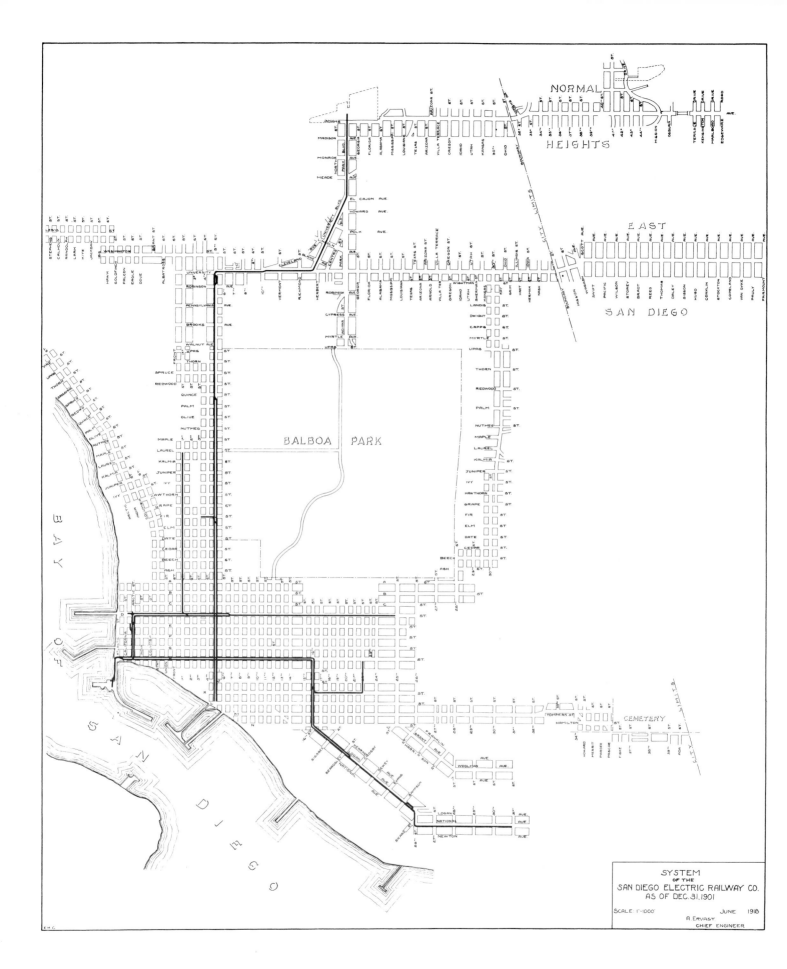

NORMAL

HEIGHTS

EAST

SAN DIEGO

BALBOA PARK

BAY

OF

SAN DIEGO

CEMETERY

SYSTEM
OF THE
SAN DIEGO ELECTRIC RAILWAY CO.
AS OF DEC. 31, 1901

SCALE: 1"=1000'   JUNE   1918
A. ERVAST
CHIEF ENGINEER

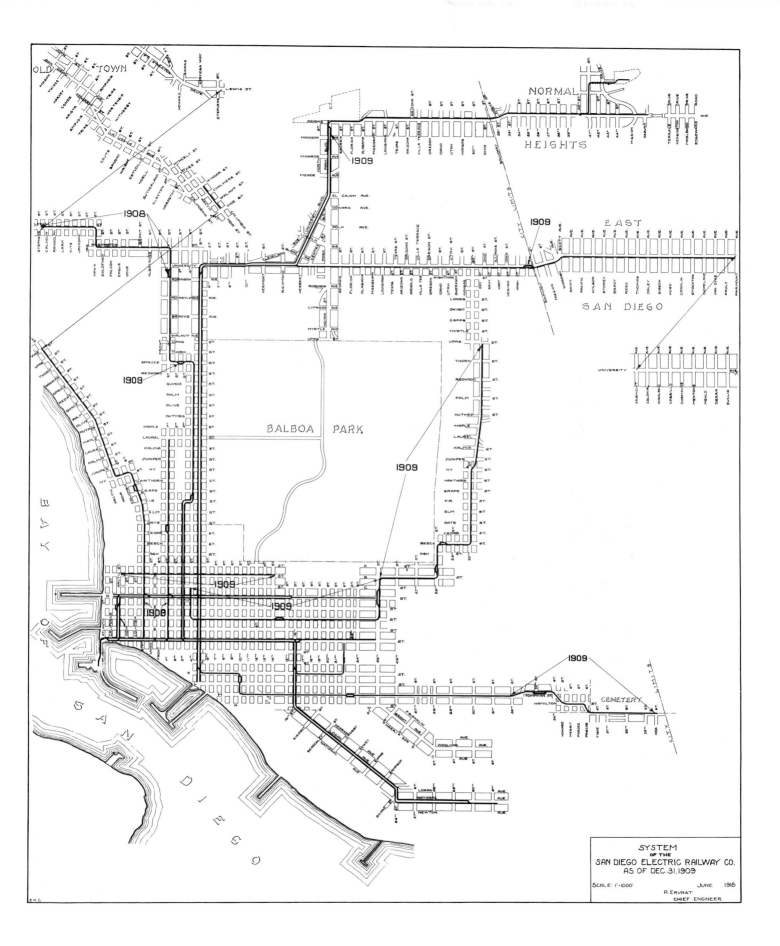

SYSTEM
OF THE
SAN DIEGO ELECTRIC RAILWAY CO.
AS OF DEC. 31, 1909

SCALE: 1"=1000'   JUNE   1918
A. ERVAST
CHIEF ENGINEER

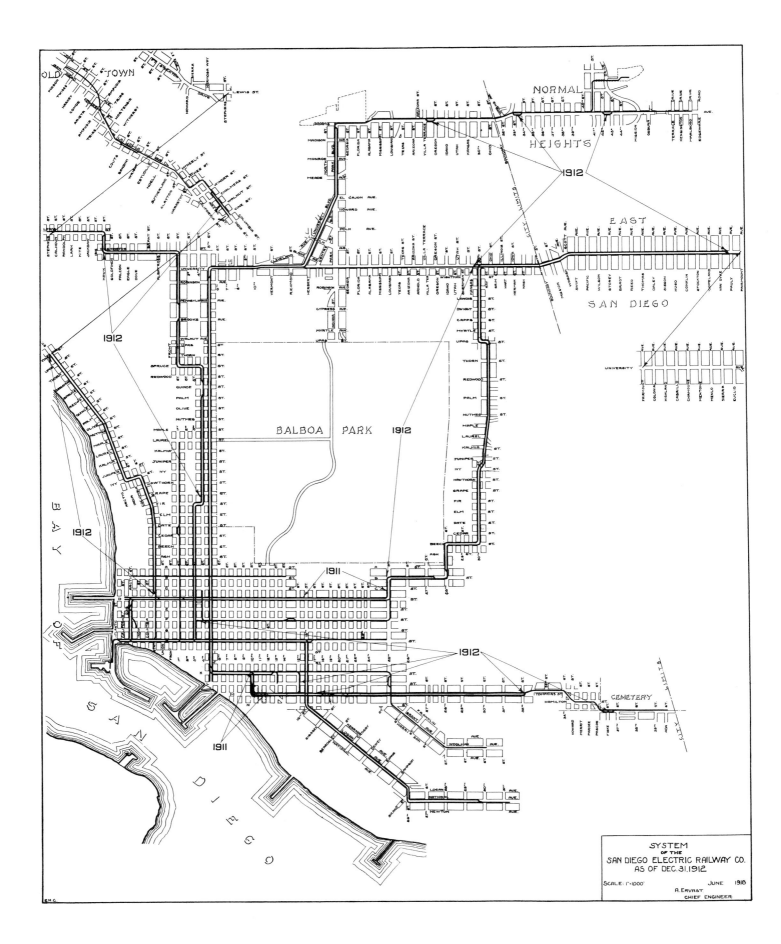

SYSTEM
OF THE
SAN DIEGO ELECTRIC RAILWAY CO.
AS OF DEC. 31, 1912

SCALE: 1"=1000'   JUNE 1918
A. ERVAST
CHIEF ENGINEER

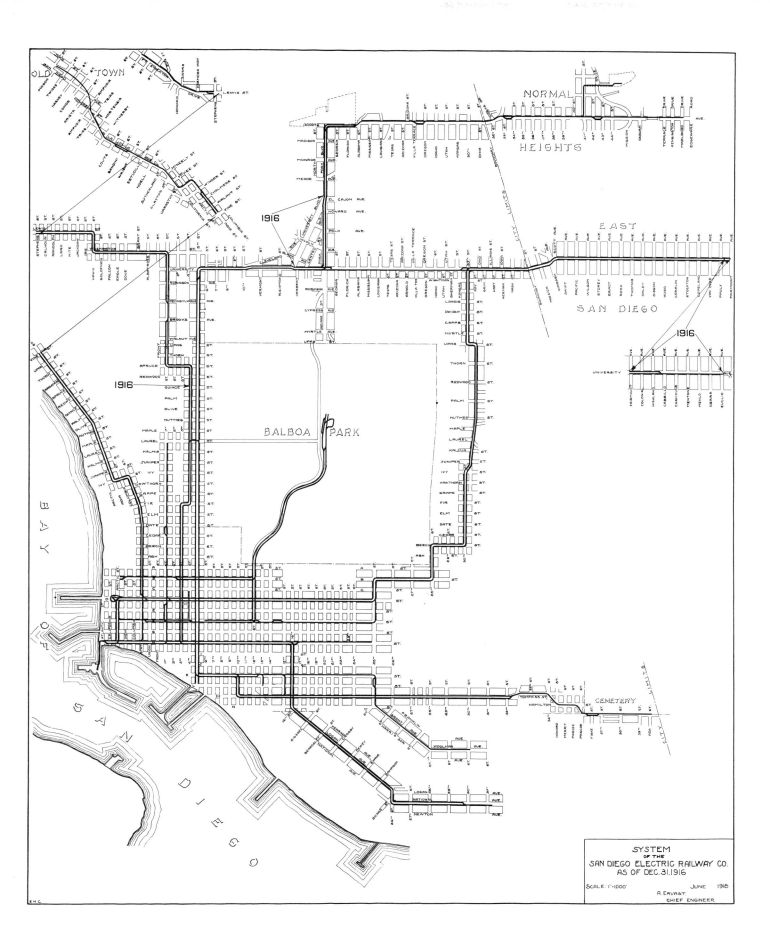

SYSTEM
OF THE
SAN DIEGO ELECTRIC RAILWAY CO.
AS OF DEC. 31, 1916

SCALE: 1"=1000'   JUNE 1918
                        A. ERVAST
                        CHIEF ENGINEER

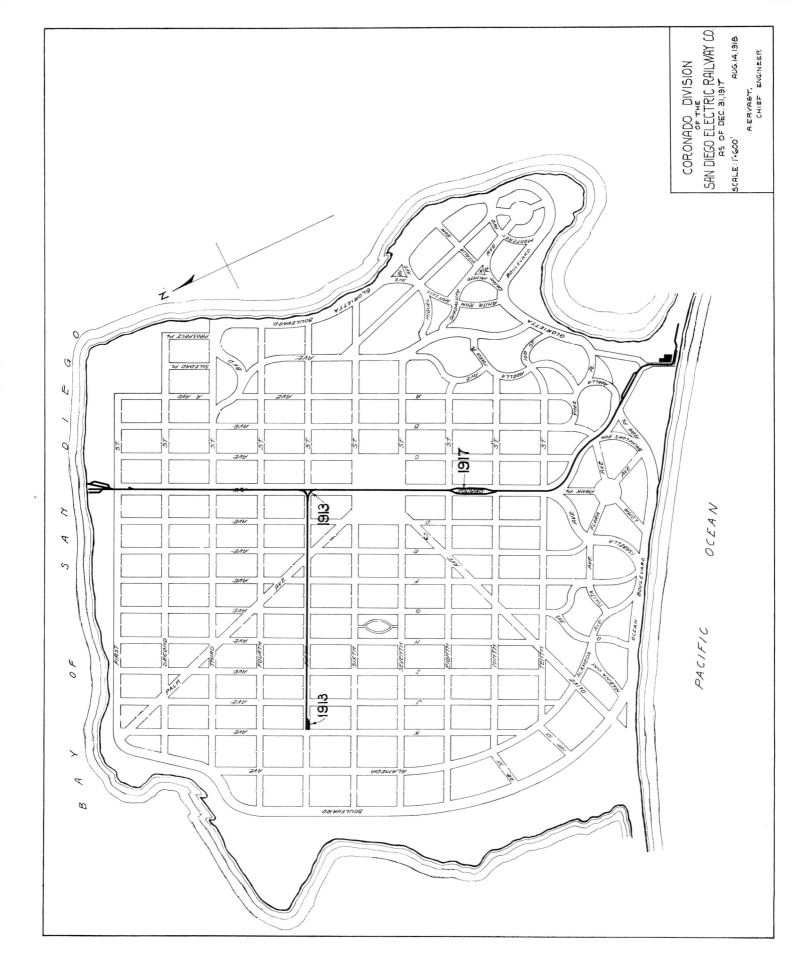

CORONADO DIVISION
OF THE
SAN DIEGO ELECTRIC RAILWAY CO.
AS OF DEC. 31, 1917
SCALE: 1"=600'   AUG. 14, 1918
A. ERVAST,
CHIEF ENGINEER

1917

1913

1913

N

B A Y   O F   S A N   D I E G O

P A C I F I C   O C E A N

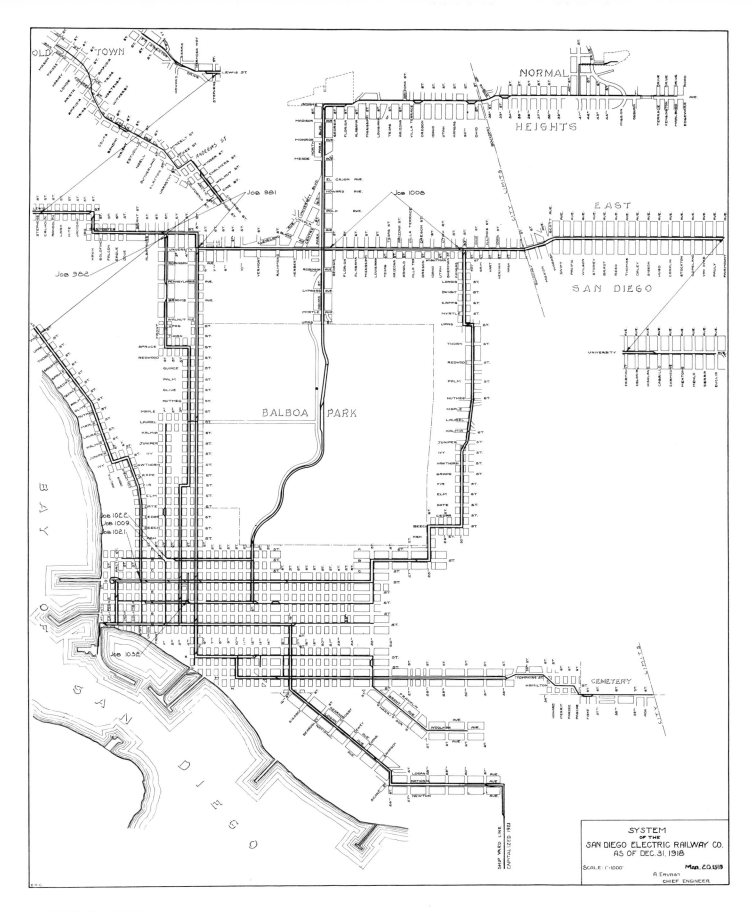

OLD TOWN

NORMAL HEIGHTS

EAST SAN DIEGO

SAN DIEGO

BALBOA PARK

BAY OF SAN DIEGO

CEMETERY

Job 981
Job 982
Job 1008
Job 1022
Job 1009
Job 1021
Job 1032

UNIVERSITY

SHIP YARD LINE
CAPITALIZED 1921

SYSTEM
OF THE
SAN DIEGO ELECTRIC RAILWAY CO.
AS OF DEC. 31, 1918

SCALE: 1" = 1000'   MAR. 20, 1913

A. ERVAST
CHIEF ENGINEER

LITHOGRAPHY - MODESTO PRINTING CO.
PRESSWORK - JOE POSTELLE
LITHO PLATES - MICKEY FERNANDES
COMPOSITION - HUNGERFORD PRESS
LAYOUT - DON DUKE
HALFTONES - AL ROSE